CHINESE VILLAGE LIFE TODAY

Chinese Village Life Today

Building Families in an Age of Transition

GONÇALO SANTOS

UNIVERSITY OF WASHINGTON PRESS
Seattle

Design by Katrina Noble
Composed in Minion, typeface designed by Robert Slimbach
Interior photographs are by the author

25 24 23 22 21 5 4 3 2 1

Printed and bound in the United States of America

UNIVERSITY OF WASHINGTON PRESS
uwapress.uw.edu

LIBRARY OF CONGRESS CATALOGING-IN-PUBLICATION DATA
Names: Santos, Gonçalo D., author.
Title: Chinese village life today : building families in an age of transition / Gonçalo Santos.
Description: Seattle : University of Washington Press, [2021] | Includes bibliographical references and index.
Identifiers: LCCN 2020055980 | ISBN 9780295747385 (hardcover) | ISBN 9780295747408 (paperback) | ISBN 9780295747392 (ebook)
Subjects: LCSH: Villages—China—Guangdong Sheng. | Rural-urban migration—China—Guangdong Sheng. | Families—China—Guangdong Sheng. | Technology—Social aspects—China—Guangdong Sheng. | Guangdong Sheng (China)—Rural conditions. | Guangdong Sheng (China)—Social conditions. | Guangdong Sheng (China)—Social life and customs.
Classification: LCC HN740.G83 S26 2021 | DDC 307.2/6095127—dc23
LC record available at https://lccn.loc.gov/2020055980

The paper used in this publication is acid free and meets the minimum requirements of American National Standard for Information Sciences—Permanence of Paper for Printed Library Materials, ANSI Z39.48–1984.∞

In memory of
my parents, Maria Manuela Duro dos Santos e João Filomeno dos Santos
my maternal grandmother, Maria José Duro
my paternal grandparents, Aurora Bela dos Santos e
Manuel Turquel dos Santos

CONTENTS

FOREWORD

For many readers, there may be something slightly disorienting about Gonçalo Santos's remarkable book. It is based on long-term fieldwork in rural China—more specifically in the rural northern parts of Guangdong. This is a place where traditional Chinese ideals of family life remain strong and where a good deal of time, money, and effort is put into traditional life-cycle rituals of various kinds. And yet these people could not be more modern if they tried. They use smart phones, of course, and communicate with each other (and with their anthropologist friend) via QQ and WeChat instant messaging; there is an intense flow of people back and forth between rural and urban places, so much so that the rural-urban contrast often seems on the verge of collapsing; in the realm of "intimate life," for example, when it comes to childbirth and eldercare, their decisions are framed in relation not only to a shared (if fragile) morality of kinship but also to a rapidly changing social, economic, and technological landscape.

In short, this book is a balancing act in two senses. Although it illustrates well China's stunning transformation in recent decades, it equally well illustrates the role that tradition continues to play in shaping Chinese lives. And although it focuses attention on the small details of everyday lived experience, especially within family settings, it equally well focuses attention on broad patterns of structural, institutional, and technological change. In this way, Santos pushes back against a certain tendency to portray China as a place in which all the old certainties have collapsed in the post-Mao era and been replaced—for better or worse—by stark new realities. But he also makes clear the extent to which new realities are indeed fundamentally changing some basic Chinese understandings of what it is to be human and of what it is to be a person caught up in networks of family and friends (or, as Santos aptly puts it, caught up in "new hierarchies of interdependence").

A particular focus here is on the technical and material aspects of life in rural Guangdong, and this is something that sets Santos's approach apart from many others in the field of the anthropology of China. We learn not only about uses of IUD and ultrasound, for example, but also about changing technologies of waste disposal. In the background is a broader modernizing project that has global echoes, of course, but that has also had a particular historical trajectory in the rural Chinese case. The people Santos worked with in Guangdong are keen to embrace modernity and development, as one would expect, and this usually means embracing technical change when it comes. But they also struggle with the everyday ethical dilemmas generated by China's wider social and material transformations, as for example when the introduction of (desired) flush toilets leads to environmental problems for the local community. Similarly, the desires and dreams these people have for their children and grandchildren often generate dilemmas that are not easily resolved.

What brings all of this together is very solid ethnography. These days, of course, many people are sharing fascinating stories about life in modern China, some of which are based in rural settings. What is less common is for an anthropologist to conduct systematic and highly detailed research in one rural community over a period of two decades—exactly at a time when it is being fundamentally reshaped. Santos's fluency in Cantonese, and the willingness of local people to share their lives and their stories with him, gives him a unique insight. Of course, the story he tells is complex—as noted above, some readers may even find it a bit disorienting. But he provides us with an empirically accurate and theoretically sophisticated snapshot of how things really are in rural China now.

CHARLES STAFFORD
London School of Economics

PREFACE

Anthropologists are well known for using small case studies to think about larger issues, and here I use the experiences of a specific village community in South China to think about larger transformations and tensions affecting the whole of rural China. These changes refer to a period that could be described as an age of transition in Chinese frameworks of governance, when China stepped up its efforts to promote large-scale technocratic projects of modernization of family life steered by the state and supported by many actors in civil society and various international organizations.

This book draws on ethnographic materials collected through longitudinal research between 1999 and 2020 with the members of a lineage village community based in northern Guangdong (map P.1): the village of Harmony Cave in the township of Yellow Flower. Most social science accounts of the effects of top-down programs of technocratic modernization in developing contexts focus on the agency of macro-level actors such as national governments and international nongovernmental organizations. My approach highlights "intimate choices" through which villagers translate larger technocratic forces and tensions into locally meaningful frameworks of modernity.

The Hedgehog and the Fox

This book builds on a well-established tradition of Chinese village studies that goes back to the work of the great Chinese anthropologist Fei Xiaotong (1939, 1992), a student of Bronislaw Malinowski at the London School of Economics in the 1930s, but it adds something to this honorable tradition. Based on two decades of longitudinal fieldwork research, it tracks the circular

MAP P.1. Research area in Guangdong, People's Republic of China

translocal movements of village households across regional and rural-urban boundaries. The individuals and families portrayed here are constantly moving across spatial boundaries, and many are labor migrants in major cities in the neighboring Pearl River Delta region, one of the most urbanized and industrialized areas in the world. This engagement with new forms of routine rural-urban mobility started in the 1980s but has increased in intensity in the last two decades, giving rise to new deterritorialized forms of village sociality that stand in stark contrast to earlier ethnographic accounts of a relatively stagnant "earthbound" village China.

Capturing these new realities of spatial mobility required a more dynamic, less bounded view of culture and the usage of multisited ethnographic methodologies (Clifford 1988; Gupta and Ferguson 1992; Marcus 1998; Ferguson 2011). This approach was also very helpful in showing that the ongoing deterritorialization of village sociality is part of a larger process of technocratization of the fabric of everyday life. The families and communities described here are not just translocal social formations; they are also patched-up assemblages of people, materials, artifacts, and ideals whose coming into being cannot be separated from the increasing salience of technoscience and technocratic expertise in the governance of rural society.

Making sense of these complexities cannot be done in a rush. This book continues to insist on the importance of long-term fieldwork, proposing a rather unique longitudinal perspective on processes of rural transformation. The decision to develop longitudinal research evolved gradually, soon after my first long-term fieldwork experience in Harmony Cave in 1999–2001, and the best way to describe this process is to evoke a famous essay by American philosopher Isaiah Berlin—"The Hedgehog and the Fox" ([1953] 2013)—in which he draws a metaphorical contrast between two categories of writers and thinkers. While the *hedgehogs* move very slowly and view the world through the lens of a single defining idea (e.g., Plato, Blaise Pascal, Marcel Proust, and Fernand Braudel), the *foxes* move very fast and draw on a wide variety of experiences to view the world (e.g., Aristotle, Michel de Montaigne, Johann Wolfgang von Goethe, and James Joyce).

As a foreign anthropologist writing about a country other than my own, I resisted the idea of approaching fieldwork research like a fox who moves from one place to the other looking for new people and new experiences to make sense of the world. I felt more attracted to the idea of moving slowly like a hedgehog, focusing on a single set of experiences for a long period, so I continued working with the people I met in Harmony Cave. I engaged in the hard work of returning for visits, building long-term relations, and, because hedgehogs can hop on cars, trains, and buses, tracking the increasing spatial movements of village households. This longitudinal approach reinforced my conviction that it is important to take the villagers' own moral aspirations and "intimate choices" into consideration when talking about rural transformations.

The Hilly Regions of Northern Guangdong

It was on a rather hot and humid sunny day back in June 1999 that I first arrived with my backpack in the township of Yellow Flower. I was twenty-five years old and it was all very exciting. This was my initiation as a young anthropologist and it felt like a great opportunity to do something that could make a difference. At the time, barely two decades since the beginning of Deng Xiaoping's reforms, China was still in the early stages of its economic ascent to global superpower status, and its countryside was still largely closed to domestic and international tourists, let alone foreign researchers. Mobile phones and Internet access had yet to become widespread, very few cars and trucks circulated on national roads, and television, newspapers, and other media had yet to develop into a large-scale business of mass entertainment. Between 1996 and 1998, I had lived in the former Portuguese colony of Macau for the sole purpose of learning Cantonese, the most widespread regional language in Guangdong. In 1998 I moved to the provincial capital, Guangzhou, to improve my spoken standard Chinese (SC)—Putonghua, or Mandarin, the official language of the People's Republic of China—and continue my studies of written Chinese at Sun Yat-Sen University, the most renowned university in South China.

My original plan was to do fieldwork in a rural community in the booming Pearl River Delta region, but I ended up shifting my site to a peripheral area in the northern "hilly regions" of Guangdong. I chose northern Guangdong because this region seemed to retain a strong sense of local identity despite the increasing number of outgoing migrant laborers seeking work in the Pearl River Delta, and the region had been recently "opened" for tourism development. I initially tried to develop fieldwork in northern Guangdong with the department of anthropology at Sun Yat-Sen University, but bureaucratic hurdles made things too complicated. I traveled to northern Guangdong to select a fieldwork location where I could stay for at least one year and chose the township of Yellow Flower (formerly Brightpath) in Yingde County because of its beautiful landscape of paddy fields and limestone mountains. I did not know anyone in the township, but this did not prevent me from taking a bus from Guangzhou to rural Yingde in late June 1999. This was not my first bus trip to rural Yingde, so I was not entirely unfamiliar with the idea of sitting on a bus full of livestock, overloaded luggage, and an improvised additional row of passengers in the corridor in between seats, but it was the first time that I was doing the journey all by myself.

There were no direct buses to Yellow Flower. Some six hours after leaving Guangzhou, I had to get off the bus right in the middle of a highway and then ride for another three hours on a three-wheeler locally known as Three-Footed Chicken—Saam-Geuk Gai in Cantonese (C). Guangdong's road network was still poorly developed, and the most isolated areas in northern Guangdong lacked asphalt roads. My three-wheeler journey on a muddy road through the hills to Yellow Flower was largely uneventful, but there was one thing that made it unforgettable. Although I am a mere 1 meter 85 centimeters tall and at the time weighed no more than 75 kilograms, I was larger and heavier than the average local adult person, so the driver of the three-wheeler wanted to charge me double the fare. I refused to pay extra but this incident suggested that I would be living in an environment in which my physical appearance would always make me stand out from the crowd. When I told the local motorcycle-taxi drivers that I was not a businessman, but just a "Western tourist" looking for a place to stay, they expressed incredulity and suspicion because they were still not very familiar with the modern notion of tourism.

This reaction of suspicion was shaped by sentiments of "cultural intimacy" (Herzfeld [1997] 2016) and shared perception of difference. Modernity is usually described as a large-scale transformation that leads to what sociologist Anthony Giddens (1991, 18) calls "the 'lifting out' of social relations from local contexts and their re-articulation across indefinite tracts of time-space." This view of modernity helps understand how increasing spatial mobility after the turn of the millennium has rendered local people more open to strangers and to other ways of seeing the world, but being more open does not necessarily mean more accepting. Modernity is as much about the "lifting out" of social relations from local contexts as it is about the reembedding of new forms and materials in local frameworks of perception. Modern forms of sociality do not take place "across indefinite tracts of time-space"; they involve processes of familiarization and domestication that allow individuals to develop a sense of complicity and cultural intimacy at multiple scales. Getting inside these networks of complicity and cultural intimacy can be very difficult, and I have to admit that my first six months in Yellow Flower were not easy.

Getting Settled in Harmony Cave

It was not very difficult to find a village to stay in—the village of Harmony Cave—but the local township government did not know how to handle my request for a temporary residence permit. My case was reported to the higher authorities of the public security bureau in Qingyuan City; and this public security bureau sent a team of ten police officers to investigate my situation. After some three hours of interrogation, they asked me to return to my entry point in China—the Macau-Zhuhai border—in order to check with the customs authorities whether my visa allowed me to visit rural Yingde. I did what they told me to do, and to my surprise, the authorities in the Macau-Zhuhai border found no irregularities in my situation. Two days later, I was back in Yellow Flower. I was able to stay in the township for fourteen months then, and I have returned on a regular basis over the last twenty years.

My entry point in Yellow Flower was the village of Harmony Cave. This book is primarily about the residents of a particular hamlet in this village: the Harmony First hamlet. These are the people who taught me how to speak local Cantonese dialect and how to farm the local rice fields, the people who welcomed me into their networks of support and cultural intimacy. I encountered strong reactions of suspicion during the first six months living there. There were rumors that I was a foreign spy coming from Macau, a foreign bandit who was taking refuge from a crime committed elsewhere, an itinerant swindler, or even a human trafficker who had come to Yellow Flower to steal people's children and sell them to foreigners. The fact that I could speak Cantonese led many villagers to think that I was a Communist Party underground agent. There is a long history of such agents coming to Yellow Flower during the Chinese civil war period, so the figure of the underground agent was still quite salient in the local imagination, especially among the older generations. Some said that I had been sent to the village to make sure the Birth Planning Policy was properly implemented or that I was to make sure the new regulations banning coffin burials were followed. These rumors were intensely debated in the first six months of my stay, but they gradually became old news as the villagers realized that I was serious about living in the countryside and learning about local ways of doing things. During my first stay, I did not have a mobile phone, and my contact with the world outside China was largely restricted to writing letters and making occasional calls through the landline phone of the post office in the market town.

During this first stay, I lived with three different households in the Harmony First hamlet. I tried to follow my hosts as much as possible in the performance of their daily tasks (figures P.1 and P.2), including farming the land, hunting snakes, catching grasshoppers, gambling, drinking rice wine, gossiping, going to local periodic markets, selling products in markets, buying piglets, killing pigs, shouldering bags full of rice to pay agricultural taxes, cooking on a firewood stove, washing my clothes in the common washing tank, taking care of the water in the fields, taking care of the children, negotiating and celebrating marriages, visiting affines (in-laws) and friends, attending "full-month" celebrations for newborns, helping a family take a pregnant woman to a clinic outside the village in preparation for childbirth, taking an elderly villager to the emergency ward of a

FIGURE P.1. Author threshing rice with host family, Harmony Cave, 1999

FIGURE P.2. Loading a bicycle with a bag of rice to pay the agricultural tax, old Harmony First residential area, 2000

higher-level city hospital, getting sick and taking myself to local village doctors, being the victim of incorrect medical injections, participating in village meetings for the construction of a village memorial door, practicing ancestor worship in lineage ancestral halls, attending deity temple rituals, joining a primary-school basketball team in the Lunar New Year competition, attending women's rehearsals of ritual wailing in funerals, attending funerals and cleaning graves, and visiting the homes of village migrants in the city. My first long-term stay in Harmony Cave was quite intense and opened the way for subsequent interactions in the following two decades.

Taking the Path of Longitudinal Multisited Rural-Urban Research

When I ended my first fieldwork in Harmony Cave in January 2001, everyone in the village knew my name, which was eventually carved onto a village memorial door that was built at the entrance to the village close to the main road. When I returned to Harmony Cave in the summer of 2005, it had become clear to me that I wanted to continue as a *hedgehog*, working with the same people, on a path of longitudinal research, but to do so I had to start commuting back and forth between the country and the city, because by the mid-2000s most of households in the Harmony First hamlet were relying on temporary labor migration to the city to earn a living. Over the years, a few village households managed to buy an apartment in the city, and some even managed to purchase an urban household—in standard Chinese (SC), *hukou*—booklet, but moving permanently to the city is not attractive to most villagers, and villagers who work in the city for much of the year still see themselves as natives and permanent residents of Harmony Cave and Yellow Flower.

Between 2005 and 2020, I returned to Guangdong for follow-up research visits in 2008, 2009, 2012, 2013, 2014, 2015, 2016, and 2017. In addition to returning to Harmony Cave and Yellow Flower, I expanded my knowledge of the villagers' migration networks in cities through repeated visits to the workplaces and the homes of village migrants living in Guangzhou and other cities in the Pearl River Delta region (map P.2). Harmony Cave was one of the first villages in Yellow Flower to have labor migrants moving to the city to seek employment in factories or to set up small-scale family enterprises (usually agricultural enterprises of vegetable gardening) in designated

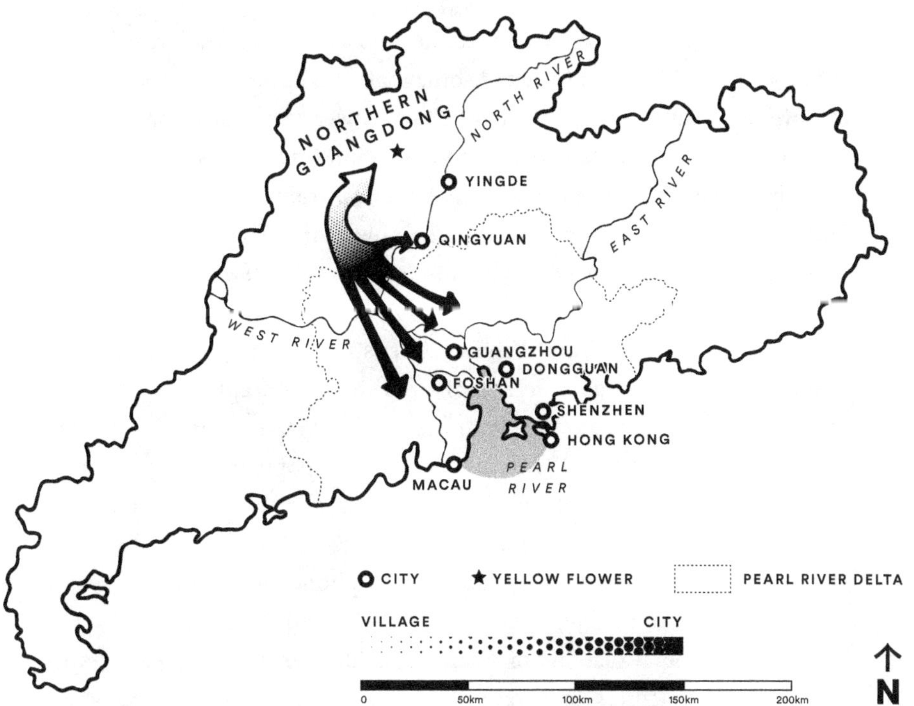

MAP P.2. Core-periphery relations and circular migration in Guangdong

periurban areas in major cities like Guangzhou and Foshan. Most village migrants favor vegetable gardening because it allows them to work as a family and to have more autonomy, as they can live together as a family in self-built zinc huts next to their vegetable plots. Much of my research in the city has involved repeated visits to villagers' vegetable gardens and to factories and factory dormitories where villagers work. I also visited the apartments that village migrants have rented or purchased in the cities.

My return visits to Harmony Cave usually took place during major ritual occasions such as Spring Festival, Tomb-sweeping Festival, lineage anniversary celebrations, and deity temple festivals. These ritual occasions are an important source of collective identity and village pride, and they offer a platform for the construction of village hierarchies and networks of social support. Most village migrants return to attend these ritual occasions, and these trips are an opportunity to catch up with gossip and reconnect to village life. Village migrants also return for more personal ritual occasions such as weddings, funerals, and other major rituals associated with one's family and close circle of village relatives. These spatial movements have been significantly facilitated by dramatic improvements in the local transportation networks and in the township's connectivity to other parts of the province. Today, there are several direct buses connecting Yellow Flower to all major cities in the Pearl River Delta, and the trip lasts no more than three hours. Buses are not the only option. Villagers can also take the fast train from Yingde City to Guangzhou or, more commonly, drive their own car or van.

Moving in space is easier also because villagers now use smart phones to communicate and make microcoordination arrangements at a distance. In the late 1990s, the township of Yellow Flower still did not have mobile phone coverage, and few villagers were familiar with the concept of the Internet. The first local Internet café—in Cantonese (C), *mong-ba*—opened in 2003 in the market town of Yellow Flower, and it was quite popular among teenagers because most homes did not have Internet access, nor personal computers or landline phones. Rates of Internet access remained low until after 2010, when there was a dramatic increase in smart-phone ownership and people started to use social media platforms such as QQ and WeChat.

This increasing availability of smart-phone devices has completely transformed local structures of rural-urban mobility and connectivity. Smart phones not only make things convenient but also allow villagers to build community and re-create a daily routine of group exchanges. These exchanges are very different from the intense regime of daily face-to-face interactions I experienced during my first fieldwork in the late 1990s, but they are helping villagers stay connected. This work of building connected lives online has led me to incorporate social media platforms in my research. I use QQ and WeChat not just to stay connected with individual villagers but also to participate in daily online group exchanges with specific families and specific lineage branches. These group exchanges allow villagers to coordinate meetings and ritual events and to share news, jokes, stories, and all kinds of comments about themselves, others, or the world in general. These exchanges can be quite funny and relaxing, and they often allow villagers to come together as a moral community commenting on larger societal developments, including larger forces of change affecting their family lives and the lives of their community.

Technocratic Governance from the Margins

This work of online moral community formation is particularly visible when major events occur such as in January 2020 when the central government announced news of a new coronavirus outbreak in the city of Wuhan, some 900 kilometers to the north, potentially more deadly than the previous outbreak of sudden acute respiratory syndrome (SARS). As the news of this new epidemic started to circulate in social media platforms not long before Chinese New Year, villagers used their family and lineage WeChat groups to learn about the lockdown of the city of Wuhan and to keep track of follow-up developments in Yellow Flower, including the local government's decision right on the eve of Chinese New Year—to shut down the borders of the township to outsiders and to enforce a ban on large public gatherings such as village banquet celebrations, village funeral gatherings, deity temple worship gatherings, and ancestor worship village gatherings, among others. It was in the context of this ban on large public gatherings that villagers were first confronted with the new technocratic realities of mourning under the emerging coronavirus epidemic state of emergency.

Two well-known village elders died around Chinese New Year, and their families were not allowed to organize a proper village funeral ceremony. The bodies of the two elders were cremated soon after death, as required by official policies of mandatory cremation enforced at the turn of the millennium to put an end to "uncivilized" and wasteful funerary practices such as the local custom of double burial (which requires the corpse to be first buried in a wooden coffin and then have the bones dug up after a few years for reburial in an urn), but the new coronavirus state of emergency led to an additional technocratic requirement: the villagers were not allowed to organize a village funeral. Because village funerals play a central role in the ritual life of local families and villages, there was a lot of debate in family and lineage WeChat groups—and I can imagine also in people's homes!—about the possible consequences of this breach of tradition. Some four months after Chinese New Year, the ban was lifted and the families were allowed to organize a proper village funeral involving hundreds of participants and the performance of "traditional" forms of ritual wailing (C: *daai-huk*) by village women and the performance of "traditional" rituals of merit (C: *gung-dak*) by Daoist-Buddhist priests to help deliver the soul from potential sufferings in purgatory or hell and transfer it either to Amitabha Buddha's Western Paradise or to a better rebirth.

The official decision to ban funeral gatherings in China was shaped by powerful political and biomedical discourses calling for the need to protect public health and prevent the spread of the pandemic, but one should not assume that these discourses are not morally questioned, adapted, and/or turned upside down by citizens in the context of specific moral communities. These moral contestations are particularly visible in communities that are living in the margins of mainstream urban society and culture. In Harmony Cave, the official ban on funeral gatherings was highly controversial, and it is clear to me that while the ban was supported by many villagers, it was also significantly contested by many others because it was perceived as a highly disruptive event. In contrast to the highly regulated and far more atomized funeral gatherings of urban families, village funerals are large-scale events that can last for days and involve thousands of people participating in complex rituals. The ban on funeral gatherings disrupted these normalized "structures of feeling" (Williams 1977), and this disruption led to moral tensions that must be treated with care. When technocratic policies (even those that are well intended) are unilaterally implemented without attending to the views of ordinary citizens, this can lead to unwanted, unexpected side effects, and I am convinced that such side effects can be avoided through the adoption of a more citizen-attuned approach to technocratic governance.

This book seeks to make a contribution to such an approach by associating it with a long-standing tradition of participatory democracy in China (Chun 2006, 2013). It is an attempt to give voice to ordinary citizens, especially those living in the rural margins of Chinese society who do not have much voice in larger national public debates on the governance of family life. The issue of lack of popular participation in processes of technocratic governance is a widespread phenomenon in most contemporary societies, North and South, East and West, because—under the influence of the global technocratic paradigm—national governments tend to favor the advice of experts over the perspective of ordinary citizens. The views of experts are of course important and should be respected as forms of authoritative knowledge, but good technocratic governance is not just about getting proper technoscientific advice to solve problems that are complex and require professional input; it is also about taking into account the views of ordinary citizens (F. Fischer 2000, 2009; Bucchi 2009; Feenberg 2010; Eubanks 2017), including those living in the margins of mainstream society and culture. This book is a contribution to larger global debates on the tension between the desire to improve and protect society through top-down technocratic governance and the desire to improve and protect society through increasing popular participation in processes of governance.

ACKNOWLEDGMENTS

Writing a book usually involves many people and a great deal of intimate choices, and this book is no exception. Many persons and institutions contributed to this book. I mention their names here solely to express my gratitude and acknowledge their part. None of the mistakes, omissions, or other shortcomings can be attributed to anybody other than myself. I owe my greatest debt of all to the villagers of Harmony Cave, especially the families of the Harmony First hamlet, for the last twenty years of delicious meals, festive celebrations, great humor, and warm hospitality. I would like to express my most sincere gratitude to everyone in the village for their openness to receive me in their homes and for their willingness to share their stories. Many other people in Yellow Flower and surrounding townships contributed to this project and I would also like to express my gratitude. I cannot mention specific names but I would like to thank everyone for their patience, care, and support over the years.

Twenty years of longitudinal research is a long time and this could not be done without the generosity of many funding institutions. The research behind the book was supported by grants from the Fundação para Ciência e Tecnologia in Portugal (SFRH/BPD/20489/2004, SFRH/BPD/40396/2007, PRAXIS XXI/BD/11184/97), the Max Planck Institute for Social Anthropology in Germany, the University of Hong Kong, and the Research Grants Council of the Hong Kong Special Administrative Region, China (GRF 17402014, GRF 17612719). I would also like to acknowledge the support provided by the Max Planck Institute for the History of Science in Berlin during a Visiting Scholar Fellowship in 2017–18 and the support provided by the Department of Life Sciences and the Research Center for Anthropology and

Health (CIAS) at the University of Coimbra during the final stage of writing and proofreading. The publication of this book was supported by funds from the Fundação para a Ciência e Tecnologia (FCT) in Portugal as part of the project UIDB/00283/2020 (Research Center for Anthropology and Health, University of Coimbra).

The idea to write this book started to take shape in Macau, where I started learning Yue Chinese and standard Chinese in the mid-1990s, and I am still very grateful to my Chinese teachers: Ms. Stella Poon, the Hau family, and Ms. Ka-In Chan. My friends in Macau are too numerous to be mentioned here, but I would like to name a few. Special thanks go to the Cavalheiro family (especially Isabel, Xana, and Manel) and to Mr. Hon-Sang Vong for their kindness and hospitality. Finally, I would like to thank Doutora Rosa Joaquim (then at the Conde São Januário Hospital) for her precious medical advice during my first stint of long-term fieldwork in the Chinese countryside. I recall one particular emergency situation in 1999 when her intervention was crucial to help me overcome the hazardous side effects of a penicillin injection mistakenly administered by staff at a rural clinic.

Moving to Guangzhou in mainland China, I would like to thank Li Xiyuan at the Center for Studies of Hong Kong, Macao and Pearl River Delta at Sun Yat-Sen University for her intellectual generosity and for opening the way for my research in the Chinese countryside. I thank also colleagues in the Department of Anthropology at Sun Yat-Sen University, including the late Huang Shuping, Ma Guoqing (now at Minzu University of China), Wang Jianxin (now at Northwest Minzu University), and Zhang Wenyi. In Nanjing, I benefited greatly from conversations with colleagues at the Institute for Social Anthropology at Nanjing University, including Fan Ke, Shao Jing, Yang Der-Ruey, Yang Yudong, Chu Jianfang, Qiu Yue, and Chris K. K. Tan. Many thanks also to Cheng Baiqing, dean of the School of Social and Behavioral Sciences at Nanjing University, for his support and hospitality. Special thanks are due to my *shixiong* Yang Der-Ruey for his unfailing support and encouragement over the years.

Outside China, I am very grateful to Charles Stafford for his careful reading and insightful suggestions on an earlier draft of the manuscript. His work has been a major source of inspiration, and I thank him also for writing the foreword of the book. Steve Harrell read an earlier draft of the manuscript with lightning speed. His suggestions got me thinking about the right questions and helped me sharpen my arguments. I owe a great deal to him. I also owe a great deal to Francesca Bray and Andy Kipnis for their constant encouragement over the years and for critical suggestions on the various chapters of this book. Michael Herzfeld has made decisive comments on parts of this book, and our conversations on the importance of spoken language during fieldwork were truly inspiring. Suzanne Gottschang and Jacob Eyferth have been intellectual companions on many levels and I owe a great deal to them. I also owe a great deal to Zhang Jun for her critical comments, her intellectual generosity, and her unstinting encouragement. This book bears the imprint of our conversations and shared projects.

Many other people left their mark in this book through conversations, joint projects, or simply comments on ethnographic materials. I list them alphabetically, though they were all equally important to the writing of this book: Erdmute Alber, Reijiro Aoyama, Rita Astuti, Maurice Bloch, Joseph Bosco, Samuël Coghe, Nélia Dias, Henrike Donner, Aurora Donzelli, Jeanette Edwards, Harriet Evans, Sandra Feio, Stephan Feuchtwang, Mareile Flitsch, Mats Fridlund, Echi Gabbert, Johanna Gonçalves, Paolo Gruppuso, Saheira Haliel, Chris Hann, Beckie Hsu, Bill Jankowiak, Kang Yi, Florian Knothe, Gray Kochhar-Lindgren, Kuah Khun Eng, Maikel Kuijpers, Teresa Kuan, Patrice Ladwig, James Laidlaw, Ling Minhua, Liu Shao-hua, Loretta Lou, Richard Madsen, Susan McKinnon, Fazil Moradi, Cristina Padez, Nuno Porto, Luís Quintais, Ricardo Ventura Santos, Ramon Sarró, Dagmar Schäffer, Martina Schlünder, Naubahar Sharif, Chiaki Shirai, Carlos Steil, Tatjana Thelen, Christina Toren, Azumi Tsuge, Cláudia Umbelino, Miguel Vale de Almeida, Susana Viegas, Wang Ruijing, Rubie Watson, Wu Xiujie, Yan Yunxiang, Karen Zachmann, and many other colleagues not mentioned here, including all the members of the Sci-Tech Asia transnational research network. There are also a few former and current graduate students whose work has left a strong impression. I list them alphabetically but I have learned a great deal from them equally: Rao Yichen, Tian Jingyi, James Wright, Jack L. Xing, and Zhong Yishan and, more recently, Raoni Arraes, Bruna Coelho, Marianne Faulstich, Ernst Loreto, and Simona-Eugenia Lenghel.

At the University of Washington Press, I was very fortunate to work with Lorri Hagman and her editorial team. I would like to thank Lorri in particular for her detailed comments on the manuscript and for her insistence on getting rid of metadiscourse and cutting down unnecessary jargon. I would also like to thank the press's readers. I have since learned their identities—James L. Watson and Ellen Oxfeld—and I could not have asked for better as they are the very best! I am very grateful for their detailed comments and critical suggestions, as well as for their encouragement to expand on the major theoretical contributions of the book. Finally, I would like to thank copyeditor Kris Fulsaas for providing incredibly detailed feedback and helping improve the clarity of the manuscript and the press's production team for their graphic input and for preparing the book cover. Many thanks to Grayscale in Hong Kong for creating the maps and figures included in this book, and many thanks also to Edelweiss in Hong Kong for her creative input and support.

Last but not least, I would like to thank my family. I dedicate this book to my parents, paternal grandparents, and maternal grandmother because they taught me a great deal about building families across borders. To my wife, Julia, it is hard to find words to express my appreciation for your being there. This book owes a great deal to her constant reminders of the need to seek simplicity and clarity and her challenging comments on many different versions of the manuscript. Our two young children, Frieda and Fabiana, taught me a great deal about the power of storytelling, and they have been incredibly understanding of my long hours of absence. I hope they will one day read the stories I tell in this book.

Parts of chapter 2 appeared in an article in *Modern Asian Studies* in a special issue on "Love, Marriage, and Intimate Citizenship in Contemporary China and India" edited by Henrike Donner and myself. Parts of chapter 3 appeared in an article in *Technology and Culture* in a special section on the history of childbirth medicalization in China and Japan edited by Suzanne Gottschang and myself. A modified version of chapter 4 appeared in the volume *Transforming Patriarchy: Chinese Families in the Twenty-First Century*, edited by myself and Stevan Harrell and published by the University of Washington Press. Parts of chapter 5 appeared in the volume *Anthropology and Civilizational Analysis: Eurasian Explorations*, edited by Johann Arnason and Chris Hann and published by the State University of New York Press. Finally, a shorter version of chapter 6 appeared in the volume *Ordinary Ethics in China*, edited by Charles Stafford and published by Bloomsbury as part of the series LSE Monographs on Social Anthropology.

LANGUAGE AND ORTHOGRAPHY

Language is a very important part of people's efforts to build connected lives, and in my research I was particularly attentive to questions of language. The official language of the People's Republic of China (PRC), Putonghua (standard Chinese, abbreviated throughout as SC), is largely based on Mandarin, a variety of Chinese that was once largely circumscribed to northern and southwestern China. Standard Chinese is the language used in the educational system, and the numbers of its speakers have increased significantly in the last four decades under increasingly far-reaching policies of educational and linguistic standardization, among other factors. But there are other spoken varieties of Chinese that are usually described as regional dialects (SC: *fangyan*), and these dialects are particularly developed in the region of South China. In Guangdong, the most popular regional dialect is Yue Chinese (aka Cantonese, abbreviated as C throughout), and the members of the village community described in this book are native speakers of a local rural subvariety of this Cantonese dialect group.

Using the term "dialect" to refer to the Yue Chinese language family may create the impression that the differences between Cantonese and Putonghua are minor. However, these two varieties of Chinese are mutually unintelligible and display differences in vocabulary, pronunciation, and grammar that are comparable to the differences between Romance languages like French and Italian. To make things more complicated, the Yue Chinese language family is itself very diverse, so there are multiple subvarieties of Yue Chinese. The most popular prestige variety of Yue Chinese is spoken in the city of Guangzhou, the capital of Guangdong, and in the Special Administrative Regions of Hong Kong and Macau. Most of the people whose lives are described in this book can understand the prestige variety of Yue Chinese, but their mother tongue is a local northern Guangdong subvariety of Yue Chinese that is not entirely intelligible to native speakers of the prestige variety of Yue Chinese who have not been exposed to it before.

This means that Yellow Flower natives are living in a linguistic environment of significant complexity. In the last two decades in particular, they have become increasingly proficient in standard Chinese through schooling, media consumption, tourism, and labor migration, and they increasingly use it in interactions with nonlocals both at home and in the city. At the same time, they continue to cultivate their knowledge of the prestige variety of Yue Chinese through engagement with the regional media industry and interaction with speakers of the prestige variety of Yue Chinese both at home and in the Pearl River Delta region. And on top of this, they continue to use Yellow Flower dialect in their daily-life interactions with relatives and members of their village and native-place networks.

If we add reading and writing to this mix, things get even more complicated. Most people in Yellow Flower are able to use Yue pronunciation (with sounds close to the prestige Guangzhou variety) to read and write standard Chinese texts. This practice of learning standard Chinese with Yue pronunciation was already in place before the establishment of the People's Republic of China in 1949, and it remained prominent locally up until the 1980s and 1990s. Since then, there has been an increasing emphasis in local primary schools on the importance of using standard Chinese pronunciation, but the tradition of teaching also the prestige Yue pronunciation remains alive.

Most Chinese words cited in the main body of the text refer to the local subvariety of Yue and are marked C for Cantonese. While there is a well-established tradition of writing texts in vernacular Yue of the prestige variety, no such tradition has evolved with respect to nonprestige local subvarieties of Yue. This poses challenges in terms of linking spoken words to specific Chinese characters and in terms of transcribing local Yue pronunciation. To transcribe local Yue words, I use the Yale System of Romanization of Cantonese without indicating the tonal accentuation. I do not indicate the tonal accentuation with diacritics and the insertion of the letter *h* because this makes words easier to pronounce by readers who are not familiar with Yale Romanization of Cantonese. A glossary at the end of the book lists all Chinese words cited in the text and their respective Chinese characters and English meanings. Chinese words cited in the text with standard Chinese (SC) pronunciation are transliterated in the standard pinyin system to transcribe these words.

A Note on the Simplified Yale Romanization System for Cantonese

Like other varieties of Chinese, Cantonese is a tonal language. This means that the relative pitch at which a syllable is pronounced plays a central role in distinguishing one word from another. Some linguists argue that the Cantonese language has seven tones and in some cases even nine or ten tones, but most current analyses assume six basic tones. Cantonese Yale represents these six basic tones using a combination of diacritics and the insertion of the letter *h* for the three lower tones (table L.1). My usage of Cantonese Yale has removed all references to tones, including the diacritics and the letter *h*. This means, for example, that instead of transcribing 你好 as *néih hóu*, it is transliterated *nei hou*.

TABLE L.1. Cantonese Tones

NO.	DESCRIPTION	YALE REPRESENTATION	
		Written	**Spoken**
1	high-flat	sī	sīn
	high-falling	sì	sìn
2	mid-rising	sí	sín
3	mid-flat	si	sin
4	low-falling	sìh	sìhn
5	low-rising	síh	síhn
6	low-flat	sih	sihn

NAMING CONVENTIONS

Throughout this book, pseudonyms and fictional names mask the exact identity and location of places, persons, and ancestors in Yellow Flower. The practice is common in anthropology and is informed by concerns with the safety and the privacy of research interlocutors.

For names of places (listed below), I coined English fictional names that are easy to remember and that retain some of the meanings, metaphors, and semantic connotations of the original Chinese names. For names of living persons, ancestors, and historical actors (listed below), I adopted the following conventions. All local surnames were transliterated from the local Yue Chinese pronunciation using the Yale System of Romanization for Cantonese with the provisions indicated in this volume's section on Language and Orthography. Names of local ancestors are Yue pseudonyms transcribed in the Yale System. For names of living persons, I sometimes use (1) a naming convention similar to the one used for the names of places, (2) Yue Chinese pseudonyms transcribed in the Yale System (e.g., A-Fai), or (3) common English given names (e.g., Candy) to facilitate the anglophone reading.

Dramatis Loci

Barrier Pond village
Big Bay township
Brightpath market town (former name of Yellow Flower market town)
Brightpath township (former name of Yellow Flower township)
Dragonpath township

Harmony Cave village
Inner Area of Harmony Cave village; also called “upper area”
New House village
Outer Area of Harmony Cave village; also called “lower area”
Red Bamboo village
Sand Island village
Sand Spine hamlet, Harmony Cave village
Seui-fong hamlet, Harmony Cave village
Seui-daat hamlet, Harmony Cave village
Temple of the Old Woman Lam
Three Mountains brigade, rural administrative area
Three Mountains village
Yellow Flower market town
Yellow Flower township

Dramatis Personae

Ancestors (in chronological sequence from oldest to youngest and including place of residence)

Yeung-mun—ancestor of Faat-bou
Faat-bou—apical ancestor of Harmony Cave village
Seui-fong—elder son of Faat-bou; ancestral head of Harmony First, Second, and Third (groups within Harmony Cave village)
Geui-long—elder son of Seui-fong
Geui-hang—younger son of Seui-fong
Maan-luk—eldest son of Geui-long; ancestral head of some families of Harmony Third
Maan-gwai—second son of Geui-long; ancestral head of Harmony Second
Maan-hin—youngest son of Geui-long; ancestral head of Harmony First and some families of Harmony Third
Seui-daat—younger son of Faat-bou; ancestral head of Harmony Fourth and Fifth
Long-cheung—eldest son of Seui-daat, ancestral head of Harmony Fourth

Yin-cheung—second son of Seui-daat, ancestral head of Harmony Fourth

Jung-cheung—youngest son of Seui-daat, ancestral head of Harmony Fifth

Living Persons (including relationships)

A-Fai (Candy's husband)—Harmony First
A-Gaam
A-Hang—Harmony First
Bright Gold (Full Elder Sister's husband)—Harmony First
Bright Image
Bright Moral
Buddha Cassia (Sister Spring's husband)
Candy (A-Fai's wife)—Harmony First
Cassia Forest (and wife)
Fortune Big (Bright Gold's close village brother)
Fortune Country (and wife)
Fortune Hero (and wife)
Full Elder Sister (Bright Gold's wife)—Harmony First
Lotus Flower
Mou-dai
Palm Sister
Sister Spring (Buddha Cassia's wife)
Sister Dawn
Splendid Omen
Third Sister

Historical Actors

Mr. Leung (a Nationalist guerrilla in Northern Guangdong in the 1940s)

CHINESE VILLAGE LIFE TODAY

Introduction

Building Families in an Age of Transition

THERE IS HARDLY ANY ASPECT OF FAMILY LIFE IN RURAL CHINA, from marriage and family planning to childbirth and child rearing, from bodily hygiene to public sanitation and moral education, that has not been subject to forces of technocratic modernization, and the reach of these forces was significantly expanded after the beginning of Reform and Opening in the late 1970s. Given the increasing trend toward the specialization of knowledge in the human sciences, there has been a strong trend to analyze separately transformations such as the impacts of scientific population governance on marriage and family planning, of high-tech medicalization on women's experiences of pregnancy and childbirth, and of intensive parenting ideologies on ideals and practices of child rearing. But these transformations are not disconnected and should be considered in conjunction, in order to highlight an important shift that started to become more visible in the last decades of the twentieth century: the increasing power of technoscience and technocratic expertise in the governance of almost every aspect of everyday life.[1]

This shift is particularly striking in China, given its remarkable journey from a poor developing country in the late 1970s to an economic superpower with leading technoscientific institutions in the twenty-first century, but the shift also reflects larger developments in different parts of the world under the impact of globalization and neoliberal capitalism.[2] This global transformation takes different forms in different contexts, but wherever it unfolds it can be identified by looking at the increasing presence of technoscience and technocratic expertise in the conduct of even the most mundane aspects of everyday life. If there were any doubts regarding the significance of this global transformation, the emergence of a deadly coronavirus global pandemic in the beginning of 2020 has dissipated these doubts: the pandemic made it clear that the world today is not just a world of unprecedented environmental uncertainties (Beck 2009, 2016; Moore 2016; Hornborg 2019; Tsing 2017; Tsing et al. 2020), it is also a world of unprecedented technocratic interventions in the governance of everyday life.

In April 2020, a few weeks after the World Health Organization (WHO) elevated the coronavirus outbreak that emerged in the Chinese city of Wuhan to the status of a new global pandemic, half of the world's population was under some form of mass lockdown imposed and/or recommended by national governments under the advice of WHO. This worldwide trend toward technocratic measures of mass confinement affected the daily lives of individuals and families around the world, and most accounts of the phenomenon have focused on the agency of macro-level actors such as national governments, expert institutions and forms of knowledge, and international organizations like WHO.

In contrast, this book adopts a bottom-up approach to consider the situated effects of similarly far-reaching technocratic interventions. This approach gives analytical priority to the situated perspectives of ordinary citizens and communities as they are subject to powerful macro-level interventions over which they have little control. People are not just passive recipients of macro-level forces of technocratic governance; they play an active role in engaging with these forces. This engagement does not take place in a vacuum but is shaped by complex collective negotiations—what I call "intimate choices"—that necessarily entail struggles and disagreements. These frictions are part of the process through which the materials and values of larger technocratic forces of governance are translated into context-specific frameworks of practice, affect, and meaning. Making sense of these processes of translation should be a priority for anthropologists and social scientists in a world in which the tension between the desire to solve problems and improve society through large-scale technocratic interventions and the desire to reclaim technocratic governance for society is an increasingly important source of social and cultural clashes.

A Twenty-First-Century Story of Intimate Choices

On the morning of May Day 2015, a longtime village friend living in Guangzhou for most of the year sent me a message on QQ (a popular instant messaging service in China) asking whether I could help his wife arrange a medical checkup in Hong Kong, where I was based at the time. I had originally met A-Fai in July 1999 during my first long-term fieldwork in his natal village, Harmony Cave. He was still a teenager back in 1999, and we stayed in close touch over the years. That morning in 2015, A-Fai revealed the big news that his wife, Candy, was eight weeks pregnant with their second child. Their first child, a beautiful baby girl, had been born ten years earlier in the township clinic in Yellow Flower, and I knew that they had been planning for quite some time to have a second.

Rural townships like Yellow Flower were never really subject to the draconian one-child-per-couple restriction of the Birth Planning Policy (SC: Jihua Shengyu Zhengce) as it was implemented in urban areas and some rural areas (Harrel et al. 2011), so A-Fai and Candy were not trying to take advantage of the new Two-Child Policy framework to be launched in 2016 in major cities like Guangzhou. Back in 2015, most couples in Yellow Flower continued to have at least two to three children, and the local Birth Planning Policy regulations allowed families to have even more children if they still did not have a male child. This means that A-Fai and Candy's plan to have a second child in 2016 had nothing to do with a sudden loosening of the local Birth Planning Policy; rather, it was about timing and family considerations. Candy had been asked to wear a surgically implanted intrauterine device (IUD) after the birth of their first child (a baby girl), but instead of removing the device after the mandatory minimum period of four years, the couple decided to keep it in place as they waited for the right time to have a second child. That time eventually arrived in 2014–15, but they disagreed on the question of the gender of this second child. Candy did not care about the gender, but A-Fai faced pressure from his natal patrilineal family (parents and elder brother) and from relatives and friends in Yellow Flower to have a male heir.

Like many other couples around the world, Candy and A-Fai faced a choice regarding their family life. This choice had to be negotiated in the context of a larger set of intimate ties and relations of interdependence, and these negotiations were themselves shaped by a wider moral and cultural landscape developed under larger forces of technocratic reconfiguration of family life in China's Reform era (beginning in the late 1970s): the Birth Planning Policy and related social movements.

When the Birth Planning Policy was first launched in 1979, the idea was to use civilizing technocratic power to enforce a new, more globally attuned, normative standard of family planning in society: one that required all couples in China to have fewer children, ideally not more than one child. This agenda was successfully enforced with varying degrees of success in most parts of China, but not without many tensions and contradictions and not without a number of unintended side effects. One of the most important of these side effects is that the stringent fertility requirements of the Birth Planning Policy contributed to reinforcing the traditional ideal of son preference (Y. Cai 2013). Under this highly restrictive policy of birth control, many Chinese families worried about not being able to have a son to carry on the family line, and many turned to historical practices such as infanticide, daughter abandonment, and giving daughters away for informal adoption to realize traditional ideals of son preference. Many also turned to newly introduced ultrasound technologies of prenatal sex screening that were used together with sex-selective procedures of abortion (Connelly 2008, 356–57; K. Johnson 2004, 2016; M. Fong 2016).

These developments help explain the rise of male-skewed sex ratios at birth from the early 1980s onward, a phenomenon that continued well into the twenty-first century despite official efforts to ban the usage of all technologies of prenatal sex selection (Attané 2012; Greenhalgh 2013; M. Fong 2016). According to official statistics, the national sex ratio at birth (SRB) grew from 109 males per 100 females in 1982 (just slightly over the average human sex ratio without selection of 103–107 males per 100 females) to numbers close to 120 males per 100 females between 2000 and 2010,[3] with Guangdong being one of the nine provinces with a SRB well above 120.[4] Since 2010, there was a gradual drop in the national SRB (Q. Jiang et al. 2017; L. Shi 2017a, 2017b), but it is clear that son preference remains culturally salient among the dominant Han ethnic majority in many parts of the country, despite the fact that since the 1990s the government has increasingly attempted to eradicate son preference and to promote son-daughter equality in family planning.

The story of A-Fai and Candy illustrates the linkages between micro-level negotiations of family planning and the complexities of macro-level agendas of technocratic reconfiguration of family life in a world that is increasingly shaped by global developments in technoscience. When A-Fai contacted me via QQ, he said he and his wife wanted a prenatal sex-screening test in Hong Kong, where the regulatory environment is more permissive (X. Liu 2017). In Mainland China, prenatal screening tests are subject to very strict regulations because doctors are not allowed to reveal the sex of the fetus, and prenatal sex screening has been illegal since the late 1980s. There is of course an underground market of prenatal sex-screening tests, but there are risks associated with these illegal services. Ultrasound technologies of prenatal sex screening are still being used today, but since the 1990s, a new generation of genetic tests emerged that can be performed with high rates of reliability from very early on in the pregnancy. The Chinese government has tried to restrict access to these genetic technologies,[5] but these restrictions are not entirely effective, and couples with resources can always order a genetic test from labs overseas or go to places like Hong Kong for testing. A-Fai wanted to take his wife to Hong Kong to do a fetal DNA analysis of her blood in order to screen the sex of the fetus. He told me that this test was very safe and could be done with a high degree of accuracy from as early as the tenth week of pregnancy, much earlier than conventional ultrasound procedures. Candy agreed with A-Fai that fetal DNA analysis was better than other methods, but she resisted testing because she opposed son preference and sex-selective abortion.

A-Fai was more influenced by the local custom of son preference, in large part because unlike Candy (who comes from Sichuan and is not fluent in the local Cantonese dialect), A-Fai is a native of Yellow Flower and is more directly exposed to pressure from immediate family, village relatives, and friends. This pressure made me think that Candy and A-Fai would ultimately be sensitive to arguments in favor of son preference because their official residence is in Yellow Flower and their vital networks of support are also there. A few days later, however, A-Fai reported that they would not go to Hong Kong because Candy felt unwell and her doctor said that traveling could increase her chances of a miscarriage. This development led A-Fai and Candy to abandon the idea of genetic testing, but this decision was made in close consultation with members of A-Fai's natal family.

Differences of opinion led to heated moral clashes, but a compromise solution was reached. Candy got what she wanted (no genetic test) but agreed to have a third child if the second baby was another girl. This "third child" solution was possible because A-Fai and Candy are officially registered in Yellow Flower and the local birth planning restrictions are not as stringent as in big cities. Candy was happy that she no longer had to think about the possibility of undergoing a sex-selective abortion, but she did not want to have a third child. She told me, however, that having a male heir is important in places like Yellow Flower, so she was ready to accommodate and sacrifice herself for the good of her conjugal family and the good of their (A-Fai's) patrilineal family.

Candy and A-Fai's decision to have a second child without using advanced technologies of prenatal sex selection was an intimate choice that involved complex moral negotiations between multiple actors. These negotiations took place in a particular context of relations of interdependence and under the influence of a larger agenda of technocratic reconfiguration of everyday practices of family planning. At the global level, expert recommendations on family planning from the 1990s onward have favored a critique of traditional ideals of son preference and related practices of prenatal sex selection, and major international organizations like the United Nations have pushed for the implementation of worldwide development programs and campaigns promoting gender equality and son-daughter equality (Bhatia 2018).

This was also the direction favored by the Chinese government (Greenhalgh 2003, 2008, 2013). In the 1990s the government launched a number of nationwide campaigns aimed at eradicating the custom of son preference, and these efforts were intensified after 2003 with the launching of a massive national campaign—Caring for Girls—sponsored by the United Nations. Candy and A-Fai were exposed to these official ideologies during their schooling years and more generally through consumption of state-controlled national and regional mass media in its various forms, but they were also exposed to more traditional ideologies of son preference, both in the context of everyday life interactions and increasingly via social media platforms. These ideologies are particularly salient in Yellow Flower due to the continuing power of lineage village structures and related ritualized practices of patrilineal ancestor worship, patrilineal inheritance, and patrilocal marriage. The ideal of son preference, however, is not confined to such rural townships and should not be seen as a remnant of "backward" traditions opposed by larger liberating forces of technoscience and modernity. Han

Chinese couples all over China have used various kinds of modern prenatal sex-screening technologies—including high-tech genetic testing—to realize the ideal of having at least one male heir, and these stories circulate widely in personal interactions and via social media. These stories reveal the existence of powerful moral forces in society that are very different from official state propaganda and that highlight the existence of a much more complex and conflictive picture of the larger moral landscape of family planning shaping the lives of ordinary people.

This moral complexity raises a number of important questions regarding the relation between micro-level choices and macro-level civilizing forces. The larger moral and cultural environment shaping the decisions of couples like Candy and A-Fai is not unified but is informed by tensions and divisions. China is a highly regimented society with an authoritarian government capable of enforcing truly draconian policies of social engineering affecting all aspects of the fabric of family life, but it is also a globalized plural society with multiple value systems that are often contradictory and cannot be captured by simplistic dichotomies opposing tradition to modernity or religion to technoscience. Rather than assuming that the larger moral landscape in China is unified and homogeneous due to the powerful social engineering efforts of the Chinese state, it is more accurate and analytically more productive to recognize that there are significant moral tensions and divisions in the larger society because people are now able to invoke a whole range of different "warring gods" to justify their everyday life decisions. These tensions and divisions are an important feature of the theories of modernity of classic social theorists such as Max Weber and Karl Marx, but as observed by sociologist Richard Madsen (2020) in an illuminating essay on "culture wars" in China and North America, such tensions and divisions have become particularly acute in contemporary globalized societies due to ongoing processes of cultural polarization, rising social inequalities, and increasing environmental uncertainties.

It is this reality of increasing moral divisions and tensions that makes the question of choice particularly important and pressing. Ordinary couples around the world are constantly being confronted with complex dilemmas regarding their family life, but it is not clear how they make their choices and how these choices are shaped by a preexisting "space of possibles" (Bourdieu 1993, 64; 1980, 107–8) or a preexisting "framework of choice" (Sleeboom-Faulkner 2010, 12–13). In the case of Candy and A-Fai, it is not clear how their choice was shaped by the existence of a strong state-driven civilizing agenda of technocratic reconfiguration of the practice of family planning. Candy and A-Fai ended up making a choice that was partly aligned with the state-sponsored civilizing agenda of family planning and son-daughter equality, but how did they make this choice? The central state has enforced a number of punitive measures to ban and outlaw the usage of technologies of prenatal sex selection, but these punitive measures do not prevent couples from resorting to underground or cross-border market opportunities for testing. It is possible that Candy and A-Fai chose not to engage with prenatal sex-selection technologies because they were exposed to official propaganda against son preference. However, A-Fai and Candy were not in agreement with one another, and theirs was not an individual choice. They have the financial means to make an independent decision as reproductive consumers or to reaffirm their sense of autonomy as a couple that is part of a larger patrilineal family collective. But they told me that such decisions are too important to be done in isolation. This led them to consult the views of their (A-Fai's) patrilineal family collective, and this consultation resulted in a complex process of negotiation that involved significant moral frictions between themselves and A-Fai's parents.

Such intimate moral frictions play a central role in mediating micro-level forms of engagement with larger macro-level civilizing forces of technocratic reconfiguration of the fabric of family life. Consideration of intimate choices moves beyond two equally extreme analytical positions in the social sciences. The first is the idea that macro-level forces and actors determine everyday life decisions by means of larger structures of subjectification and social control. This view is particularly strong when thinking about societies with authoritarian governments as in China, where the state is well known for its capacity to enforce far-reaching, coercive technocratic interventions in society. However, even the most coercive macro-level intervention in society has to be mediated by complex moral negotiations at the micro level. It is by looking at this work of micro-macro mediation that we can discern how top-down forces are translated into locally meaningful frameworks and assemblages of family life.

The second extreme analytical position is the idea that in contemporary societies, important decisions like the one made by Candy and A-Fai are increasingly a matter of individual choice because of the impact of larger macro-structural processes of privatization, mass consumerism, and more generally the growth of individualism. As consumers of reproductive technologies, ordinary couples like Candy and A-Fai are increasingly "interpellated" (Althusser 1971) to make individual choices and to develop their own moral narratives around these choices, but this idiom of individual choice does not provide an adequate model to capture the complex processes of negotiation involved in important decisions regarding matters of reproduction and family life. Consideration of intimate choices takes into account the increasing centrality of questions of individual agency in contemporary societies, while showing how moral collectives, social obligations, and networks of social support continue to play an important role in decision-making processes.

Beyond Individualization

The individualization paradigm grew out of a larger movement in the social sciences questioning the classic tendency to favor structural forces over individual agency. This critique is very useful but it has also contributed to reinforcing a master narrative of social transformation that shows little awareness of the limits of universalizing ideologies of individual autonomy and self-realization. This narrative goes back to the writings of classic social theorists who analyzed the rise of industrial modernity as a moment of historical rupture that opened the way for the rise of affective individualism and the decline of traditional patriarchal family and community structures.[6] This emphasis on the liberating individualizing effects of modernity has continued to inform the writings of mid-twentieth-century structural-functionalists and modernization theorists like Talcott Parsons and William Goode, and it eventually found its way into the writings of a more recent wave of theorists of individualization.

Writing about the transformation of intimate life at the turn of the millennium, Anthony Giddens (1991, 1999) and Ulrich Beck (1992; Beck and Beck-Gernsheim 1995, 2002, 2013) argued that processes of neoliberal restructuring and globalization from the 1980s onward have led to the growth of affective individualism and to the decline of conventional mid-twentieth-century heteronormative family models based on rigid roles and obligations.[7] This theory of individualization in late modernity was meant to reflect the post-1980s weakening of the conventional nuclear family in Euro-American societies, but the model has proved useful to raise questions about changes in different parts of the world. While anthropologists and historians questioned the excessive emphasis on individual agency and argued that there are significant variations in global patterns of family and social transformation,[8] supporters of the individualization thesis continued to hold on to the master narrative of a converging worldwide process of structural disembedding that encourages individuals to challenge rigid "traditional" expectations and take more control of their own biographical trajectories.

This emphasis on individualization was very influential in studies of family and intimate life in Reform-era China and inspired a powerful critique of earlier research agendas that were too centered on Orientalist notions of Chinese and Asian collectivism. The work of anthropologist Yunxiang Yan entitled *Private Life under Socialism* (2003) was particularly influential (see also Y. Yan 2009b, 2010, 2013a, 2013b, 2015b, 2016). Yan's book is concerned with the rise of the individual as a central social category in rural family and community life, linking this transformation to larger macro-structural forces of individualization under China's compressed modernity. Tracing the beginning of this macro-level dynamic of individualization to the May Fourth movement and the progressive reformist ideals that emerged during the first decades of the twentieth century,[9] the book draws particular attention to the highly compressed changes that occurred under socialism and above all during the first two decades of the Reform period, covering important topics such as the growth of individualistic values, the decline of rigid family hierarchies and extended family ties, the collapse of collectivist ideologies, the rise of smaller child-centered families, and the emergence of new forms of intergenerational solidarity.

Since the publication of Yan's monograph in 2003, the focus on issues of individualization has become popular, extending to studies of Chinese urban society, sexuality, education, mass consumption, migration, religion, moral change, and digital communication.[10] This research on individualization has highlighted the increasing importance of idioms of individual agency and personal autonomy in contemporary China, but it has also overstated the extent to which individuals have become detached from larger moral expectations, social obligations, power relations, and cultural traditions (Harrell and Santos 2017; Santos and Harrell 2019).[11] Yan has tried to address this point by drawing attention to the specificities of the Chinese path of individualization, noting that under compressed modernity the individual has been pushed by the combined force of the market and the state to bear more responsibilities and be more competitive but has failed to gain true autonomy because China lacks a strong cultural tradition of individualism and does not have in place the necessary legal and political provisions to nourish a sense of individual autonomy (Y. Yan 2010, 2015a, 2015b, 2016, 2017, 2018). Yan's point that this is individualization without true individualism helps us understand the increasing influence of state-centric neofamilist ideologies of social responsibility under Xi Jinping in what seems to represent a complete reversal of the progressive ideals launched by the May Fourth movement in the first decades of the twentieth century.

Recent literature on family, marriage, and sexuality in contemporary China has tried to address some of these tensions in order to move the discussion forward. Deborah Davis and Sara Friedman's introduction to *Wives, Husbands, and Lovers* (2014) suggests that the rather rigid norms that have long governed the heteronormative institution of marriage are being replaced by new values of personal fulfillment that allow for much greater individual variation. This focus on processes of marital deinstitutionalization echoes the general orientation of the individualization thesis, but Davis and Friedman assert that the "traditional" concept of the multigenerational (patrilineal) family is not being deinstitutionalized to anywhere near the same degree. This qualification is insightful, but the resulting model is still too simple to make sense of the great variety of marital and intergenerational relations in contemporary China.

In the introduction to *Transforming Patriarchy* (Santos and Harrell 2017), Stevan Harrell and myself propose a more nuanced, ethnographically grounded model capable of making sense of China's diverse landscape of family forms and intimate transformations. In some respects, there has indeed been a dramatic weakening of institutional structures, but in other respects, earlier patriarchal norms and procedures—virilocal marriage (in which the woman moves into the community of the husband's natal family), women's responsibility for housework, patricentric kin terms—seem to prevail, even if in a slightly modified form. Still other developments present themselves as moral tensions: the decline of son preference and the increasing emphasis on the value of daughters stand in contradiction to the emergence of increasingly male-biased sex ratios at birth,[12] and the rise of a more individualistic culture of dating, marital choice, and divorce goes hand in hand with the continuing ability of the elder generation to influence their children's heteronormative marital trajectories as well as their divorce experiences.[13]

Analyzing this moral double bind requires moving beyond the "iron cage" of master narratives of individualization. If the strength of the individualization paradigm lies in its attention to everyday life practices and questions of individual agency, its weakness lies in the rather one-sided assumption that modernity entails a macro-structural process of disembedding of individuals from the constraining authority of larger collectives, institutions, and traditions. This master narrative fits well with the general orientation of Euro-American cultural discourses of liberal individualism and with global consumerist ideologies of individual choice, but it is not very helpful for capturing the moral tensions and divisions experienced by individuals and communities around the world under the impact of larger forces of technocratic modernization and globalization.

One way to make sense of these moral tensions is to engage with theoretical approaches in the humanities and social sciences that conceptualize modernity as a process of normative reconfiguration of society that is contentious and conflictive by definition and thus involves complex negotiations between multiple actors. These negotiations can be studied at both the macro level, in the context of larger national and transnational exchanges and formations of power, and at the micro level in the context of everyday life interactions in specific contexts. Examination of intimate choices combines the micro and macro levels of analysis. Instead of assuming that the family life of ordinary rural couples like A-Fai and Candy is ultimately determined by the workings of larger macro-level forces of change, an examination of their choices shows how the impact of macro-level forces is mediated by micro-level negotiations taking place in the context of specific communities and networks of relations.

The Technocratic Governmentality Paradigm

Technoscience and technocratic expertise are increasingly central in the governance of everyday life in contemporary societies. The extent of this phenomenon was recently underlined during the global COVID-19 pandemic when a significant proportion of the world's population was placed under extreme forms of quarantine and social distance epidemic management that not only posed significant restrictions on the conduct of everyday life activities but also empowered individuals, families, and other civil-society actors to engage in new moral projects of self-formation and self-fashioning. The COVID-19 pandemic opened the way for the production of new kinds of subjects, and this process of subject-making or of "subjectivation" (Foucault cited in Laidlaw 2014, 101–8) is not simply a matter of becoming a subject through subjugation to certain powerful forces—it is also a matter of becoming a subject through active processes of reflective self-formation. Making sense of these two dimensions of processes of subjectivation requires the development of a more decentered, pluralistic understanding of how technocratic power and governance work in contemporary societies. This approach is associated with a large body of literature that one might call the technocratic governmentality paradigm and that was largely inspired by the work of French philosopher and historian of ideas Michel Foucault (1977, 1978, 1979, 1988, 1991, 2009).

Foucault's basic insight was to make the case that the development of modern forms of governance in Europe from the eighteenth century onward were shaped by the increasing salience of a type of governing rationality, "governmentality," which is concerned primarily with shaping the conduct of the larger population and promoting its improvement and optimization by means of numerous technocratic interventions with diverse and, quite often, unpredicted effects. One of the major points of Foucault's research on governmentality was to question conventional repressive and state-centric visions of modern government and to replace these visions with a more pluralistic model of governance in which the work of governing the life of the population is not just performed by state institutions and agencies but involves a whole ensemble of quasi-state and nonstate authoritative discourses and institutions based on the power of science, technology, medicine, and other forms of expert knowledge. These governing rationalities and technologies have repressive and disciplinary elements, but they also include more positive elements of individual and collective self-cultivation. They target all aspects of the fabric of everyday life including health care, welfare, education, social work, criminality, spirituality, and so on, and their governing effects are complemented by the actions of citizens and other actors in civil society who are themselves turned into active participants in the process of technocratic government.

This more pluralistic non-state-centric conception of technocratic power has inspired a whole tradition of post-Foucaultian studies of governmentality in anthropology and related disciplines. By and large, these studies have come to be dominated by studies of neoliberal governmentality focusing on the logic of technocratic government under increasing forces of privatization and destatization, devolution of risk onto the "enterprise" or the individual (now construed as the entrepreneur), and "responsibilization" of individuals who are increasingly "empowered" to govern their economic, social, and personal selves or else increasingly punished for not being able to govern themselves properly.[14]

The case of China has proved particularly challenging for students of neoliberal governmentality because its engagement with the global neoliberal order in the last four decades has taken place under the management of an authoritarian Communist Party regime that shows no signs of weakening its control of the economy and its stranglehold over civil society. Like many developing countries, China has benefited from the technical and financial support of the global aid industry, but this engagement did not come at the expense of the authority of the central state; it only helped reinforce the state's vertical spatialization. To give just one example, without the support provided by WHO and the UN, the Chinese Communist Party (CCP) would never have been able to build the vast "biobureaucracy" (Kohrman 2005) that was required to enforce the Birth Planning Policy from the late 1970s onward, and this biobureaucracy was only a pre-digitech precursor of the mass surveillance state system that is now emerging with the support of digital technologies that could not have been developed without international aid and foreign support.

The continuing authoritarian nature of the Chinese state poses an important dilemma to neoliberal governmentality scholars: is the fabric of everyday life in China still largely governed by a strong element of state coercion, surveillance, and repression, or are there signs that post-Mao China has embraced a more pluralistic model of technocratic governance that is increasingly concerned with "empowering" individuals and communities to become more active agents of governance? The work of anthropologist Susan Greenhalgh (2008, 2010, 2020; Greenhalgh and Winckler 2005) remains central in this debate. Writing about international mainstream media discourses on the Birth Planning Policy, Greenhalgh (2010, 8–9) criticizes the "cold war era coercion story," a master narrative that assumes that state coercion is the single most important factor behind China's population politics. Greenhalgh (1988, 1994) does not deny the importance of state coercion and official repression, but she argues that the conventional state-coercion narrative fails to acknowledge an important political shift from a Maoist mobilizational and Stalinist bureaucratic framework of population control to a series of comprehensive reforms from the 1990s onward that favored the emergence of more indirect techniques of governance based on the market, technology, and the legal system, as well as on communities, families, and individuals themselves (Greenhalgh 2008, 2010, 2020; Greenhalgh and Winckler 2005). To be sure, the Maoist-Stalinist approaches to population control were not entirely discarded after the 1990s, but Greenhalgh notes how the emergence of "softer" techniques of governance in this period signals the consolidation and expansion of a new form of technocratic power that is exercised not only for the repressive end of enhancing population control but as well for the more positive end of optimizing the population's life, health, welfare, and prosperity. This new project of population administration and citizen cultivation is supported not just by state organizations but also by a widening range of quasi-state and nonstate actors that is neglected by conventional state-coercion narratives (see also Greenhalgh and Zhang 2020).

Greenhalgh is right in noting that Reform-era China has developed a more pluralistic framework of governmentality that retains an element of tight authoritarian control, which has been significantly tightened under Xi Jinping and is now increasingly mediated by digital technologies of mass surveillance. She is also right in noting that the problem with the narrative of state coercion is that it tends to lay too much emphasis on the governing actions of the CCP and its strategies of domination and disciplinary control, conveying the misleading impression—as anthropologist Veena Das (2007, 59) puts it—that "the experience of becoming a subject [in China] is exhausted by that of subjugation" to the authoritarian rule of the CCP. For Greenhalgh (2010, 2020), the Reform period has witnessed the emergence of a more pluralistic technocratic framework of power that is increasingly mediated by a whole ensemble of quasi-state and nonstate professional institutions and organizations that are often subject to party-state controls and are expected to serve the party by lending their expertise to the making of official policies and plans (Cao and Suttmeier 2017). This more pluralistic model of government (in Foucault's extended sense) continues to have an authoritarian and repressive dimension, but it is also empowering Chinese citizens and communities to engage in an increasingly diverse range of individual and collective projects of self-formation and subjectivation. This point about the linkage between power structures and ethical processes of self-cultivation is very insightful because it conceptualizes the Birth Planning Policy not simply as a mechanism of social control but also as a tool of moral education, self-cultivation, and self-governance.

Greenhalgh's pioneering analysis of the Birth Planning Policy as a technocratic platform of governance that establishes close linkages between structures of subjectification (or of domination) and structures of self-formation can be generalized to other aspects of Chinese contemporary frameworks of population governance (Greenhalgh and Zhang 2020), but this emerging model of technocratic governmentality cannot be adequately captured by the term "neoliberal." What is interesting about China is that its engagement with global frameworks of neoliberal governmentality and technocratic modernization was informed by the basic principle that it is possible to learn from the technocratic agendas of modernization promoted by "Western" countries and "Western"-dominated organizations without committing to the underlying "Westernizing" discourses and ideologies embedded in these agendas. Although China has been describing itself as a nation-state for well over a century, it remains essentially what historian Martin Jacques (2009) calls a "civilization-state" in terms of history, culture, identity, and ways of thinking. What civilization-states do, essentially, is to promote and defend one way of life against all alternatives, and the CCP looks at the social and economic achievements of the last four decades in light of this civilizing ambition to promote "the Chinese way of life." This helps explain why every new paramount leader since Deng Xiaoping has endeavored to make a conceptual contribution to the ideological enterprise of constructing a new "socialist civilization" (Dynon 2008, 2014; Pieke 2016) based on the power of science and technology but retaining core Chinese characteristics.

Greenhalgh's emphasis on the pluralistic dimensions of Reform-era technocratic frameworks of governance applies also to the CCP's civilizing agenda during this period. It would be a mistake to assume that only the CCP is responsible for setting the standards for what counts as the new socialist civilization with Chinese characteristics; this civilizing mission involves a whole range of quasi-state and nonstate actors as well as citizens and citizen communities who are subject to normative expectations to behave in ways that express a civilizing sense of social responsibility. This more pluralistic non-state-centric approach to China's civilizing technocratic power is useful to bring into focus the work of ordinary citizens and citizen groups as active ethical subjects and agents of government. The problem here is that there are many different kinds of citizens and citizen groups, and most studies of technocratic governmentality in Reform-era China tend to direct attention to the point of view of privileged social groups such as scientists, party cadres, engineers, and medical doctors—the groups that benefit the most from the technocratic power structures during the Reform period.

A Bottom-Up Approach to Civilizing Technocratic Power

The intimate-choices approach follows Greenhalgh and others in arguing that Reform-era China's authoritarian structures of power and social control have become increasingly plural and dependent on a whole range of globalized discourses and institutions of science, technology, and other forms of technical expertise to govern the conduct of the larger population. This framework of technocratic governmentality has a strong civilizing dimension that is not restricted to the actions of state organizations or to the actions of professional institutions of technocratic expertise but, rather, is extended to ordinary citizens and communities and their efforts to engage with normative standards of action to develop their own projects of individual and collective self-cultivation. This book builds on the efforts of an emerging body of studies in the anthropology of science and technology in China to bring into focus the everyday negotiations shaping the workings of technocratic frameworks of governance. More than an everyday life approach to civilizing technocratic power, I am here calling for an approach that takes into consideration the perspective of populations that are structurally situated in the margins of dominant national social institutions and organizations.

This bottom-up approach from the margins seeks to expose the limitations of analytical models that are too centered on the views of privileged social actors and institutions, and it seeks to make a contribution to ongoing efforts in the humanities and social sciences to counter increasing global and regional structural inequalities by giving more visibility to what sociologist Boaventura de Sousa Santos (2014, 2018) has called "epistemologies of the South," including forms of knowledge (and, I would add, ways of doing things) developed by people in different parts of the world in their engagements and struggles with dominant globally circulating Northern cultures of technocratic modernization (see also Escobar 2018, 2020). My usage here of the opposition North and South is not geographical. The South is not a location with a latitude coordinate, but a relational condition of marginality in a larger system of power relations (Tsing 1994, 2005). Just as "the South" can be found in countries associated with the global North, so "the North" can be found in countries commonly linked to the global South.

Up until quite recently, China has been depicted as a developing country, but it is becoming increasingly difficult to maintain this classification in light of China's increasing economic power and influence in world affairs. China still has a large "peasant" population and a relatively low income per capita by global standards, but the reforms of the last four decades have improved the fortunes of many hundreds of millions of Chinese people, and the Chinese economy is already the second largest on the planet. This transformation reflects China's engagement with Northern ideologies of development and technocratic modernization, and the CCP justified this engagement with the values of science, technology, and progress. This civilizing mission was already in place before the Reform period, but what is meant today by science and technology is more sophisticated and specialized than before; it is also more elitist, as it no longer includes things like peasant wisdom and local knowledge. Today, as anthropologist Stevan Harrell (2020, 22) shows, the phrase "science and technology" refers to a network of increasingly world-class universities and research institutes that not only address "pure" and "applied" problems but also act as a signifier of development—of the advanced state of China's urban civilization and its education system, contrasted to the continued "backwardness" of peasants and minorities, and of China's march of progress toward resuming its rightful status as the world's leading civilization-state.

This ideological opposition between "advancement" and "backwardness," urban and rural, Han and non-Han can take many different forms depending on the specific context, but it usually involves a celebration of expert knowledge and a devaluation of everyday forms of knowledge. It is not a coincidence, for example, that one of the major figures behind the launching of the Birth Planning Policy in the late 1970s was a male rocket scientist called Song Jian who knew a lot about abstract mathematical equations but very little about the practicalities of contraception, family planning, and childbirth. Greenhalgh's research on the story of this missile scientist and his mathematical equations teach us a lot about the workings of elite research institutions and their linkages to the central government (Greenhalgh 2003, 2008). This is a very important contribution, but it is a different kind of project than focusing on ordinary people's experiences and negotiations of the Birth Planning Policy in different parts of China. It is not enough to study macro-level technocratic frameworks of governance where they are being produced and negotiated; we also need to understand how such macro-level frameworks of power are entangled in complex user-mediated negotiations at the micro level. Because there are many different kinds of users, it matters from which perspective we explore everyday articulations of globalized assemblages of technocratic governance. Making sense of micro-macro intersections of technocratic governance from the perspective of marginal populations is particularly challenging because it points to the existence of profound gaps between the views of elite actors and institutions in Chinese society and the views of ordinary citizens and citizen communities. These gaps force us to think more carefully about an important tension that will likely be an increasing source of conflicts in twenty-first-century China: the tension between the desire to improve and protect society through top-down technocratic governance and the desire to improve and protect society through increasing popular participation in processes of governance.[15] How can we find ways of overcoming this tension, and how can we give more visibility to the views of more than 500 million rural citizens in public technocratic debates on the future of rural China?

This bottom-up approach to the workings of civilizing technocratic power combines the insights of constructivist approaches to family and kinship in anthropology with feminist approaches in social studies of science and technology. From the new anthropology of kinship and family (Carsten 2004; McKinnon and Cannell 2013), I borrow the idea that human practices of marriage, gender, and family are normative constructions that are not given but are subject to complex negotiations in specific sociocultural and politico-economic environments. One common assumption about these negotiations is that they are largely confined to the private sphere of "the home," but this is an analytical mistake. It is more accurate to look at these negotiations as a private-public endeavor that involves multiple actors across multiple circuits and arenas.[16] From feminist approaches in social studies of science and technology,[17] I borrow three major ideas: first, that changes in everyday practices of family, gender, and intimate life are shaped by developments in science and technology; second, that this dynamics of "co-production" (Jasanoff 2004) involves the construction of "socio-technical ensembles" (Bijker 2010) requiring the mobilization of a large amount of materials, people, ideals, resources, and artifacts; and third, that the construction of these intimate assemblages entails processes of negotiation and contestation that can be studied from many different perspectives, including the perspective of housewives or working women who are not experts and do not occupy a powerful position in society.

The focus on negotiation and contestation is a central aspect of attention to intimate choices. There is a well-established scholarly tradition in social studies of science and technology focusing on processes of "technopolitical" negotiation and contestation (Hecht 1998; Mitchell 2002), but most studies tend to focus at the macro level on experts, developers, and policy makers. This macro-level approach is also pervasive in studies of processes of "technopolitical" reconfiguration of everyday practices of family, gender, and intimate life. For example, writing about the global biopolitics of the modern intrauterine device (IUD), sociologist Chikako Takeshita (2012) shows how the scientific development of the IUD in the 1960s was shaped by American elite prejudices against women of color and the lower classes (see also Drucker 2020). These biases were built into the initial configuration of the IUD, but they did not prevent the IUD from spreading globally from the 1960s onward. One reason for this is that IUD researchers, activists, and government officials worldwide invested a significant amount of effort and resources in "translating" the device as a contraceptive method that is adaptable to local communities of female users. These "translation" efforts were crucial to turn the IUD into a "politically versatile technology"—that is, a technology that can reach many different kinds of people because it is adaptable to different kinds of politics and social interests. There is much to be learned from Takeshita's analysis of the changing meanings of the IUD as it travels in space and time, but her research is primarily concerned with macro-level forces and discourses shaping the global circulation of the IUD. The approach presented here does not dismiss the significance of macro-level forces and discourses, but situates these forces and discourses in the context of micro-level processes of negotiation involving ordinary users, their families, and their networks of social support. I am calling here for a new anthropology of everyday articulations of technoscience and technocratic governance.

One of the advantages of this micro-macro approach is that it highlights the moral agency of ordinary users and communities in the face of increasingly powerful technocratic forces of modernization and globalization. The Birth Planning Policy once again offers a good illustration of this point. In the implementation of the Birth Planning Policy in northern Guangdong from the late 1970s onward, local rural populations were able to retain a remarkable degree of moral autonomy in their engagement with larger technologies of power and disciplinary control. To be sure, local rural populations were largely powerless in countering the overall direction of change dictated by the Birth Planning Policy, but the enforcement of this policy went hand in hand with the emergence of a local subculture of family and intimate life that is not entirely dominated by the values promoted by higher-level state organizations and other major actors and institutions in Chinese society. This subaltern process of cultural creativity can be read as evidence of moral agency, but one should be careful not to romanticize the moral unity of local rural populations. Significant moral disagreements exist within local rural communities, and these internal moral frictions play an important role in shaping local forms of engagement with larger forces of technocratic modernization and globalization. These concerns are relevant to long-standing debates on subaltern resistance (Scott 1985, 1990; Abu-Lughod 1990; Ortner 1995, 2016; Appadurai 2013), as well as to more recent debates on moral transformation and subject formation in contemporary societies (Mahmood 2005; Laidlaw 2014; Keane 2016), an important topic in the growing field of the anthropology of ethics.

Attention to intimate choices contributes to recent debates in what has been called the "ethical turn in anthropology" (Fassin 2014; Mattingly and Throop 2018). First, it highlights the often-neglected role of technoscience in the making of contemporary projects of moral transformation and self-cultivation, especially those concerned with family and intimate life (see also Boellstorff 2015). Second, it contributes to the development of a dialectical approach to subject formation that overcomes conventional dichotomies between freedom and constraint, technology and society, autonomy and belonging, individual and collective. The intimate choices approach sides with recent critiques of classic approaches to morality as a collective system of rules or values,[18] but it does not overstate the significance of individual choice and individual moral autonomy, a common assumption under contemporary forces of neoliberal globalization, technological progress, and consumer individualism (Gammeltoft 2014). Rather, it argues that individual subjectivities and individual projects of self-fashioning are most productively situated in the context of larger frameworks of sociality, structures of inequality, and networks of interdependence at multiple levels.

CHAPTER 1

Harmony Cave Families

Transition to the Twenty-First Century

A VILLAGE COMMUNITY IN THE TWENTY-FIRST CENTURY EXTENDS well beyond the classic genealogical and territorial unit defined in conventional village studies. The village of Harmony Cave is not a bounded lineage community but an open field of social and spatial networks with changing configurations and changing patterns of rural-urban interaction. China has witnessed rapid urbanization and rising rates of rural-urban migration after the beginning of Reform and Opening. In Guangdong, where the reforms began much earlier than in other provinces, the development of the Pearl River Delta region from the 1980s onward, including vibrant cities and special economic zones like Shenzhen and Zhuhai, next to Hong Kong and Macau, respectively, went hand in hand with a large-scale phenomenon of rural-urban migration with far-reaching social and economic implications. This rural-urban migration affected rural families and communities in Guangdong and in other parts of China, leading to a radical reconfiguration of the fabric of village life. In northern Guangdong, as shown by the example of Harmony Cave village, the normalization of rural-urban migration to the Pearl River Delta region was shaped by larger civilizing forces of technocratic modernization, involving intimate choices by villagers, families, and communities regarding their engagement with changing infrastructures of mobility and digital communication. These complex negotiations inspired the development of an increasingly translocal model of rural livelihood that challenges the rather static methodological and theoretical frameworks of conventional village studies (Marcus 1998; Xiang 2007; Ferguson 2011).

Research on labor migrants and rural-urban migration in Reform-era China tends to favor the perspective of cities and urban governance, not that of villages and rural governance.[1] This analytical privileging of cities and urban governance cannot be separated from a globally powerful media narrative describing China's rural-urban migration as a form of rural exodus that is leading to a depleted if not disappearing countryside. Such a narrative is useful to make sense of stories of rural abandonment, but it overlooks the fact that a significant proportion of rural migrants in China continue to maintain strong ties to their home families and communities. These ties provide rural migrants with an important safety net that allows them to cope with the uncertainties of labor migration and that makes possible the continuing contributions of labor migrants to the growth of urban economies, while allowing cities to minimize the development of massive shantytown slums in the age of mass migration. But it is not enough to ask how rural-urban migration changes urban landscapes and economies. How are increasing rural-urban migration and mobility in the age of digital connectivity leading to the emergence of new frameworks of rural sociality? Answering this question exemplifies how the new villages of twenty-first-century China have become patched-up formations or assemblages constructed out of increasingly complex rural-urban mobilities and entanglements in the context of new "power geometries" (Massey 1994) and structures of social and spatial inequality.

In his classic book *Xiangtu Zhongguo* (SC), literally "earthbound China," first published in 1947, Chinese anthropologist Fei Xiaotong (1948, 1992) argues that "traditional" Chinese rural society was built around a strong sense of attachment to ancestral soil (see also Fei 1939; Fei and Chang 1945). This vision of rural China remains crucial to understand social solidarity in present-day lineage villages like Harmony Cave, but the attachment to ancestral soil has been significantly deterritorialized. Up until the last decades of the twentieth century, such places were based on a territorial notion of village community that was close to Fei's classic formulation. People lived in tightly knit residential areas that involved daily face-to-face interactions, and everyone depended on village land to make a living. Moving into the twenty-first century, the village community is no longer a territorial assemblage in Fei's classic sense. Villagers no longer depend on shared ancestral land as a major source of livelihood, and many choose a translocal mode of livelihood that involves circular movements between the country and the city. Villagers continue to attach a strong value to the ancestral village, but few actually reside in the physical space of the village for much of the year. They continue to interact with one another on a regular basis, but this interaction is no longer based on face-to-face neighborly exchanges but on social media exchanges. At the same time, there is still a strong obligation to attend major communal ritual events back in the ancestral village, which continues to be seen as the core site for the ritual celebration of shared identity. This ongoing attachment to a shared sense of collective ritual identity offers a potential model to think about the fate of kinship-territorial formations like lineage villages in the current age of hyper spatial mobility and digital communication.

The Village of Harmony Cave and the Township of Yellow Flower

Harmony Cave village is nestled in the beautiful landscape of limestone mountains and rice-paddy fields of Yellow Flower township in the northern "hilly regions" of Guangdong, some 200 kilometers north of the city of Guangzhou (see map P.1). The local landscape retains a strong rustic component due to the combined presence of limestone mountains, rice-paddy fields, and traditional mud-brick village compounds. The local karst landscape was formed from the dissolution of soluble rocks like limestone and is characterized by underground drainage systems with sinkholes and caves. Many irrigation water canals provide water to the local rice fields during the wet season, but the township has only one major waterway, a small river that flows into the much larger Lian River, the largest tributary of the North River flowing into the Pearl River Delta system in southern Guangdong. The small river flowing through Yellow Flower is not navigable by large boats but it is large enough to add an important layer of beauty to the local karst landscape, which includes spectacularly scenic areas that are often compared to the world-famous landscape of Guilin. For this reason, Yellow Flower has recently become a major tourist destination, attracting growing numbers of domestic visitors.

Yellow Flower is under the jurisdiction of the city of Yingde, a county-level division of the prefecture-level city of Qingyuan. The main waterway running through Yingde County is the North (Bei) River, a major tributary of the Pearl River, and in the last ten years the county benefited from the construction of a major highway and a high-speed train line. The principal varieties of Chinese spoken in Yingde County are Cantonese and Hakka (Yingde Xian 1965). In Yellow Flower, there are no Hakka-speaking communities, but most rural townships east of Yellow Flower include a high percentage of Hakka-speaking communities. In June 2018, Yellow Flower had an official population of roughly 56,000 individuals.[2] This is a medium-sized township. Most rural townships in China range between 10,000 and 100,000 individuals. There are about 110 "natural villages" (C: *jiyin chyun*) in Yellow Flower, but these are often not administrative units. The key administrative units at the township level are "village committees" (C: *chyun-wai-wui*)—meaning a small cluster of neighboring villages—and "village groups" (C: *chyun-man siu-jou*), meaning a small natural village or a residential hamlet within a natural village. Yellow Flower has eleven village committees—the "brigades" (C: *daai-deui*) of the Maoist period—and more than 270 village groups—the "production teams" (C: *saang-chaan-deui*) of the Maoist period. There is also one "neighborhood committee" (C: *se-keui geui-wai-wui*) responsible for the governance of urban planning and development in the market town.

Harmony Cave belongs to the village committee of Three Mountains and was first incorporated in this "brigade" in 1951, soon after the Communists rose to power. In 2018 Three Mountains included six "natural villages" (most of them single-lineage villages), with a population of more than 3,000. This population is small by Yellow Flower standards. Some village committees have more than twenty villages, with a population greater than 5,000. Three Mountains has only two large villages, Harmony Cave and Three Mountains, each with a population of less than 1,000. Harmony Cave is a single-lineage community surnamed Chan and is divided in five village groups: Harmony First, Harmony Second, Harmony Third, Harmony Fourth, and Harmony Fifth. These village groups were created in the 1950s as part of the process of collectivization, when they were called production teams, but their formation was based on deeper agnatic divisions within the village: on one side are residents of Harmony First, Harmony Second, and Harmony Third, who see themselves as the descendants of the eldest son of the founding village ancestor; on the other side are residents of Harmony Fourth and Harmony Fifth, who see themselves as the descendants of the youngest son of the founding village ancestor.

This book is primarily concerned with the aspirations, activities, and trajectories of the households of Harmony First, in whose clay-brick housing compound I resided when I first arrived in Harmony Cave in 1999 (see figure P.2), and for this reason I developed closer ties with members of this village group in the following two decades. By 2018, Harmony First had a population of around 220 individuals, and their close agnatic relatives—Harmony Second and Harmony Third—had populations of about 120 and 160, respectively. These three village groups combined had a total population of about 500, slightly more than the total population of their two rival village groups: Harmony Fourth (around 250) and Harmony Fifth (around 170).[3]

Most villages in Yellow Flower are localized lineage communities with a single patronymic.[4] The local term for this type of village is "single-surname village" (C: *tung-sing-chyun*). These villages can be described as local associations or organizations that are based on a claim of shared patrilineal descent from a founding ancestor or ancestors. Many villages have written genealogies to demonstrate this claim of shared descent, and those that do not have written genealogies preserve knowledge of descent lines through oral memory and naming practices. The claim of shared descent is reinforced by customs of communal ancestor worship and by ownership of communal property such as land and other economic assets. In addition to having strict rules of patrilineal inheritance and heirship, these single-surname villages are shaped by strict rules of village patrilocal exogamy. This means that village brides are still expected to move into their husbands' families and communities, and most girls in Harmony Cave and other local villages end up marrying into families and communities from the same township or from neighboring townships. Newly married brides today are no longer living under the shadow of their mothers-in-law/parents-in-law but join their husbands in requiring the establishment of a separate family "stove" and the construction of a separate house in the village or elsewhere. Newlywed couples no longer have to reside in the village on a regular basis, but there is still the expectation that their social, ritual, and economic life will be patricentric in the sense that it will revolve around that of the husband's larger patrilineal family and his ancestral lineage village.[5]

Most lineage communities in Yellow Flower were founded during the Qing period (1644–1911), but the earliest administrative records of the township go back to the beginning of the Ming dynasty (1368–1644) (Yingde Xianzhi 2006). The name Yellow Flower was officially recognized in 1705 under the emperor Kangxi and then again in 1836 under the emperor Daoguang. Many villagers say that the local limestone mountains were once covered by a wildflower locally known as "yellow flower," hence the name Yellow Flower. The township area was directly affected by the counterinsurgency campaign fought by the Communists against the nationalist guerrillas in Guangdong province during the civil war period, a good reminder of how local history was always linked to larger national and global transformations. The township was effectively "liberated" in 1950, and a new local government was established in 1951.

In 1958 the name of the township was changed to Brightpath, and a new higher-level administrative category—the "people's commune" (SC: *renmin gongshe*)—was created. This administrative category was salient in the 1960s during high socialism, but was replaced by "district" (SC: *qu*) soon after the beginning of decollectivization in the 1970s. In 1987 the *qu* was turned into a "home town" (SC: *xiang*) and in 1993 into a "township" (SC: *zhen*), the current administrative term. In 2004 the township of Brightpath was expanded to incorporate a neighboring township, and the new megatownship was renamed Yellow Flower, the Qing designation of the region. The township economy has been growing quite steadily in the last four decades. The same can be said of the core-urbanized area of the township: the market town of Brightpath (now called Yellow Flower). After the beginning of the process of decollectivization in the late 1970s, Brightpath started to hold a periodic market on every day of the lunar calendar ending in four or nine, and this tradition of periodic markets is still alive at a time when the local economy is becoming increasingly diversified and shaped by a growing consumer market and tourism industry.

Village Genealogical History and Generational Markers

The founding patrilineal ancestor of the village of Harmony Cave is called Faat-bou. According to existing genealogical records, his patrilateral great-grandfather settled sometime in the seventeenth century in the Yellow Flower region, and his ancestry can be traced back to an official surnamed Chan, named Yeung-mun, who moved to Guangdong from western Fujian in the first decades of the Ming dynasty (which began in 1368). Yeung-mun first settled in eastern Guangdong in the East River area, but he later moved to the North River area in northern Guangdong. He initially settled in the township of Big Bay, north of Yellow Flower, but one of his grandsons later moved to Yellow Flower and continued his grandfather's line in this region. In the first decades of the twentieth century, an ancestral hall was constructed in Yellow Flower to honor the memory of the ancestor Yeung-mun, and this ancestral hall was renovated in 1999 and completely rebuilt in 2013. The council of elders in charge of this ancestral hall has completed a detailed written genealogy of Yeung-mun and his descendants in 2010. The founding ancestor of the village of Harmony Cave—Faat-bou—is included in this written genealogy as one of Yeung-mun's descendants (Chan Lineage Association 2010).

When I first lived in Harmony Cave between 1999 and 2001, I wanted to understand the generational history of the village and its various residential areas starting from the founding ancestor, but there were no written records, so I started to compile oral genealogies of the various agnatic branches of the village. In 2004 I completed a diagram that contained detailed information on the genealogical history of the village and its various residential hamlets. This diagram, the first written genealogy of the village, was greatly appreciated by village elders, to whom it was shown in the form of a giant 100-centimeter-by-21-centimeter poster. I have since revised and updated this diagram in response to feedback from villagers. The most recent version spans about eighteen generations. If we accept that the average time between two consecutive generations is twenty years, the passing of eighteen generations amounts to more than 350 years.[6] This means that Faat-bou must have settled in the Harmony Cave region in the early to mid-seventeenth century (a period of dynastic transition and demographic turmoil in the whole of China), but it is difficult to know for sure what happened, because it is not always easy to differentiate fact from fiction when it comes to oral or written genealogies.

There are no written records describing the social and spatial arrangements of the village in its first hundred years of existence, but my interviews with elder villagers suggest that starting from the seventh generation—sometime in the early nineteenth century—the village established itself as a corporate descent group, and this transformation was marked by the adoption of a corporate system of naming based on lineage generational markers to indicate the passage of generational time. This means that from this period onward, all new male descendants were given a "formal name" (C: *syu-meng*, literally "book name") to be used in stone inscriptions and other ritual records, and this formal name included a generational marker that was taken from the following poem, here transcribed in the local Cantonese language with a tentative English translation line by line:

Jaan jiu sing ging wan chyun ji jik yin ming.
赞朝成景运传子值贤名.
Help the country continue its beautiful journey and produce descendants who will establish a reputation of virtue and talent.

Yau yiu gwong yu jou kei cheung wing haau sing.
有耀光虞祚其昌永孝声.
Bring honor to our ancestors and extend the prosperity of our lineage for all eternity.

Ji nang sing ging buk siu hing gai wo ming.
嗣能承敬卜肇庆继和鸣.
Continue the meritorious achievements of the ancestors and celebrate these achievements on a regular basis.

Cheung sau jou wing jaak san fung yin sau ying.
长守祖荣泽新峰衍秀英.
Protect the glory and the longevity of our lineage; hope for an even greater success of the new generations.

This poem works as a mnemonic device to help villagers remember the system of generational markers adopted by the village as a corporate descent group sometime in the first half of the nineteenth century. The first generational marker to be added to the formal name of a male villager was the first character of the poem, *jaan* (赞), and this character was soon followed by *jiu* (朝), *sing* (成), *ging* (景), and so on. Each time a village family has new male descendants, the formal name of these descendants will include a new generational marker taken from the poem cited above. As of 2018, the village had already used the first ten generational markers as indicated in the first line of the poem. At some point in the future, the village will reach the last character of the poem, *ying* (英), and a new set of generational markers will have to be created to continue recording the great achievements of lineage descendants and the passage of generational time.

This custom of using generational markers in lineage naming practices has a long history in South China.[7] By the Ming dynasty, as shown by anthropologist Rubie Watson (1985), many village communities in Guangdong started to define themselves as corporate descent groups with a founding ancestor, and as part of this process, they started to use generational markers in the names of all new male descendants. This practice was an attempt to construct a sense of agnatic solidarity among village "brothers and uncles" (C: *hing-dai suk-baak*) by creating a shared universe of naming practices and generational time markers. But the usage of a shared system of generational markers was also instrumental in articulating an idiom of reproductive competition between village families and lineage branches.

A lineage branch that has been consistently fast at acquiring the necessary wealth to renew itself with fresh male progeny will occupy a more advanced position in the system of generational markers. This has implications for the way villagers address one another in the course of daily life. During my first stay in the village between 1999 and 2001, there were already a few young boys with the generational marker *ji* (子). According to local customs, these boys had to address all male villagers whose names had the generational marker *ging* (景) with the term for "great-grandfather" (C: *gung-taai*) because the boys' generational marker, *ji* (子), is three generations younger than *ging* (景). This practice was at times a source of embarrassment for the villagers with the generational marker *ging* (景) because some of them were not old enough to look like a great-grandfather. They were addressed as great-grandfathers not because of their age but because they lagged behind in terms of generational markers, and this lagging behind followed from the fact that their family line had not been very successful at speeding up the process of patrilineal social reproduction. Lagging behind in terms of generational markers is a source of family embarrassment because it suggests that one's family line struggles to reproduce itself over the generations. By contrast, having an advanced generational marker is a source of family pride because it suggests that one's family line is resourceful enough to reproduce itself at a fast pace over the generations and thus contribute to the expansion of the family and village line.

This logic of predatory expansion played an important role in shaping the development of the village as a lineage community from the nineteenth century onward.[8] By the first half of the twentieth century, the village of

Harmony Cave was divided in two major lineage branches named after two major patrilineal ancestors: Seui-fong (the eldest son of the founding village ancestor) and Seui-daat (the youngest son). These lineage branches had a territorial dimension in the sense that they corresponded to two different village hamlets built side by side in an auspicious location at the foot of a small group of figure-shaped limestone mountains. Both hamlets faced a large plain of agricultural fields that included a seasonal irrigation stream. This stream, which still exists, originates in the mountain range northeast of the village. The choice of village location was based on feng shui considerations, as was the decision to have all village doors facing east. I was told on several occasions by older villagers that village doors have to face east because this is the only way to assure that "the water coming into the village does not flow away" (C: *seui lau-loi, ng-hai lau-jau*). It is not clear when this decision was first made, but feng shui considerations played an important role. In feng shui, the cosmic breaths that constitute the efficacy of a site are blown about by wind and held by water. If the water moves too fast or in the wrong direction, the cosmic breaths will be taken away. A village without enough wind- and water-held cosmic breaths will not be able to prosper and produce many children. In those days, securing a good reserve of wind- and water-held cosmic breaths was crucial to secure prosperity and a large (male) progeny, but it was not enough.

Village Life on the Eve of the Communist Revolution of 1949

Key concerns for village families in the first half of the twentieth century included food insecurity, disease, banditry, feuds, disputes, and social inequality. Local peasant families relied on multicropping rice farming to make a living (Santos 2006b, 2009, 2010, 2011), but they did not own the land, and the village area often did not have enough water to cultivate two annual crops of rice. Only a few privileged families were able to eat rice meals with any regularity. Most families relied on a diet of sweet potatoes and taro. Subsistence farming was not the only source of income. Many families engaged in various forms of paid labor, commerce, and handicraft industries to make a living.

Older villagers interviewed in the late 1990s recalled the existence of local periodic marketing structures in the first decades of the twentieth century. These local markets—despite poor transportation networks and physical isolation—were connected to market towns farther north, and these marketing networks were in turn connected via the North River to a larger marketing system centered on the city of Guangzhou and the Pearl River Delta region. There are still some material cultural traces of these earlier marketing networks. In the mountain area north of Harmony Cave, I found evidence of old mountain paths connecting the Yellow Flower region to the neighboring market town of Big Bay, a Hakka-speaking township located farther north, close to the North River. Villagers from the Yellow Flower region were attracted to Big Bay because the periodic market there was bigger than in Yellow Flower and thus offered more business opportunities. My interviews in the late 1990s with older villagers suggest that these old mountain paths connecting Yellow Flower to Big Bay were very active in the first half of the twentieth century. Back then, most travelers walking on these mountain paths were men, and it was not always possible to travel safely outside village territory.

During the Chinese civil war period in the 1940s, the Yellow Flower region became a major hideout for the Nationalist guerrillas, and the village of Harmony Cave played a central role in the counterinsurgency campaign fought by the Communists in northern Guangdong. A prominent member of the Nationalist guerrillas, Mr. Leung, was hiding in Harmony Cave when the Communist People's Liberation Army (PLA) arrived in the village area in January 1950, a few months after Mao Zedong proclaimed the foundation of the People's Republic of China. There were many casualties as a result of the confrontations between the Nationalist guerrillas and the PLA. Older villagers interviewed in the late 1990s recall that Mr. Leung and his village associates kept all villagers captive and used rifles and pistols to fight the Communists. As the confrontations progressed, Mr. Leung managed to leave the village through a secret passage in the mountain caves. He was supposed to go to a neighboring township to call for reinforcements, but he never returned.

The story goes that he managed to take a boat to the Pearl River Delta region and later on to Hong Kong. After Mr. Leung's escape, the confrontations lasted for a few more days, and after that, the Communist army invaded the village and put an end to the resistance. The army managed to identify three of Mr. Leung's associates, who were executed by a firing squad a few weeks after the end of the hostilities. It proved more difficult to identify the names of other villagers connected to Mr. Leung, so a collective punishment was imposed on the whole village: *all* male villagers over sixteen years old were sent to a labor camp in Shaoguan for a few months to be educated in the teachings of Chairman Mao Zedong.

Collectivization and the Origins of Inner-Outer Spatial Opposition

The early 1950s were times of radical change. In 1950 the official process of land reform and class labeling was initiated. In 1951 the "brigade" of Three Mountains was created and included six single-surname villages (see note 4). In 1953 the village of Harmony Cave was divided into five "production teams" that ended up reproducing preexisting agnatic kinship ties within the village (figure 1.1).[9] The members of the first three production teams—Harmony First, Harmony Second, and Harmony Third—are basically the descendants of Seui-fong (the eldest son of the founding village ancestor), and the members of the last two production teams—Harmony Fourth and Harmony Fifth—are the descendants of Seui-daat (the youngest son of the founding ancestor). Figure 1.1 shows additional overlaps between production-team boundaries and preexisting agnatic kinship groups. Seui-fong had three grandsons, and these three grandsons are the ancestral heads of Harmony First, Harmony Second, and Harmony Third. Maan-hin (the youngest grandson of Seui-fong) is the ancestral head of Harmony First and some Harmony Third families; Maan-gwai (the second grandson of Seui-fong) is the ancestral head of Harmony Second; Maan-luk (the eldest grandson of Seui-fong) is the ancestral head of a few Harmony Third families. A similar logic applies to the production teams of Harmony Fourth and Harmony Fifth. Seui-daat had three sons, and these three sons are the ancestral heads of Harmony Fourth and Harmony Fifth. Long-cheung and Yin-cheung (the two eldest sons of Seui-daat) are both ancestral heads of Harmony Fourth. Jung-cheung (the third son of Seui-daat) is the ancestral head of Harmony Fifth.

The newly formed production teams of the 1950s displayed significant points of intersection with previous agnatic kinship formations, but these production teams also opened the way for new socialist ideals and frameworks of social and economic organization. These collectivist units introduced immediate organizational changes in the lives of villagers, but these

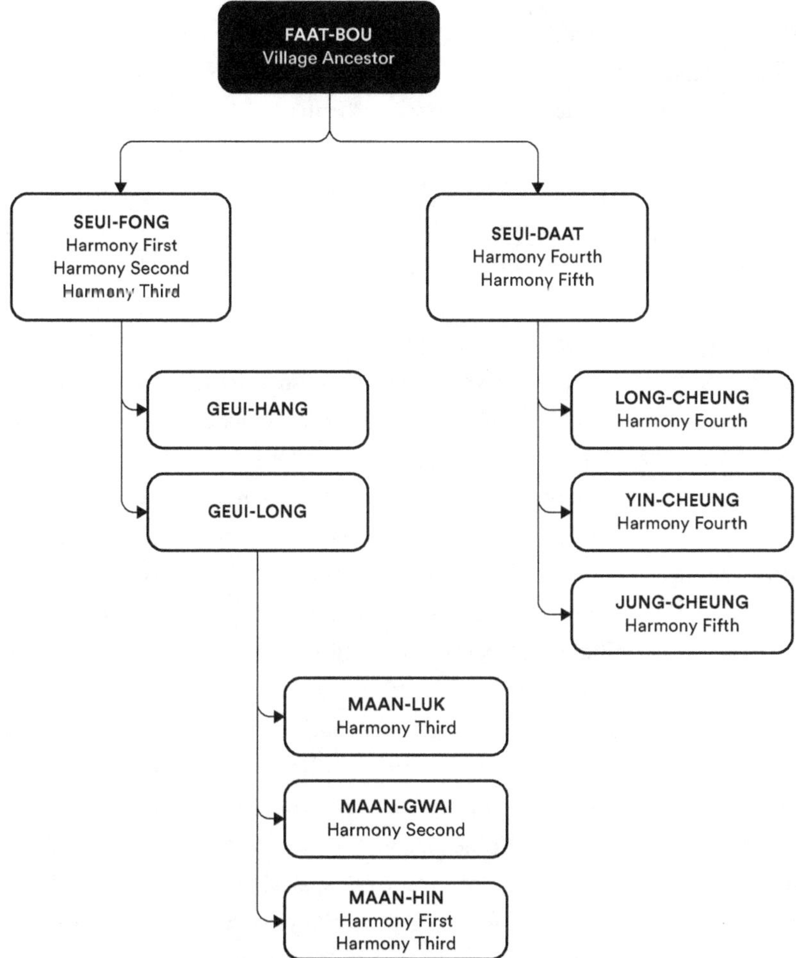

FIGURE 1.1. Harmony Cave lineage branches and production teams

changes were not as radical and revolutionary as conveyed by socialist propaganda. It is true that village life became increasingly subject to the power of cadres and state structures, but most state representatives at the brigade level or at the production-team level were ordinary villagers with short-term training courses. It is also true that the process of socialist collectivization significantly undermined the power of "traditional" structures of social organization based on lineages and deity temple associations, but the shift to high socialism was gradual. In the 1950s, villagers started to work together as members of production teams, but there were still plots of land distributed at the household level. Moreover, there were no major changes in residential arrangements, as the village continued to be spatially organized around two major ancestral hamlets: the hamlet of Seui-fong (the eldest son of the founding village ancestor) and the hamlet of Seui-daat (the youngest son of the founding village ancestor).

It was only after the beginning of the Great Leap Forward that this ancestral pattern of residential organization was disrupted. In 1958 the name of the township was changed to Brightpath, and a new higher-level administrative category—the "people's commune"—was created with the goal of stepping up the process of collectivization and the extraction of local resources through higher-level centralized procurement. This period of high socialism was an important turning point in the spatial history of the village. The leadership of the brigade of Three Mountains announced a series of ambitious plans for the construction of new village housing, new agricultural processing stations, and a new irrigation-water reservoir as part of a larger drive to promote the socialist modernization of the local agricultural economy. This civilizing project would require the relocation of a significant number of Harmony Cave residents from their ancestral hamlets to a new residential hamlet to be located in an area south of the ancestral village location that would also host the new primary school and the new administrative headquarters of the brigade of Three Mountains. The move to the new residential hamlet of Sand Spine was very controversial in Harmony Cave, and it inspired the emergence of a clear-cut spatial and conceptual differentiation between two very different parts of the village: the older Inner Area (C: *leui-dai*), also called the "upper area" (C: *seung-bin*), and a newly developed Outer Area (C: *ngoi-bin*), also called the "lower area" (C: *ha-dai*).[10] This was an important turning point in the history of the village (figure 1.2), and it involved intimate choices: while those who stayed in the older "inner area" continued to stand for tradition and for preserving ancestral ways of doing things, those who moved to the newly developed "outer area" called for change and embodied the new revolutionary ideals of a civilizing project of socialist modernity.

The Inner Area of the village was where the founding ancestors of Harmony Cave first settled. Back in the 1950s, few villagers would question the sacredness of this location, and its superiority was justified not just on the grounds of ancestral genealogical considerations but also on the basis of

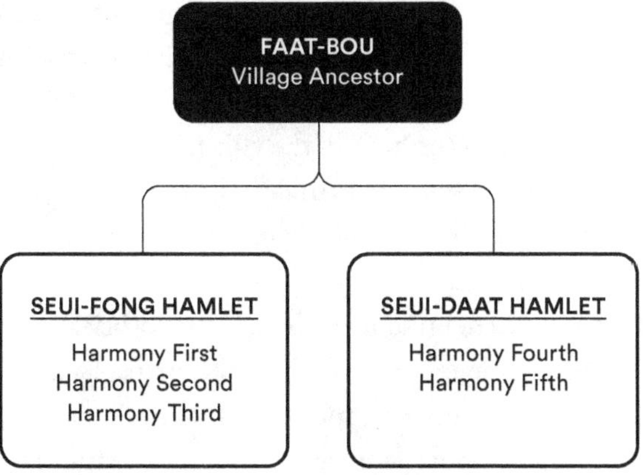

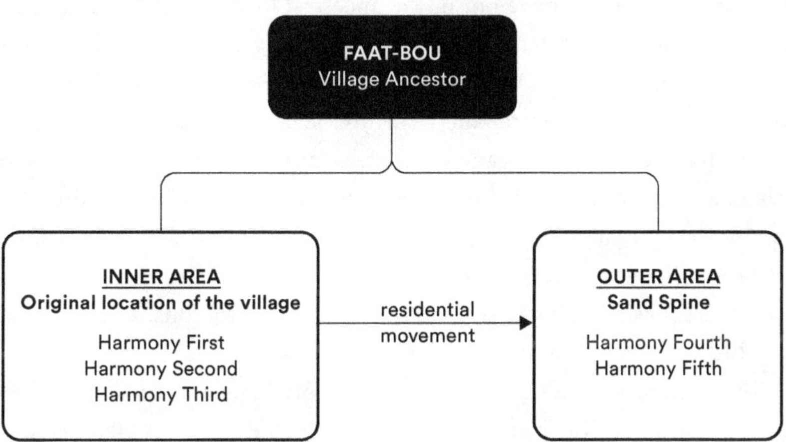

FIGURE 1.2. The rise of Harmony Cave's Inner Area–Outer Area opposition, before and after 1960

feng shui considerations, both practical and cosmological. The Inner Area was regarded as the ideal location for residential settlement first of all because of its favorable location in a quiet, shaded area at the foot of a small group of 200-meter-high limestone mountains. A more cosmological feng shui explanation was that the Inner Area was optimally located for access to the right kinds of cosmic breaths. In light of these feng shui considerations, many in the village opposed the decision to move out of the Inner Area, and there were concerns about how the move to the Outer Area (the area of flat dry land south of the Inner Area) would bring misfortune to the village.

The man who had been the head of the village at that time told me during several conversations and interviews undertaken between 1999 and 2013 that brigade cadres played an important role in countering these rumors said to be based on unfounded superstitious beliefs. These cadres argued that the Inner Area lacked space to build new upgraded mud-brick housing, and this lack of space made it imperative to find an alternative location for the construction of a new residential hamlet called Sand Spine. The Sand Spine project attracted the support of a significant group of village households, including most households from the production team of Harmony Fourth and some from Harmony Second. These villagers agreed with brigade cadres that more housing was needed and that the Inner Area lacked space to build adequate housing. These villagers also agreed with brigade cadres that the only solution was to move out of the ancestral location of the village, and they thought that constructing a new residential hamlet in the Outer Area could only bring progress. Moving to Sand Spine would place villagers in a location that is more central and closer to the heart of the new cultural and political center of the brigade of Three Mountains, next to the primary school and the brigade's headquarters. This new location would also bring significant advantages in terms of access to various brigade-level resources, allowing villagers to stay at the forefront of new infrastructural developments like power networks, agricultural processing stations, and new roads suitable for bicycles and motorized transportation.

The construction of the Sand Spine residential area was finalized in 1960 during the Great Leap Forward. This was a period when excessive centralized procurement of local resources led to a situation of food shortage that was worsened because villagers were physically exhausted from work in multiple projects of infrastructural development, including a large mountain reservoir constructed in 1958–59 (Santos 2011). The construction of the Sand Spine residential area revealed profound social divisions between villagers that transcended existing social differentiations in terms of lineage branch affiliation and production-team membership. There emerged significant disagreements between villagers residing in the hamlet of the descendants of Seui-fong, a lineage branch that included the production teams of

Harmony First, Harmony Second, and Harmony Third. All the members of Harmony First and Harmony Third refused to move to Sand Spine, but some members of Harmony Second agreed to move to the Sand Spine residential area in the new Outer Area of the village. There were also significant disagreements between villagers residing in the hamlet of the descendants of Seui-daat, a lineage branch that included the production teams of Harmony Fourth and Harmony Fifth. Almost all members of Harmony Fourth decided in favor of moving to Sand Spine, but Harmony Fifth refused to move to Sand Spine in the new Outer Area. This team preferred to build a new residential hamlet close to the old Inner Area of the village, and the construction of this residential hamlet was completed in 1960. This hamlet was called Loyal Prosperity to commemorate the achievements of Jung-cheung, the name of this team's venerable ancestor.

The local economy started to recover from the shocks of the Great Leap Forward sometime in the early to mid-1960s when sideline private plots were restored and agriculture was thus partly decollectivized. This was also the period when the larger state-coordinated project of engineering a Green Revolution in agricultural productivity started to gain momentum (Santos 2011). Key technical changes during this period include the introduction of new high-yielding semidwarf rice varieties developed by Chinese researchers back in the mid-1950s.[11] Another important technical change was the introduction of modern chemical fertilizers, herbicides, and pesticides, but it would take decades before these products became widely available in the township. Still in the 1960s, the introduction of electricity in the core urbanized areas of the local market town allowed the emergence of the first mechanized agricultural processing stations. This technological change had a tremendous impact on local agricultural practices as well as on practices of food consumption (for example, people started to eat husked, polished rice that was much whiter). By the late 1960s, new farming machinery such as tractors started to appear, but the most successfully disseminated machines during this period were manual, including new models of pedal-powered rice threshers (not to mention bicycles, which started to become popular for carrying both passengers and cargo).

In the Harmony Cave area, the 1960s was also the period when the effects of the mountain reservoir built in 1958–59 started to become more visible due to the expansion of irrigation networks and cultivated area. Average rice yields started to climb from the mid-1960s onward and soon reached an unprecedented 500–600 *jin* (SC for a weight measurement of one-half kilogram) per *mu* (SC for a field measurement of one-fifteenth hectare) in the first crop and slightly less in the second crop—leading to an annual production of 900–1,000 *jin* per *mu*, or about 6.7–7.5 metric tons per hectare (Santos 2011, 489). These economic transformations took place at the same time as the Great Cultural Revolution (1966–76), a period that played an important role in shaping the overall configuration of the local society primarily through the effects of mass campaigns. When Mao died in 1976, village households were still producing agricultural products for both collective self-consumption and centralized state extraction. Unable to sell their products in local markets or to engage in sideline petty-capitalist activities, village households had little control over their economic activities; they worked for larger production teams and had a significant share of their production output extracted by the state for urban consumption. Yet the rise in local productivity levels together with the expansion of farmland area and the attainment of higher levels of crop production were sufficient to assure the basic food security of a fast-growing population.

This population growth did not lead to radical changes in the social and spatial organization of the village, but reinforced the Inner-Outer spatial opposition created during the Great Leap Forward. The 1960s and 1970s marked a period of significant economic and demographic competition not just between production teams but also between the two key residential areas of the village: the Inner Area and the Outer Area. Under Mao, more children meant more agricultural labor, and more labor meant more production output and more accumulated work points crediting work performed, so there was a strong incentive for villagers to marry early and give birth to many children. In the early 1970s, the central government launched official campaigns promoting *wan, xi, shao* (SC), meaning "later marriage, longer birth interval, and fewer births," but these campaigns did not have much impact in the Yellow Flower region. Local family planning ideologies remained strongly pronatalist, but there were economic and demographic inequalities between production teams, with some production teams being more successful than others in terms of access to resources and fertility levels. A similar dynamic of inequality affected the development of the two major residential areas of the village, with the Outer Area doing slightly better than the Inner Area. Many villagers told me that the main reason for this was that the households residing in the newly developed Outer Area were more closely aligned with brigade-level power structures and were favored in terms of access to resources in the local redistributive economy. This helps us understand why the Outer Area experienced a slightly higher rate of population growth during the 1960s and 1970s.

Village Life in the Age of Labor Migration

By the late 1990s, when I first arrived in Harmony Cave, a new way of conceptualizing and experiencing the spatial opposition between the Inner Area and the Outer Area was emerging. The construction of the Sand Spine residential area in 1960 created a conceptual spatial opposition between the "progressive" socialist values of the Outer Area and the "backward" feudalist values of the Inner Area, but this opposition was subject to a number of important changes after the death of Mao in 1976. Decollectivization allowed villagers to regain a number of economic freedoms. Production teams were turned into village groups without any shared production responsibilities. The land was redistributed at the level of the household, and village families started to engage in an increasingly diverse range of income-earning activities involving monetary transactions. By the mid-1980s, villagers in Harmony Cave and the whole of Yellow Flower township started to engage in labor migration to cities in the neighboring Pearl River Delta region, a development that reflected the region's geographic location in the province of Guangdong.

This province was favored by the central government to be "one step ahead" (Vogel 1990) of the rest of China in the process of Reform and Opening due to its proximity to Hong Kong and Macau. As early as 1980, Deng Xiaoping announced the creation of the Special Economic Zones of Shenzhen and Zhuhai (next to Hong Kong and Macau, respectively), and in the mid-1980s, a number of liberalizing economic reforms were implemented in most major cities in Guangdong (Whyte and Parish 1984; Ikels 1996). These reforms led to spectacular changes in terms of urbanization, infrastructural development, and economic growth, and in 1992, Deng Xiaoping declared during his Southern Tour in Shenzhen, "Let some people get rich first!" an expression that captured the spirit of the new civilizing project of post-socialist modernization emerging in Guangdong and the rest of China.

The main goal of this new civilizing project was to stimulate the growth of urban economies through the devaluation of agricultural work and the development of the necessary infrastructural networks of mobility to facilitate the transport of goods and commodities and the circular migration of cheap "peasant" labor from the country to the city. This new civilizing project relied on various technocratic measures to maintain, if not intensify, the inequalities between rural and urban areas that had developed during the previous decades of high socialism, while introducing a new component of mobility and interconnectivity. Under Mao, the spatial movements of the population were strictly controlled, and households were classified by function within a system of agricultural and nonagricultural status divisions. These divisions masked differential access to state resources and allowed the central government to extract resources from agricultural households and communities to feed the privileged urban populations.

Under Deng Xiaoping and after, the household (SC: *hukou*) registration system was kept in place, and with it the caste-like system of distinctions between agricultural and nonagricultural households (K. Chan 2010). The central government continued to devalue agricultural work and extract agricultural resources from rural communities, but there was a new framework of subjectification: rural citizens were now being encouraged to migrate to the city to seek work, but they were not given full access to urban citizenship entitlements. For the central government, this was a cheap and potentially stable way to feed the growth of urban economies, but for the villagers—who did not have much say in these new developments—this posed a number of intimate choices and dilemmas of subjectivation regarding the desirability of engaging with a new model of livelihood based on labor migration and the desire to strive for economic prosperity.

Reassembling the Inner Area–Outer Area Opposition

In Harmony Cave, and in most villages in Yellow Flower township, the village factions that favored engaging with labor migration ended up prevailing, and local engagement with labor migration allowed many village households and families to make enough money to move out of their fast-decaying clay-brick homes (C: *nai-jyun nguk*) in tightly knit village compounds and to build more modern, fully detached houses made of solid construction materials. These houses have multiple stories (usually two or three) and are square-shaped buildings with a flat terrace on top (figure 1.3). Although not very big or extravagant in design, they are known in the local Cantonese language as *lau* (C), literally "mansions," a term that captures the

FIGURE 1.3. Building a modern house with multiple stories, Harmony Cave, 2000

symbolic significance of these buildings in the local imagination. The first Harmony Cave "mansions" were constructed in the late 1990s, and most of these modern houses were built in the Outer Area of the village, close to the brigade's headquarters. This was a housing revolution that added new meanings to the "old" symbolic opposition between the Inner Area and the Outer Area. As more and more modern houses were built in the "outer area," this part of the village became increasingly associated with economic success through labor migration. If in the 1960s the term Outer Area was associated with the "progressive" values of high socialism, by the late 1990s and the early 2000s it was increasingly associated with the "progressive" values of the new post-socialist era of money and labor migration.

This transformation was gradual and involved complex intimate choices made by villagers, families, and communities. Local attitudes about rural-urban migration started to change in the late 1970s and the early 1980s with the beginning of decollectivization and economic liberalization. Guangdong has a long history of practices of migration, including long-distance migration to North America, western Europe, and Southeast Asia (J. Watson 1975; M. Chen 2013), but the Maoist-implemented national household registration system introduced significant restrictions on the movement of people across rural-urban boundaries. Under Deng Xiaoping, some of these mobility restrictions were loosened and there emerged a phenomenon of informal rural-urban migration. Harmony Cave was one of the first villages in Yellow Flower township to discover the economic advantages of engaging in rural-urban migration.

In 1981 a young married man from Harmony First, A-Hang, managed to get permission from local officials to visit affinal relatives (in-laws) in Nanhai, a city in the Pearl River Delta region. The details of this trip were arranged by landline phone at the post office in the market town. In those days, the village brigade still did not have access to electricity or to telephone communication, and moving from one place to another was complicated. Local roads were still very narrow and muddy, and there were still no commercial bus services connecting the township to the city, so A-Hang bicycled his way out of the hills to a national road and boarded a truck that took him to the city of Nanhai. It took him two days to arrive at his final destination. His relatives lived in a rural neighborhood in Nanhai, but they were no longer farming, so A-Hang rented a large portion of their agricultural land and started to cultivate rice and vegetables to sell in local redistribution markets. A-Hang's wife soon joined him in Nanhai, and they prospered during the first few years of their business.

The villagers to follow A-Hang's footsteps were from Harmony First. This is not surprising, for two reasons. The first is that A-Hang's family was attached to the production team of Harmony First, and he favored sharing his knowledge and experience with people from his own production team. The second reason is that the families that form the core of the production team of Harmony First are closely related in terms of agnatic descent, and when the local economy was liberalized in the late 1970s and early 1980s, they were already in possession of the necessary skills to cope with the challenges and uncertainties of launching a family business. Their advantage was historical. Many of the families that form the core of the production team of Harmony First have a history of successful business activities in the period before the Communist Revolution. This history generated a number of deeply ingrained economic habits, skills, and dispositions that were significantly repressed during the Maoist period[12] but that remained alive (albeit in a dormant form) through informal processes of intergenerational transmission of skills. After Reform and Opening, this economic "habitus" (Bourdieu 1977, 1979, 1980) was allowed to come to life once again, playing an important role in guiding Harmony First villagers to venture into the Pearl River Delta region in order to develop successful forms of economic entrepreneurship and family business.

The first group of Harmony First villagers to follow A-Hang's footsteps in 1983–84 included six couples who developed a model of work and living arrangements that would prove influential for future developments. These couples were successful in setting up their own agricultural enterprises in the same area in Nanhai. They focused on growing vegetables rather than rice because vegetables grow faster and are thus more suitable as cash crops, and they built zinc huts in the middle of their vegetable gardens, working and living on their rented agricultural land (figure 1.4). Vegetable gardening is very intensive and requires multiple workers. Doing it alone is difficult, so it works best as a family endeavor, but not all elders found it easy to cope with long-distance traveling and to adapt to the new ways of life in the vegetable gardens. For this reason, when couples left the village, they preferred to leave their children (if they had any) under the care of their patrilateral grandparents.

This first wave of village migrants included a small number of young unmarried men who ventured to the city to look for factory work. This was the time when the industrial output of the Pearl River Delta region was starting to take off in what was a very early stage of its economic ascent as the world's factory floor. One of these village men got a job in a slaughterhouse

FIGURE 1.4. Zinc hut in a vegetable garden, Guangzhou, 2015

in the rural outskirts of Nanhai. Another found work in a palm broom factory also in the same area. These men sought employment in areas that allowed them to reside in the vegetable gardens of fellow villagers. This was a good way to save money on housing, but it was also a way to benefit from social support. A similar phenomenon shaped the migration strategies of village couples planning to set up a vegetable gardening enterprise. Most migrant couples preferred to rent land in areas not too far from the vegetable gardens of other fellow villagers in order to benefit from various forms of social support. This migration pattern led to the emergence of a number of satellite village communities in the Pearl River Delta region.[13] The one in Nanhai was the first, but others quickly followed.

A second wave of village migrants in 1985 and 1986 was still largely circumscribed to the village group of Harmony First. Some of these migrants favored going to Nanhai, but others started to explore other cities in the Pearl River Delta, such as Guangzhou and Foshan. The work patterns chosen by migrants were similar. Couples were primarily interested in vegetable gardening in periurban areas that had land specifically allocated for that purpose, preferably with fellow villagers nearby. Single men, by contrast, wanted jobs in factories or with other employers who would not ask questions pertaining to official restrictions regarding rural-urban migration. In 1985 the National People's Congress passed the Identity Card Bill of the People's Republic of China, which allowed the issuing of temporary residence permits for rural migrants. These permits rendered rural-urban migration legal but did not put an end to rural-urban segregation. Going to the city with a temporary residence permit as opposed to doing it illegally did not make much difference in terms of rights and entitlements. In both cases, village migrants retained the status of "second-class citizens" because as holders of a nonlocal "agricultural" household booklet, they did not have access to urban welfare services and privileges, and they could not easily acquire a local "nonagricultural" household booklet.

Additional waves of village migrants in the late 1980s and throughout the 1990s included the first batch of young unmarried women seeking individual paid work in factories and other workplaces in the cities (Pun 2005; H. Yan 2008; Gaetano 2015). This transformation went hand in hand with changes in local attitudes toward female education. In the 1980s and 1990s, under the influence of the nine-year compulsory education law of 1986, the number of young village girls attending primary school and middle school increased, thereby nurturing a female desire to pursue a life of migrant work.[14] The rate of female illiteracy among village women born in the 1970s or earlier is still high, but most village women born and bred during the Reform period have undergone some form of basic schooling. This educational revolution went hand in hand with a dramatic transformation in women's spatial mobility. Before the 1980s, the daily life of most village women was largely circumscribed to the physical space of the village and the surrounding agricultural fields.[15] In the 1980s and 1990s, village women started to venture on their own to places outside their village and township, and by the late 1990s, female rural-urban migration had already become normalized, along with increasing local emphasis on labor as a result of migration as the main source of family income.

This emphasis on labor migration led to the development of a translocal model of livelihood with far-reaching consequences (see map P.2). In a number of classic studies of agrarian transformation in Algerian society in the 1960s and 1970s, Pierre Bourdieu (1979, 2013; Bourdieu and Sayad 1964) uses the term "depeasantification" to refer to processes of social change associated with increasing "peasant" engagement with urban economies. Most villages in the Yellow Flower region are clearly being affected by dynamics of "depeasantification" in Bourdieu's sense, but this did not lead to the hollowing out of local rural society (cf. H. Yan 2008; Murphy 2002, 2020). Quite the contrary, it spurred the emergence of a new local rural society based on increasingly tight linkages to urban centers. Choosing to engage with labor migration allowed villagers to move away from subsistence farming, but the link to agriculture remained in place. This link is first of all a matter of livelihood. Most village migrants working in the city continue to earn a living through agricultural practices such as vegetable gardening, and most villagers who stay in Yellow Flower township continue to work in the agricultural sector, either by setting up their own independent business or by working for major agribusiness companies operating in the region. But the villagers' continuing attachment to agriculture is not just a matter of livelihood; it is also a matter of lifestyle. Many village families (including families with migrant workers) usually have someone in the village taking care of a few plots of village ancestral land and cultivating key food items like rice, peanuts, and sweet potatoes, among others, to help reduce living expenses and secure access to good-quality food.

This continuing attachment to agricultural practices goes hand in hand with a strong attachment to "traditional" notions of "native place" (C: *ga-heung*). From the very beginning, one of the main goals of village migrants was to make enough money in the city to improve living conditions back home. Labor migration allowed village families to develop new forms of housing that departed quite significantly from local architectural traditions and practices. Up until the 1980s and 1990s, most villagers in Yellow Flower township lived in fragile clay-brick houses that were not freestanding but were part of larger tightly knit village compounds. The new modern houses that emerged in the age of labor migration are bigger, more robust, and more self-contained than earlier clay-brick structures. In Harmony Cave, the first modern house was constructed in 1997 by a well-to-do family from Harmony First, soon followed by two similarly designed houses. Four years later, in 2001, there were already six modern houses in Harmony Cave, most of them built with savings earned through labor migration. By 2010 at least 50 percent of all village households were already living in a modern house, and the numbers have since continued to increase.

This housing revolution had a profound effect on the way villagers conceptualized the opposition between Inner Area and Outer Area. Harmony First families dominated the first phase of the housing boom in the 1990s and the 2000s, but there were also many new houses constructed by Harmony Third and Harmony Fifth families. Most new houses were constructed in the Outer Area, close to the primary school and the brigade's headquarters, and this collective investment on the expansion of the Outer Area represented a major symbolic and material intervention in the "old" opposition between Inner and Outer Areas. The construction in the 1960s of the residential area of Sand Spine created the Outer Area as a space for future village development, and this expansion embodied a set of political rationalities that represented a radical socialist break with the architectural traditions of the older Inner Area of the village. A similar break with the past started to take place in the 1990s and the 2000s with the construction of the first modern houses in the Outer Area of the village, but the guiding ideology of this new village project of modernization was no longer a philosophy of socialist planning and redistribution but instead a whole new set of post-socialist ideals based on money and economic success. This led to the emergence of a new

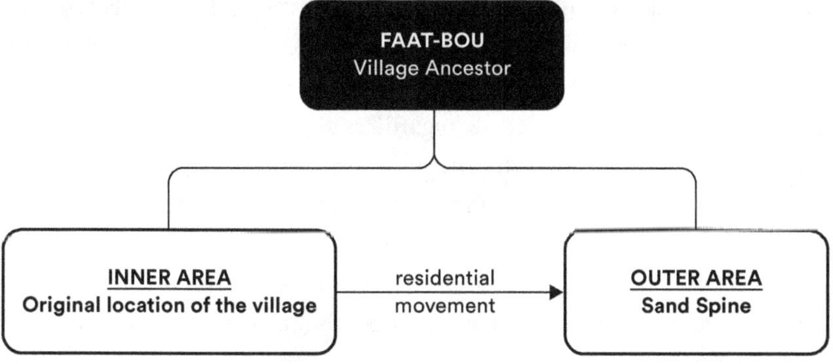

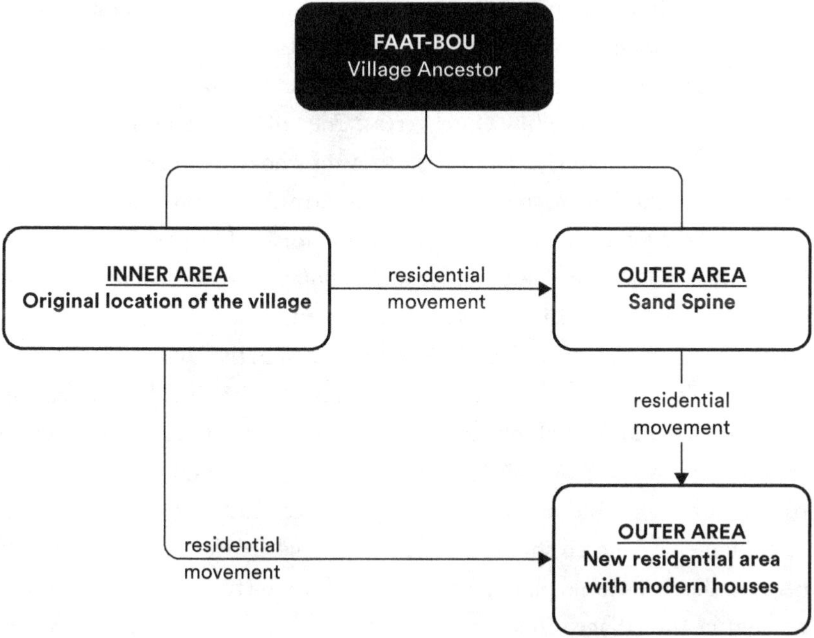

FIGURE 1.5. Changing residential arrangements in Harmony Cave, 1960s–1980s and 1990s–2000s

elite residential area of modern houses in the Outer Area of the village that included "mansions" built by village households from different village groups and agnatic branches (figure 1.5). The main factor behind this "mixing" was the emergence of increasing socioeconomic status differentiations in the village. Successful migrant workers (regardless of production team and lineage branch) wanted to distinguish themselves from other villagers by building a new house in the Outer Area of the village. This was a strategy of collective spatialization of socioeconomic status, and this spatial differentiation imposed itself on top of a preexisting layer of kinship-territorial differentiations. There were significant tensions underlying this project of socioeconomic differentiation.

Not everyone agreed with the decision to locate the new houses in the Outer Area, and I had the opportunity to participate in many of these intimate negotiations during my first stay in the village between 1999 and 2001. These debates often took place in the context of informal interactions, but there were also more formal negotiations. In the summer of 2000, I was invited to join a village panel to manage the construction of a new village memorial arch to commemorate the achievements of village ancestors. One of the main issues of contention was the location of the memorial arch: should it be built in the "old" part of the village (the Inner Area) or in the "new" part of the village (the Outer Area)? The village panel was dominated by male villagers from Harmony First, some of whom had recently built new houses in the Outer Area, so it is probably not surprising that the panel decided in favor of the Outer Area. The arguments put forward by panel members to justify this decision were very similar to those offered by Harmony First villagers to justify their decision to locate the construction of their new houses in the Outer Area: The village arch should be located in the Outer Area because of this area's convenience for transportation. At the time, the local township government had initiated the construction of a new asphalt road connecting the market town of Yellow Flower to the city of Yingde, and this road would run right through the middle of the Outer Area. The village panel argued that the memorial arch should be located somewhere close to this new road because the road would play an important role in the future economic development of the village. This decision met significant opposition within the village (also within Harmony First), but the memorial arch was ultimately constructed close to the new road in the Outer Area, next to the residential area with new houses.

Village Life in the Age of Hypermobility and Rural-Urban Interconnection

Twenty years have passed since the village memorial arch was inaugurated in the fall of 2001. Since then, the political project of turning the Outer Area into the core area of the village experienced a new wave of transformations. As more and more villagers sought work outside the village, the economic center of the village shifted to the market town of Yellow Flower and the various Pearl River Delta cities, and this led to further changes in home ownership strategies. Villagers continued to build new houses in the territory of the ancestral village, but there emerged a new trend to get a house or an apartment in the local market town, either because of business reasons or simply out of convenience: proximity to shuttle buses, schools, and markets, among other services. This trend toward getting a house or apartment in the market town (or even in a neighboring city) goes hand in hand with the development of a highly mobile lifestyle that was made possible by improvements in transportation networks and by increasing access to private cars (see J. Zhang 2019 on the rise of automobility in Reform China). Increased mobility has furthered the dynamics of village deterritorialization that were initiated by labor migration. This process of village deterritorialization has resulted in the development of a translocal mode of livelihood with flexible residential arrangements. The Outer Area of the village is no longer restricted to Sand Spine (built in the 1960s) or the area close to the village arch with new modern housing (emerged after the late 1990s); the Outer Area of the village now includes the market town of Yellow Flower and just about any urban area where villagers reside or work for much of the year (figure 1.6).

This dynamic of residential flexibility is a key component of the process of village deterritorialization shaping the lives of villagers in the twenty-first century, but it has raised important moral dilemmas for villagers and a new set of intimate negotiations. These negotiations were intensified in the last decade and have led to a renewed emphasis on the importance of returning to and taking care of the Inner Area of the ancestral village. This has inspired the renovation of several ancestral halls and residential hamlets in the older Inner Area of the village, and these endeavors were partly supported by government funds for rural development. The main issue at stake is a return to the Inner Area not as a daily residential space but as a space of collective

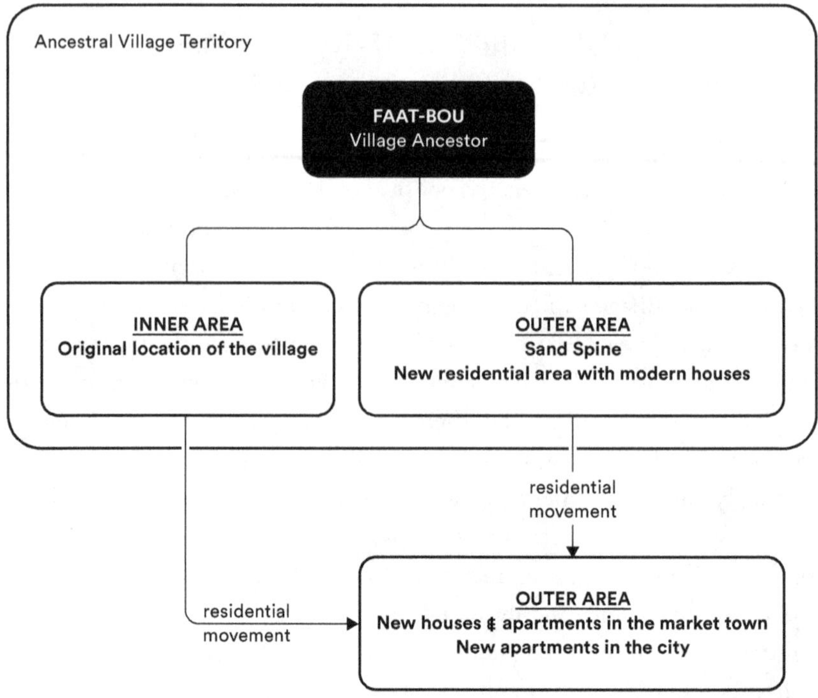

FIGURE 1.6. Moving beyond the territory of the ancestral Harmony Cave village, after 2000

memory and a site for collective ritual activities. Most village families continue to be dispersed in space and across the rural-urban continuum, and this translocal mode of livelihood has decreased the intensity of face-to-face interaction between villagers. At the same time, the increasing use of new technologies of communication has allowed villagers to keep in touch and even mimic intense face-to-face interactions by means of a daily routine of intense social media exchanges at a distance.

Labor Migration, Economic Diversification, and Household Income

Starting from the mid-2000s, labor migration effectively became the main source of income for most village families in Yellow Flower township. As a high-profile township official told me during an informal conversation in February 2015, "Every rural township in Guangdong has its own dominant economic strategy.[16] Village folks in Yellow Flower rely to a very large extent on income derived from labor migration. At least 40 to 50 percent of the local village population is working in the city for much of the year, and this migrant population usually has a level of education no higher than middle school. Setting up a vegetable-gardening enterprise remains the most popular option for migrant couples, and factory work together with service work remain the most popular options for youngsters." He continued, "Some townships favor a different strategy of rural development. In the neighboring township of Dragonpath, the majority of the village population stays at home doing a local business. Most village families invest money on orchards, planting fruits like mandarin orange. In Dragonpath, family earnings are on public display in people's orchards. In Yellow Flower, family earnings are hidden in bank savings or somewhere else outside the village in people's vegetable gardens; family earnings are not on public display at home because of labor migration." These differences are not just the product of diverging local official policies of development but also reflect complex micro-level intimate negotiations.

Today, labor migration remains an important source of family income in Yellow Flower township, but there is a trend toward economic diversification that is sponsored in large part by growing outside sources of investment. Village families continue to cultivate part of their agricultural land for household consumption, but a significant part of this land is now being rented to major agribusiness companies investing in large-scale plantations of tea, fruit, or bonsai trees. This transformation started in the mid-2000s, when the Guangdong authorities began promoting the relocation of smog-producing industrial facilities from the Pearl River Delta region to more peripheral areas like northern Guangdong.

This policy encouraged many large-scale agribusiness companies to move their operations into impoverished townships like Yellow Flower. This process of relocation requires paying fees to local township authorities, but it also involves negotiating access to land with local village groups. Although village land is distributed at the level of the household, the land continues to be treated as a collective asset, and in most cases agricultural companies cannot sign rental agreements with individual households. In 2010 the whole village of Harmony Cave agreed to rent out a significant portion of its agricultural land (including wetlands, dry land, and mountain land) to a major company of "ecological agriculture" and organic tea production belonging to the Takson Group. Two separate eight-year agreements were signed: one with Harmony First, Harmony Second, and Harmony Third (the descendants of Seui-fong), and another with Harmony Fourth and Harmony Fifth (the descendants of Seui-daat). In 2018 the Takson Group signed a new eight-year agreement with both village groups. The company agreed to pay an annual fee of ¥500 (US$75) per *mu* to the descendants of Seui-fong and the descendants of Seui-daat. The company also agreed to pay an additional fee to the local township government, but this number is not public. The company reached similar agreements with other villages, and as of 2018 it was responsible for the cultivation of 3,000 *mu* (200 hectares) in Yellow Flower township as part of its corporate strategy for promoting economic sustainability and poverty reduction in the countryside.

This is not the only type of negotiations going on between villagers and agribusiness companies. Not all companies coming to Yellow Flower township develop their business in line with national and local officials' visions of "ecological agriculture." Most companies are not so ecologically minded and there were even a few cases of illegal logging companies and mining companies engaging in environmentally disastrous operations in the township. But the most representative type of not so ecologically minded company in Yellow Flower is Guangdong Wens Foodstuff Group. This company does not rent village land or hire local villagers to work on large-scale projects of agricultural development. Instead the company outsources its farming operations to local farmers and provides equipment, expert consultancy, and insurance against risk. Farmers working for Guangdong Wens have some degree of managerial autonomy because they are not working directly under a boss, but they have to sell their pigs or chickens to Guangdong Wens at prices that are partly set by the market, partly set by the company. Many farmers told me in 2016 that they no longer enjoy as much freedom as they had in the early 2010s because Guangdong Wens has imposed increasingly stringent regulatory frameworks due to a number of high-profile food scandals in Guangdong and nationwide. The income of farmers working with this company varies quite significantly, depending on market price fluctuations and on the final quality and volume of their harvest. In Harmony Cave, there were at least fifteen families in 2018 subcontracting farming operations from Guangdong Wens, and I visited most of these pig farms and chicken farms in 2018. One thing I noticed during this visit is that all farms are located as far away as possible from village residential areas due to increasing concerns with the environmental hazards produced by these farms.

These changes in the local economy have facilitated the diversification of local economic strategies, and this has in turn facilitated the return of many village migrants to the township. Many villagers are no longer willing to go through the hardships of labor migration for a long period of time, so after a few years working in the city, they return to the township to set up a local business, quite often an agricultural business such as working for Guangdong Wens or else setting up an independent agricultural enterprise such as an orchard plantation. As several Harmony Cave friends reminded me during a return visit to the village in 2017, the countryside nowadays is a better place to make money and earn a living than two decades earlier (C: *yi-ga nung-chyun hou wan-chin gwo yi sap nin chin*). One important factor contributing to this climate of economic optimism is the growth of the local tourism industry.

Although Yellow Flower was officially opened for tourist commercialization as early as the late 1990s, the township has never delivered in this respect until quite recently. In the early 2010s, tourist numbers started to rise steeply due to improvements in regional transportation infrastructures connecting the township to surrounding cities, and these changes led to growth in the number of local hostels, hotels, tourist shops, and restaurants. The new trend in the township is for villagers to set up rural hostels (C: *nung-ga-lok*) to cater to the growing tourism industry, especially during major Golden Week public holidays like Labor Day (May First), National Day (October First), and Chinese New Year (usually in January or February). The nationwide mobility restrictions imposed during the first half of 2020 because of the COVID-19 pandemic negatively affected the local tourism industry as well as the income of the local migrants working in urban areas, but it is still too early to say what the long-term impact of the pandemic will be on the local economy. The dramatic growth of the tourism industry after the turn of the millennium is part of a larger set of changes pointing to a profound structural transformation in the local economy. If it is true—as my Harmony Cave friends put it in 2017—that the countryside is now a better place to make money and earn a living than two decades earlier, it is also true that living costs are higher and "people's material aspirations have increased quite significantly" (C: *yi-ga jeui-kau ge ye do-jo hou do*). In the early 2000s, the average monthly income of a factory worker laboring twelve hours a day was less than ¥1,000 (US$120), and the average annual income of a migrant couple working as vegetable gardeners was about ¥10,000 (US$1,200). This income level is very low by present-day standards, but villagers were more frugal and less consumption-driven than they are today, so they managed to save a significant portion of their annual income, and they needed only ten to fifteen years' worth of savings to be able to upgrade their housing and build a two-story "mansion" costing as little as ¥70,000 (US$8,400).

Today, the logic of the local economy is completely different. There was a significant increase in average income levels, but villagers are less frugal and costs are higher. A factory job in the city now pays between ¥3,000 (US$450) and ¥5,000 (US$740) per month, depending on the quality of the work and the total number of work hours, and working for a small restaurant in Yellow Flower market town now pays as much as ¥2,000 (US$295) per month. Migrant couples working as vegetable gardeners can make between ¥30,000 (US$4,500) and ¥50,000 (US$7,400) per year, and this is also the average annual household income in Yellow Flower township. These numbers point to a twofold to fivefold increase in average income levels when compared to the early 2000s. But while it is true that income levels have increased in absolute terms, it is also true that living costs are higher, material aspirations have increased, and villagers are spending far more money as consumers. Consumption levels are so high—when compared to the early 2000s—that a household with an annual income of ¥30,000 (US$4,500) can hardly save any money. It takes an annual household income of ¥50,000 (US$740) for one to be able to save as much as one did in the early 2000s. But saving ¥10,000 (US$1,200) every year is not a lot of money nowadays. Building a new village house with two stories has risen in cost from ¥70,000 (US$8,400) to ¥300,000 (US$45,000) including fittings, interior decoration, and furniture. Household savings are often no longer enough to purchase a new village house or a new apartment in the market town. Most households need the support of relatives and friends to be able to secure this kind of money.

Rebuilding the Ancestral Village in the Age of Digital Interconnection

The numbers above place Yellow Flower village communities in the rural periphery of the larger regional economy of Guangdong province, reflecting growing socioeconomic inequalities between the wealthy Pearl River Delta region and the northern hilly regions of the province (Y. Zhang, Tong, and Liang 2018). But the numbers above also point to growing socioeconomic inequalities in local society, which are still reflected in housing. The total number of Harmony Cave families living in new modern houses has been increasing steadily since the turn of the millennium, but at least 15 to 20 percent of all village households are still living in clay-brick housing structures. There is also an increasing diversification of housing arrangements. Many families favored building their new house in the Outer Area of the village, but there is a growing tendency to move out of the village and settle in a new house or a new apartment in the local market town or even in a neighboring city. This tendency toward getting a house or apartment outside the village has intensified in the last decade and has furthered the dynamics of village deterritorialization initiated by the process of labor migration, but villagers continue to show a strong sense of symbolic attachment to the physical territory of the ancestral village and, among villagers who grew up in the 1980s and 1990s, there is a growing sense of nostalgia about the past and the tranquility of having a simple village life. In January 2019, just before Chinese Lunar New Year, a village friend and amateur poet, A-Gaam, sent me a poem via the social media platform WeChat that helps capture the double bind faced by village migrants caught in between the increasing uncertainties of work in the city and the self-mocked nostalgic memory of a simple life of subsistence agriculture back in the tranquility of one's home village (pronunciation in Cantonese):

Gam-maan choi-ga daai dit, seung faan ga-heung jung faan-syu.
今晚菜价大跌，想返家乡种番薯。
Tonight the market price of vegetables has dropped, and I feel like going back to my home village to cultivate sweet potatoes [for self-subsistence].

Heung-ha hung-hei hou,
乡下空气好，
The air of the country is so good,

Jung-cheut dou si bou.
种出都是宝。
Whatever is planted turns into a treasure.

Faan-syu haau yat haau,
番薯烤一烤，
Roasting sweet potatoes,

Sik-yun man yau-mou.
食完问有无。
Once we are done eating [sweet potatoes] one can always ask for more.

Wu-tau haau yuk bou,
芋头烤肉煲，
Taro barbecue pot,

Sik-baau tou sou-sou.
食饱肚扫扫。
Once the stomach is full it will clear things away.

The message of the poem is quite simple: Life is nice and simple back in one's home village if only one could go back, but one cannot really go back. Regardless of whether one is working as a self-employed vegetable gardener in the city or as a subcontractor for an agribusiness company in Yellow Flower, the reality is similarly harsh: everyone is busy working harder and harder under increasing uncertainties, no guarantees of pay, and increasing costs of living and family reproduction.[17] Under these circumstances, it is tempting to cultivate a sense of nostalgia for the past, and in the last decade, this sense of nostalgia is starting to lead to a renewed emphasis among villagers on the importance of taking care of the traditional Inner Area of the ancestral village. This emphasis is taking place at the same time as the fast-paced dynamics of village deterritorialization described above and is adding a new traditionalist twist to local forms of engagement with larger civilizing visions and narratives of Reform-era modernity.

To be modern from the 1980s and 1990s onward was to make enough money to build one's own house with two or three stories, but by the turn of the millennium, when the first new village "mansions" were constructed, it became clear that the place to build one's new mansion and thus to express one's modernity was the Outer Area of the village. Since then, village households continued to associate modernity with building a modern house in the Outer Area of the village, but the meaning of the term "Outer Area" was gradually expanded beyond the ancestral village to include the local market town and various neighboring cities. This process of village deterritorialization has raised questions about the future of village unity and safety, leading to complex internal negotiations that starting from the 2010s resulted in the emergence of a new counteremphasis on the importance of creating an alternative vision of modernity that seeks to combine the pursuit of spatial mobility and economic income with the ritual celebration of ancestral traditions and spaces. This new narrative of modernity has already inspired the renovation of several ancestral halls and residential hamlets in the older Inner Area of the village (figure 1.7).

The year 2010 marked the rise of this more "traditionalist" vision of modernity and village development, and once again the village group of Harmony First was instrumental. In the late 1990s and early 2000s, Harmony First played a key role in promoting the construction of a large number of new modern houses in the Outer Area of the village, but by 2010 this village group decided to change its views on the course of development. Confronted with increasing traffic on the main road close to the primary school and the

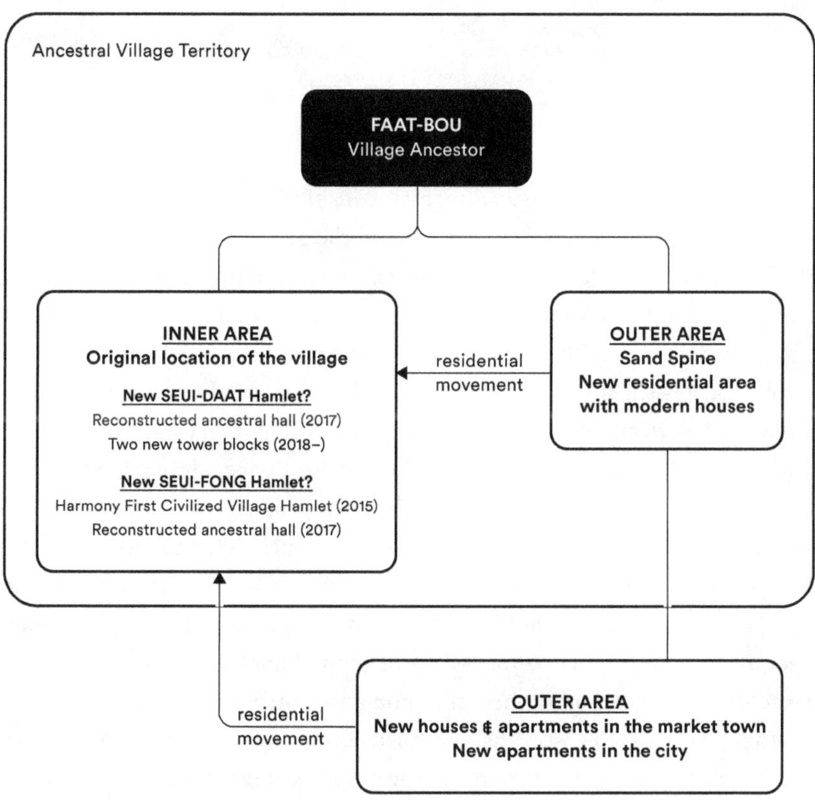

FIGURE 1.7. Reconstructing the inner area of the ancestral Harmony Cave village, after 2010

FIGURE 1.8. Demolishing the old Harmony First residential area, 2012

brigade's headquarters, the leading members of this village group started to advocate for a return to the Inner Area on the grounds that this part of the village had a better feng shui and was quieter and more secluded. It was at this point that the group decided to apply to a national rural development program called "Civilized Village" (SC: Wenming Cun) to gain access to governmental subsidies to help improve housing conditions (Perry 2011). Villagers had to submit a construction plan developed in close consultation with the local government, including a detailed budget showing how villagers would match governmental subsidies. The project was approved in 2011, and a brand-new Harmony First hamlet was concluded and inaugurated a few years later in 2015 (figure 1.8). The village groups of Harmony Second and Harmony Third did not join this Harmony First project, but two years later, in 2017, they joined forces with Harmony First to renovate and reconstruct the ancestral hall of their common ancestor: Seui-fong.

This project of ancestral hall reconstruction is symptomatic of a larger dynamic of ritual competition between lineage branches. A few months before the inauguration of the reconstructed ancestral hall of Seui-fong (the ancestor of Harmony First, Harmony Second, and Harmony Third), the village groups of Harmony Fourth and Harmony Fifth celebrated the reconstruction of the ancestral hall of their common ancestor: Seui-daat. Both ancestral halls were built in the Inner Area of the village, and the consecration of these ancestral halls in 2017 was an important part of the return to the Inner Area initiated in 2015 with the construction of a brand-new Harmony First "Civilized Village" hamlet.

This return to the Inner Area was marked by a few more recent developments. In 2018 the village groups of Harmony Fourth and Harmony Fifth announced the construction of two tall residential buildings in the Inner Area of the village in what was a response to the "Civilized Village" project of Harmony First. In 1960 Harmony Fourth had moved to Sand Spine and Harmony Fifth had moved to a small residential compound close to the Inner Area. These two village groups lived in separate residential areas between the 1960s and the 1990s. In the 2000s, a number of economically successful families from Harmony Fourth and Harmony Fifth started to build new modern houses, but the location of these new houses was scattered (some were constructed in the Inner Area, others in the Outer Area). In the early 2010s, prominent members of these two village groups started to engage in conversations about the renovation of the ancestral hall of their common ancestor: Seui-daat. These conversations opened the way for a larger debate about village group housing and about a possible residential return to the Inner Area of the village. There was, however, a problem of space. The land owned by the two groups in the Inner Area was insufficient to allow the construction of individualized new housing for all the members of the two village groups. The two groups had faced this problem in 1960 before moving to Sand Spine, but back then, they did not have at their disposal the technology to build tall buildings with enough apartments to accommodate everyone. In 2018 the leaders of the two village groups signed a deal with a professional construction company to build two tall blocks of apartments right next to the ancestral hall of Seui-daat: one block is managed by Harmony Fourth, the other by Harmony Fifth. In 2019, in response to this initiative from Harmony Fourth and Harmony Fifth, the leaders of the village group of Harmony First started to discuss plans for the construction of one tall block of apartments right in the middle of the Harmony First "Civilized Village" hamlet, next to the ancestral hall of Maan-hin, their ancestral head.

This return to the Inner Area reveals a strong commitment to the notion of a shared ancestral village. Villagers are increasingly concerned with practices of communal ancestor worship, as suggested by the renovation of the ancestral halls of Seui-fong and Seui-daat in the Inner Area, but they are also spending a significant amount of savings on other communal ritual activities such as those based on local deity temple associations. These organizations have lost much of the authority and the political functions they had in the pre-Communist period, when local society was profoundly fragmented and divided by territorial feuds, but they are still an important source of collective identity, and they offer some protection from the vagaries of the market economy. They are an important source of social solidarity in the local society, but villagers are no longer interacting with one another in tightly knit forms of daily village sociality. Many of the newly built houses in Harmony Cave are empty or are occupied only by elders and young children because of the high rates of labor migration. Village migrants have developed a highly mobile lifestyle that involves frequent movements between village, market town, and city, and they often have few opportunities for regular face-to-face interaction, which increasingly is restricted to major ritual occasions, such as weddings, funerals, and full-month banquets, and major communal festivals like lineage celebrations and deity temple ritual celebrations.

This is not to say that villagers do not keep in touch with one another. Mobile phones have played a key role in long-distance communication since the 2000s, and the increasing availability of smart phones in the 2010s onward allowed villagers to re-create a daily routine of intense group exchanges in the virtual world of social media platforms (Wallis 2013; Law and Peng 2006, 2008). Most villagers are regular participants in WeChat groups, with daily exchanges between members of different circles of proximity, including close family, extended family, village group (lineage branch), and old classmates, among others. These exchanges are at times very intense, but one does have to show up all the time online and the exchanges are no longer based on face-to-face interactions. Such daily virtual exchanges allow villagers to maintain a sense of community and shared origins, but this sense of community and shared origins is no longer a territorial assemblage in Fei's classic sense. Villagers no longer depend on shared ancestral land as a major source of livelihood, and they no longer live in tightly knit residential areas. Village migrants have developed a mobile model of livelihood that involves constant rural-urban movements, but this translocality did not lead to a complete rejection of territory and shared ancestral origins. Villagers continue to attach a strong value to the ancestral village. The ancestral village has become a major site for the ritual celebration of shared identity, and there is also a strong obligation to attend major communal ritual events.

CHAPTER 2

Love and Marriage

The Challenge of Scientific Birth Planning

LOVE, MARRIAGE, AND FAMILY PLANNING ARE NOT NECESSARILY experienced as a tightly connected whole, but in Yellow Flower township, they are often presented in daily conversations and ritual activities as if they are part of a larger unified set of social obligations. These gendered, heteronormative functions fulfill the work of familial social reproduction as prescribed by local traditions of family and lineage organization. But what happens to local practices when they start to be governed by very powerful technocratic notions of scientific birth planning supported by state organizations as well as by a widening range of quasi-state and nonstate actors?

China's explicit engagement with transnational neo-Malthusian ideas goes back to the late nineteenth century, but this engagement was fragmentary and largely inconsequential at the policy level. The origins of the reformist agenda of family planning go back to the establishment of a Family Planning Commission within the State Council in 1964, but the scale of this civilizing agenda was significantly amplified after the launching of the Birth Planning Policy (SC: Jihua Shengyu Zhengce) in the late 1970s. This took the form of a strict One-Child Policy in major cities like Beijing and Guangzhou (a Two-Child Policy since 2016 and a Three-Child Policy since 2021), but there were significant variations in implementation across the country, especially in rural areas. In rural northern Guangdong, it took the form of a highly flexible two- to three-children policy, and its implementation required the use of significant coercive force on the bodies of villagers, especially women, by means of medical technologies such as mandatory intrauterine devices (IUDs) and procedures such as sterilization and abortion.

The moral clash between local patriarchal family arrangements and the technocratic values of the Birth Planning Policy was particularly violent between the 1980s and the 2000s, and its influence lingers in contemporary village society. In the mid-2010s, the central government started to loosen its nationwide restrictions on marital fertility, but it continued to control biological reproduction and the bodies of ordinary villagers, especially women, by means of regular medical checkups and contraceptive technologies such as IUDs. Most scholars and commentators analyzing the societal impact of the Birth Planning Policy highlight the agency of the central government and the support of international organizations (White 2006; Scharping 2003; M. Fong 2016). This approach is very insightful but is somewhat monolithic because it places too much emphasis on the capacity of the central government to make interventions and change the behavior and the minds of ordinary citizens and citizen communities.

This state-centric narrative fails to acknowledge that the implementation of the Birth Planning Policy involved the active participation of many quasi-state and nonstate actors and institutions, including ordinary communities, families, and individuals (Greenhalgh 2003, 2008, 2010, 2020; Greenhalgh and Winckler 2005). The active role of ordinary citizens and communities in the implementation of the Birth Planning Policy is particularly visible in rural communities and areas that remain strongly attached to their traditional values of family and lineage organization. In Cantonese-speaking northern Guangdong, these traditions continue to place a strong emphasis on lineage organization and the importance of having many patrilineal heirs. This continuing attachment to pronatalist, male-biased reproductive ideals has shaped the choices and negotiations of villagers and village communities as they engaged with larger official technocratic frameworks of population governance.

Under the Birth Planning Policy agenda, family planning practices in China were increasingly subject to globalized articulations of technocience and technocratic expertise, but there is still a limited understanding of how these macro-level forces were themselves entangled in complex user-mediated negotiations at the micro level. Motion is important to make sense of the coming together of larger sociotechnical ensembles of power and chains of transformation, but as anthropologist Anna Tsing suggests in her famous study (2005, 4) of global (dis-)connection in the Indonesian rain forests, "There is no motion without friction." Friction is not just what gets in the way of motion; it is also what makes movement possible. Friction—as Tsing defines it—refers to "the awkward, unequal, unstable, and creative qualities of interconnection across difference" (ibid.). Friction is what makes global connection powerful and effective, and it also gets in the way of the smooth operation of global power. Friction makes possible the movement of global neo-Malthusian technologies of family planning to impoverished rural areas in Guangdong province, but it is also what gets in the way of this development, what disrupts and reconfigures circulation of new visions of technocratic modernity.

The following case study features a family from the Harmony First hamlet, seen through the lens of two different generations: one born in the 1950s and 1960s, the other born in the 1980s and 1990s.[1] All families are unique and this family is no exception, but its generational shifts illustrate larger processes of transformation in Yellow Flower township and in many parts of village China. The generation born in the 1950s and 1960s experienced love and marriage in the 1960s, 1970s, and 1980s in line with local patriarchal traditions and under the influence of earlier socialist legal reforms, but their family planning practices were subject to dramatic forces of technocratic reconfiguration after the 1980s and 1990s under the influence of the Birth Planning Policy. Local resistance to the policy began to decline only in the first decade of the twenty-first century when the generation born in the 1980s and 1990s started to have children. This generation continues to embrace "traditional" patriarchal values of family planning, but they want to have fewer children and are more concerned with personal happiness.

Love and Marriage in the 1970s and 1980s

Bright Gold (born 1962) is the male head of one of the households I know best in Harmony Cave, as I lived with his family for six months during my first stay in the village and have remained in close communication by means of phone exchanges and regular visits for nearly two decades. When I first got to know the family between July 1999 and January 2000, it included Bright Gold, his wife, and their four young children (three sons and one daughter). Bright Gold has no brothers, and his parents passed away in the 1980s. He has four sisters, but when I first arrived in the village, these sisters had long ago married out to neighboring lineage communities.

Reflecting the continuing hold of "traditional" ethical frameworks of "valuing males and belittling females" (C: *jung-naam hing-neui*) in the 1960s and 1970s, Bright Gold (as the only son) was the only child of the family to be allowed to undergo formal schooling. Back then, few boys made it beyond primary school, but Bright Gold managed to enroll in a local "people-run" middle school, obtaining his senior middle degree in 1978. Three years later, in 1981, he married an illiterate girl from a neighboring lineage community whom he had first seen in 1978 while working in the rice fields of an affinal relative. He and his wife, Full Elder Sister (born 1960), told me proudly on several occasions that theirs was not an arranged marriage as in the "old society" (C: *gau se-wui*). There was of course a matchmaker, and their parents and close village relatives had a strong say in the marriage, but the choice of marriage partner was not entirely imposed on them, and they were at least partly involved in the process of matchmaking.

Bright Gold told me that he agreed with his parents and close lineage relatives that Full Elder Sister was a good match because she clearly had a good "foundation" (C: *gan-gei*): her own physical constitution and family history suggested that she would be able to work hard in the fields and to give birth to many sons, a major concern for Bright Gold's father, who married late in life and managed to have only one son. Full Elder Sister made up her mind about Bright Gold only after making a secret premarital visit to his village in the company of a small group of young women from her natal village. This customary practice of "visiting the house (of the prospective groom)" (C: *mong-nguk*) helped her acquire detailed information about Bright Gold and his family before agreeing to move to the next stage of the marriage negotiations.

A key part of these negotiations focused on the contents of "corporeal body money" (C: *yuk-san-chin*), a traditional form of brideprice payment given by the groom's parents to the bride's parents. Even today, such negotiations involve a series of exchanges between the parents of the two sides, but back in the 1970s and 1980s, these exchanges were largely controlled by parents and left little room for the development of intense premarital contact between groom and bride. In those days, young adults did not engage in what today is called "dating" (C: *paak-to*) on national TV shows, and premarital sex and "love relationships" (C: *lyun-ngoi gwaan-hai*) had yet to become a subject of public discussion. Most importantly, romantic love was not considered a key factor when choosing a marriage partner. Social background, labor skills, and brideprice payment, to give a few examples, were far more important. The fact, however, that youngsters did have at least a partial say in whom they married represented an important departure from earlier practices.

Most marriages in the 1930s and 1940s were completely dictated by parents. Parents usually negotiated the marriage of their children at a very young age, and if this was not possible, the marriage would be arranged by parents at a later stage and would often involve "blind arrangements" whereby the groom and bride would see each other for the first time only on the day of their wedding. In the 1930s and 1940s, it was possible to have only one official wife, but it was common for wealthier households to establish polygynic households involving the cohabitation of a "big wife" (C: *daai-po*), the official wife, with a "small wife" (C: *sai-po*), a concubine with a lower status.

Starting from the 1950s, these intimate structures were significantly transformed, in large part because of the New Marriage Law of 1950 and various socialist mass campaigns promoting the practice of "free monogamous marriage" through a policy of compulsory official registration of marriage.[2] Old bachelors like Bright Gold's father would never have been able to marry and have a family of his own without the New Marriage Law of 1950. The law challenged the local custom of keeping widows under the control of the patrilineal family of the deceased husband, and this allowed many widows to have the option of remarrying, usually without any brideprice exchanges involved. At the time, not everyone was willing to marry a widow because of the local belief that widows are "ghost-wives" (C: *gwai-po*) who bring bad luck, but old bachelors like Bright Gold's father were more inclined to favor this "unlucky" option to the alternative of remaining unmarried for the rest of their lives. In 1952 Bright Gold's father agreed to marry a "ghost-wife" from a neighboring village, but she died during the birth of their first child (a baby daughter) in 1954. In 1955 Bright Gold's father agreed to marry a second "ghost-wife," also from a neighboring village, who gave birth to three additional daughters and one son (Bright Gold). We thus see that Bright Gold and his sisters would never have been born without the changes brought about by the New Marriage Law and its support for a notion of monogamous marriage based on the willingness of the two individual parties involved.

Official commitment to encouraging marriage and family life based on free individual choice was intensified after the beginning of Deng Xiaoping's reforms in the late 1970s. An important turning point was the Second Marriage Law of 1980, which was officially promulgated in 1981, the very year when Bright Gold and Full Elder Sister registered their marriage. This law, which redefined marriage as a voluntary contractual relationship grounded on emotional affection, made divorce much easier under certain circumstances. Many anthropologists have argued that this legal change inspired a nationwide turn toward the increasing salience of affective ties and individual satisfaction in heteronormative frameworks of love, marriage, and family life (Y. Yan 2003; Jankowiak and Li 2017; Davis 2014b). This transformation was gradual and affected different parts of China in very different ways. In rural areas like Yellow Flower township, the turn toward the increasing salience of affective ties and individual satisfaction was not immediate and remained limited for much of the 1980s and 1990s. However, one aspect of the revised law had a more immediate and visible impact in Yellow Flower: its definition of marriage in light of an emerging national policy of neo-Malthusian family planning and population control designed by the newly established National Family Planning Commission.

Having Children and Building a Family in Times of Transition

First implemented by the central government in 1978–80, not long before Bright Gold and Full Elder Sister registered their marriage, the Birth Planning Policy was meant to have a profound impact on nationwide practices of marriage and family. There had been previous efforts during the 1960s to call for the implementation of similar models of family planning on a national scale, and in the early 1970s the central government started to promote mass campaigns of birth control and family planning under the heading "later-sparser-fewer (children)" (SC: *wan, xi, shao*);[3] but never before had the central government approached the governance of family planning on the basis of a national system of compulsory birth quotas or had family planning been elevated to the status of a central component of national policy.

When the Second Marriage Law was promulgated in 1981, it referred to "birth planning" as a national duty. Villagers in Harmony Cave started to hear about this as early as 1980–81 when local brigade cadres and local brigade midwives were first instructed by township officials about the concept of "birth planning" (SC: *jihua shengyu*). There is a long tradition of discourses and techniques concerning family planning in Chinese rural communities (Skinner 1997; F. Bray 2013a), but the concept promoted by the new policy emphasized fertility restriction and criticized the practice of son preference. The basic idea behind this new vision of "birth planning" was that reproduction is not a right or an entitlement but a privilege granted by state authorities to heteronormative married couples on the basis of a system of birth quotas whose ultimate goal is to reduce the number of births and increase the total number of one-child families. Failure to meet this system of birth quotas entailed various kinds of penalties and punishments.

When Bright Gold and Full Elder Sister got married in 1981, the local economy was experiencing a period of significant growth following decollectivization in the late 1970s. This economic growth is reflected in changes in local brideprice payments. Before the Communist Revolution and in the years immediately after, local brideprice payments included a monetary component—as suggested by the local term "corporeal body money"—but the overall value of brideprice was primarily calculated in terms of rice and other agricultural products. In the 1960s, there was an attempt to eradicate the notion of brideprice, and a few marriages took place without any brideprice payments, but brideprice returned in full scale in the 1970s, taking an increasingly monetized and inflated form after decollectivization began in the late 1970s (Parish and Whyte 1978; Siu 1993). In the early 1970s, when Bright Gold's eldest sister married, her parents received a brideprice of ¥220 (US$100). In the mid-1970s, when Bright Gold's second sister married, the going rate of brideprice was already ¥500 (US$230). By the late 1970s, when the brideprice of Full Elder Sister was negotiated, Bright Gold's parents had to pay ¥920 (US$400) to her natal family. Brideprice inflation continued in the 1980s and 1990s at a time when Bright Gold and Full Elder Sister were struggling to build a family of their own.

Bright Gold and Full Elder Sister had all their children during the first ten years of marriage, a pattern that is still common today in Yellow Flower township. Their first child (a boy) was born in 1982, the second (a boy) in 1984, the third (a girl) in 1987, and the fourth (a boy) in 1991. This was a decade of dramatic economic growth that witnessed important technological and infrastructural developments such as the arrival of electricity supply. Many local village households started to engage in temporary labor migration to the neighboring Pearl River Delta region, and for Bright Gold and Full Elder Sister, the 1980s was also a defining decade in other respects. Bright Gold's parents died (his father in 1983, his mother in 1985), leaving the couple with no options for child care if they decided to engage in temporary labor migration. Migration continued to intensify in the 1990s, and by the late 1990s it had become the most popular livelihood strategy in the village and had established a clear-cut pattern: while unmarried young adults (both male and female) favored working as unskilled wage laborers in factories, married couples preferred to be self-employed vegetable gardeners, on rented land in periurban areas.

During the 1990s, Bright Gold and Full Elder Sister continued to engage in subsistence farming and seasonal forms of wage labor such as construction. When I first lived in their house, in July 1999, they were struggling economically, but their problems were not just economic. They also had frequent domestic quarrels, whose origins went back to the early 1990s soon after the birth of their fourth child (their youngest son), when disagreements arose about what their main strategy of livelihood should be. In clear contrast to Bright Gold, who believed that they should remain at home and lead a quiet life farming and taking care of the children, Full Elder Sister thought that they should adapt to the spirit of the new times—the times of "getting rich first" (SC: *xian fu qi lai*)—and focus on "earning money" (C: *wan-chin*), not "plowing the fields" (C: *gaang-tin*). In her view, staying at home farming had no future. She thought that Bright Gold should go out of the village to make money while she should remain there farming and taking care of the children. For Full Elder Sister, this was the best way to rise above the poverty line and provide for their children. With a bit of luck, they would make enough money to build a new "modern" two-story house and move out of the decaying clay-brick communal housing complex where they had lived since the early 1980s.

After several years of quarrels, some of them quite ugly, Full Elder Sister decided in 1997 to leave the village with their eldest son (then about fifteen years old). Divorce was not really an option for her,[4] so she decided to seek work in the city to show her discontent. This was not just an act of domestic rebellion; it also reflected her strong personality and echoed important changes in local society. Twenty years earlier, Full Elder Sister would not have been able to leave her husband to seek work in the city: the political economy did not encourage rural-to-urban migration, married women ventured outside the village area only during ritual festivities, and there was little infrastructural support (roads, buses, etc.) for those seeking to move out. Her decision to leave the village was by no means easy, and she would never have been able to make this decision without the support of her husband's close patrilineal relatives in the village. They too thought that Bright Gold's failure to "assume responsibility" (C: *fu-jaak-yam*) as the household's breadwinner was unacceptable. In their view, Full Elder Sister leaving Bright Gold alone at home with the young children was the only way to make ends meet.

This move was an important turning point in the power relations in their household, as she became the family's main breadwinner, but it did not improve their conjugal interactions. By the end of her first year away from the village, Full Elder Sister was commonly referring to Bright Gold as a loser in front of their children. Bright Gold faced mounting pressure to change his behavior, and he fell ill in late 1998.

I first heard about this illness soon after moving into Bright Gold's home in July 1999. I was told that the illness was serious enough to keep him in bed for several weeks, and I heard Full Elder Sister on the phone complaining about the money she had to spend on doctors. However, I soon started to realize that there was more to this illness than met the eye. One morning, after checking the water levels in the rice fields, Bright Gold and I set out for the surrounding hills to herd his cow. One of the main topics of conversation that morning was sexuality and the resurgence of female prostitution in the local countryside, and he ended up confiding that he and his wife (both in their late thirties) had not had satisfying sexual relations since the early 1990s. This was the first of a series of discussions spreading over a period of almost twenty years—some of them in the presence of his wife—that fundamentally changed my views on local family life.

Coping with Neo-Malthusian Birth Planning Technologies in the 1990s

Their troubles had started soon after the birth of their fourth child in 1991 and were closely linked to the Birth Planning Policy. At the time, a number of birth planning regulations were already in place in Yellow Flower township. Nationally, there were significant variations in policy implementation, including significant differences between Han Chinese and ethnic minorities, between rural areas and urban areas, and between central and peripheral areas. In major Han Chinese–dominated cities, the policy usually took the form of a very strict "one-child policy," but this was not the case in rural areas, where there were significant variations (Harrell et al. 2011).

In Yellow Flower, the policy was first announced in the late 1970s, but it was not vigorously enforced until 1988. The fact that the policy finally reached this relatively out-of-the-way township in full force in the late 1980s reflects larger trends in policy implementation at the national level. The period from the early 1980s to the late 1990s was when the Birth Planning Policy was implemented in its strictest and cruelest form in China, and the countryside was no exception. The 1980s and 1990s were decades of intense clashes between the authoritarian stipulations of the Birth Planning Policy and a "strong society" in which villagers sought to retain some control over their reproductive practices (White 2006, 2010; K. Johnson 2004, 2016). This dynamic of state-society tensions is evident in the history of the Birth Planning Policy in Yellow Flower until the turn of the millennium.

As in other parts of the countryside, the Birth Planning Policy in Yellow Flower has always allowed families to have more than one child. This was the case when the policy was first announced in the late 1970s, and it continued when the policy started to be more vigorously enforced from the late 1980s onward. After 1988, the policy allowed two to three children, and if these children were all girls, local families could give birth to more children as necessary until a son was born. Between 2005 and 2016, I interviewed several local officials involved in policy implementation at the township level during the 1980s and 1990s, and they all agreed that the adoption of a relatively flexible and permissive policy framework in Yellow Flower was a deliberate strategy to minimize popular resistance to the policy. They told me that the gap between official ideologies and local patriarchal ideals was too big. Some kind of policy compromise was required to allow couples to achieve the local minimal acceptable offspring set—two sons and one daughter—to satisfy normative village expectations. The work of implementing this policy was not just circumscribed to township officials and local employees of the National Family Planning Commission; it also involved medical doctors, rural clinics, village cadres, All

China Women's Federation representatives, and village informers, among many others. These various actors and institutions were part of larger networks of material and social interaction that pushed for the institutionalization at the local level of patriotic frameworks of family and population governance.

One key factor in this process of institutionalization was the introduction of a system of punishments that was not just administered by officials and bureaucrats; it was also managed and mediated by medical professionals and technologies of birth control, including technologies such as IUDs for women (surgical insertion in the uterus of a stainless steel ring IUD that cannot be easily removed without professional aid) and procedures of sterilization for both men and women (conventional incisional vasectomy with local anesthesia and conventional tubal ligations with general anesthesia). A third major technology of birth control was abortion, but my focus here is on IUD insertion and sterilization, two key tools of neo-Malthusian family planning that are widely used in much of the developing world (Connelly 2008; Takeshita 2012). Condoms and birth control pills did not play a major role in the development of the local Birth Planning Policy because it was assumed that these technologies were too dependent on user initiative, motivation, and discipline. Local policy-makers also assumed that urban-style "birth-planning certificates," wherein the bearer of the certificate pledges not to give birth to "unplanned children," would be completely ineffective because local people wanted to have many children and would not honor their pledge. Moreover, the most common penalties for breaking a birth planning pledge (including withdrawal of employment rights and benefits) would have little effect on a population that even today continues to make a living largely outside the formal economy.

Returning to the story of Bright Gold and Full Elder Sister, in 1991, when their fourth child was born, the local Birth Planning Policy allowed village couples to give birth to two children, but stipulated the payment of a compulsory "unplanned birth fine" (C: *chiu-saang-fai*) for any extra birth. The policy also stipulated the mandatory sterilization of one of the parents after the birth of the fourth child. The only exception to this rule—given the local emphasis on the importance of having a male child to carry on the family line and take care of the parents in old age—were couples with no male child after their fourth attempt. Bright Gold and Full Elder Sister did not qualify for exemption.

When their fourth child was born in 1991, they were trying to have not a first male child but a third male child. This desire was not unusual back in the early 1990s due to the continuing hold of local traditional ideologies of family planning that prioritized having many male heirs to strengthen the patriline of one's family and village, but not all families could afford to pay the requisite unplanned birth fines. Bright Gold and Full Elder Sister managed to have so many unplanned children (including their third and fourth) without putting themselves in significant financial trouble because they had a close relative well positioned in the local village political hierarchy who helped reduce the size of their fines. In those days, getting these kinds of favors was not difficult. What was really difficult, if not impossible, was to obtain exemption from mandatory sterilization after the birth of the fourth child because the responsibility for this aspect of policy implementation was in the hands of higher-level township officials, with whom villagers had limited connections.

Officials usually implemented this mandatory sterilization by making a surprise household visit. Soon after the birth of the fourth child of Bright Gold and Full Elder Sister, a small group of officials showed up on their doorstep to tell them that one of them had to be sterilized. The couple offered little active resistance, as they had heard many stories of family property destruction. The officials allowed them to choose who would be sterilized, and they decided that Bright Gold should be the one to bear the heavy responsibility. During the late 1980s and early 1990s, many couples opted for male sterilization (vasectomy). There were rumors that this surgical procedure was easier to reverse than female sterilization (tubal ligation), and many villagers wanted to leave open the possibility of having more (unplanned) children.

This belief in the reversibility of male vasectomy procedures was linked to the material specificities of local surgery practices. Local vasectomy procedures usually involve a skin incision in the scrotum area, but earlier techniques blocked the flow of sperm simply by using a string or a clip to tie the vas deferens. Many villagers were convinced that this tying technique was easy to reverse, and there was talk of successful cases of reversal, so in the mid-1990s the local medical clinic started to use a more complex surgical procedure that involved cutting and tying the vas deferens, followed by tying the loose ends.[5] Many villagers told me that this change to this surgery technique, which was believed to be more permanent, together with the enforcement of a new wave of harsher birth planning penalties, affected the popularity of male sterilization. Female sterilization thus started to become more popular than the practice of male sterilization, a local trend that has continued well into the twenty-first century and that echoes larger national trends.[6]

Bright Gold's vasectomy was performed at the local township clinic on the same day of the officials' surprise household visit. Birth-planning officials lectured him on the gravity of the country's population problem while praising him for his patriotic willingness to be sterilized for the sake of the nation and the "quality" of the population. Bright Gold told me that these officials were very insisting, and he admitted that their repeated grilling convinced him that he was doing something "righteous," something important for the "good" of the country. As the Chinese anthropologist Fei Xiaotong (1992) famously noted, Chinese hegemonic moral frameworks tend to define the individual in a relational manner, and the self exists only in a hierarchically ranked web of interpersonal relations known as a "differential mode of association." Inside the relational individual, there is the divided self, which contains a small self, centered on personal desires and interests, and a big self, bearing the interests of a collectivity—be it the family, the kin group, or the nation-state. When the two are in conflict, the "small self "or *xiaowo* (SC) must submit to the "big self" or *dawo* (SC) (Y. Yan 2015a, 2017). When Bright Gold agreed to undergo a "patriotic sterilization," he used this kind of moral reasoning, which made him feel that he had no choice but to submit his small (individual) self and the small self of his family and lineage group to the larger self of the nation-state and its greater destiny. Bright Gold returned to the village a few hours after the conventional incisional vasectomy procedure as the doctors promised, but the pain in his testes did not go away as quickly as he had been told; after a few months, it started to become clear that the procedure would have a lasting negative effect on his health.

This experience of compulsory sterilization due to birth planning policy infractions is not exceptional in the local context. Ever since the beginning of its announcement in the early 1980s, the local Birth Planning Policy generated significant popular discontent, and the vegetable gardens of local migrants working in the Pearl River Delta region played an important role in local responses to this state-driven "civilizing mission" as it became more powerful in the late 1980s and early 1990s. These gardens offered a means of escaping annual birth planning inspections, and they allowed local women to give birth to unplanned children away from the controlling eyes of birth planning officials. The gardens also allowed village families to earn enough money to pay for unplanned births, delay the timing of sterilization, and have more than the official birth quota of two to three children.

This transgressive approach to local birth planning regulations remained quite widespread even after fines became more costly in the mid-1990s. There are many factors behind this collective pattern of individualized transgression, but of particular importance is the continuing influence of a strongly pronatalist and male-biased lineage ideology of family planning that stipulated a minimal acceptable offspring set of at least two sons and one daughter. These patriarchal ideals of family planning effectively encouraged village couples to have many children, sometimes more than five or six. When decollectivization was initiated in the 1970s, local reproductive practices were still strongly pronatalist and male-biased, and this continued in the 1980s and 1990s because children (sons especially) continued to be regarded as major social and economic assets. Without any exception, all village couples who had their children in the 1980s and 1990s—the age cohort of Bright Gold—chose to transgress birth quotas up to the point that the husband or the wife faced compulsory sterilization, and they *all* did it knowing or at least suspecting that this surgical procedure could have a negative impact on their well-being.

Constructing a Gendered Ethics of Compulsory Sterilization

In standard Chinese and English-language biomedical textbooks written for users based in affluent countries and cities, both vasectomy and tubal ligation are usually regarded as common low-risk surgical procedures.[7] My observations over a period of almost two decades suggest that postsurgical complications (for both men and women) have not been as uncommon in Yellow Flower as some biomedical textbooks suggest. Textbooks not only tend to reduce the patient to a physical body devoid of complex emotions and a complex mind—a point that was suggested to me by several medical professionals, including my own wife, who is specialized in perinatal osteopathy—but they also fail to take into account issues of social and cultural context. They assume, for example, that surgery is voluntary and that patients are always advised to consider how the long-term outcome of a vasectomy or a tubal ligation might affect them both emotionally and biologically. This is certainly not the case for people like Bright Gold who were sterilized under significant pressure by state officials. Textbooks also tend to assume that the quality of medical services is high and equally available to everyone. However, the average quality of rural township clinics such as the one in Yellow Flower leaves much to be desired in terms of the quality of medical service provision, and if villagers face any postsurgery problems such as sepsis and infection, they will not receive medical assistance unless they pay for it, and they often do not have enough money.

Bright Gold's descriptions of his symptoms seem to fit what standard biomedical textbooks often refer to as postvasectomy pain syndrome—a poorly understood complication leading to constant or occasional pain in the testes—but this is not the way Bright Gold described his condition to me. Referring to this surgical wounding, Bright Gold told me on several occasions that it affected his capacity for bodily development (C: *faat-yuk*) very negatively. His descriptions of this process drew heavily on local medical beliefs based on key doctrines of traditional Chinese medicine combined with elements of local popular religion.[8] According to these ideas, *qi* (C: *hei*), a vital energy or life force usually inherited from one's patrilineal ancestors, circulates in the body through a system of pathways called meridians. Health is an ongoing process of maintaining balance and harmony in the circulation of this vital energy or life force, and this work of balancing requires fine-tuning the interaction between two opposing yet complementary *yin-yang* forces that are seen to structure all life.

Bright Gold told me that the surgical procedure imposed on him by local officials provoked a dangerous polarization in his bodily equilibrium in terms of yin-yang interactions, hence the occasional pain in his testes and his overall lack of energy and strength. The first postsurgery symptom (occasional pain in the testes) is rare in Yellow Flower, but lack of energy and strength is one of the most commonly reported side effects of local practices of vasectomy. Most local men who have undergone sterilization report having lasting symptoms of abdominal pain and lack of energy after the surgery, and they say that these symptoms are particularly acute when doing hard physical work. Women too report symptoms of abdominal pain and lack of energy post–tubal ligation, but local patriarchal family values stipulate that the wife, not the husband, should be the one to bear the side effects of sterilization, because husbands have to earn money and do more physical work, so it is better for the economic well-being of the family if the wife agrees to undergo sterilization.

I first learned about this gendered ethics of sterilization when I started interviewing local village women in the early 2000s about their experiences of sterilization. Each time I asked why their husbands did not volunteer for sterilization, the answers formed a pattern that remained still in place through the 2010s. Sister Dawn, a thirty-six-year old married woman (originally from Harmony Cave) who was sterilized in the local township clinic in 2006 one week after giving birth to her second son, explained in 2016: "I agreed to do the sterilization because my father-in-law asked me. He said that men are the ones who earn money and they usually have to do more physical work than women. After sterilization, men become weaker physically, their waist is no longer very strong, and they are no longer able to exert themselves and do a lot of work to earn money. This is not good for the family."

Sister Dawn also said that she deeply regretted having agreed to the tubal ligation because she was in the process of divorcing her husband and she might have wanted to have another child. Later, in 2020, she told me via WeChat that she had finally managed to divorce her husband after years of quarrels and living apart. She felt wronged because she thought she worked harder than her husband during the marriage, but her complaints did not go as far as questioning the foundations of the gendered ethical system behind her father-in-law's request. She said that ultimately someone has to bear the burden of sterilization, and she agreed with her father-in-law that it is better to choose the one who does less physical work. Men usually do heavier physical work, but her husband never did much work after they married, including physical work, and for this reason, he—*not* she—should have undergone sterilization.

Bright Gold told me on several occasions in the early 2000s that the surgery had not just affected his bodily equilibrium but had spilled over to other realms of his life. He started feeling depressed about the idea of being "sterile," and his sexual performance was negatively affected. In his view, this loss of energy-virility created a further imbalance in his household because, in addition to the couple's previous disagreements, their sexual life was affected and they could no longer look forward to the possibility of having more children. Like most villagers, Bright Gold usually talked about sexuality (especially issues related to sexuality within the family) primarily as a reproductive duty, not as a pleasure activity,[9] but his remarks on the possibility of having more children reveal important disagreements with Full Elder Sister about reproductive ideals.

Both agreed that success in life is also evaluated in terms of reproductive achievements, but when their fourth child was born in 1991, their ideas of what counts as a minimal acceptable offspring set were very different. Full Elder Sister thought that four children were enough, but Bright Gold disagreed because—like most men of his generation—he was more committed to local traditional ideologies of family planning and lineage expansion. These ideologies bear striking resemblances to Marxian-Maoist conceptions because they approach economic growth as a sustained process of demographic expansion in which more children (especially male heirs) mean more family and lineage members, and more people mean more resources, more labor, and thus more power and wealth. For Bright Gold, children meant power. Having four children was good, but he wanted to have another. Full Elder Sister's position was closer to that of the local birth planning regulators. She told me during a private conversation in 2001 that, because she was not very keen on having a fourth child, when their third child was born in 1987 she accepted being fitted with an IUD despite painful side effects like heavy bleeding and cramping because she was not very keen on having another child. After removal of the IUD, when their fourth child was born in 1991, she told her husband that she did not want to have more children because it would only bring them more poverty. She was against the practice of mandatory sterilization, but she told me in 2005 that her husband's sterilization did help her achieve the goal of not having any more children. Had she given birth to a fifth child in the mid-1990s, she would not have been able to leave the village in 1997 to work in the city.

Changing Frameworks of Love and Marriage in the Twenty-First Century

Bright Gold and Full Elder Sister confirmed my analysis when we discussed these issues in person in 2012 and 2015. Bright Gold is now a grandfather in his fifties, and he prefers to describe his sterilization experience in terms of its negative effects on his ability to work hard and earn money. In 2003 he joined Full Elder Sister in the Pearl River Delta region to help her run a small-scale vegetable gardening business together with their three sons. Like many other migrant families from Yellow Flower, they live in a large zinc hut on the grounds of their market garden, and they return to the village several times a year, especially for festive occasions. Bright Gold is still capable of agricultural work, but he does only light tasks. His wife and children often say that he is totally useless when it comes to selling vegetables and getting the numbers right. They also mock him for not being able to ride a motorcycle (a basic male skill in the countryside) and for being afraid to venture by himself outside their market garden. Bright Gold still insists—to the despair of his wife and children—that he would prefer to return to the village to lead a peaceful life of farming, but his worries and energies are now focused on the poor health of his wife, who had a stroke in 2008 that significantly diminished her physical ability to do agricultural work, and on the future of his eldest son, who is now more than thirty-five years old and has no marriage prospects.

Bright Gold's younger children have slightly better prospects, but they do not entirely fit the image of China's second generation of migrant workers that is reproduced in state media. Lotus Flower, their only daughter, is closer to this idealized image of a new generation of rural migrants trying to become more connected to urban society and urban lifestyles. Both she and her husband, whom she married in December 2015, attended a Guangzhou university with the support of family and relatives. They are exceptional cases. Most local youngsters—including all of Lotus Flower's brothers—tend to drop out toward the end of primary school or the end of middle school in order to make a living as migrant workers. They usually start working in factories to earn money to get married, and it is often in these sweatshops that they meet their future wives or husbands, usually girls or boys from the same home township or from a neighboring one. Most marry in their early twenties or their mid-twenties and plan to have their children within ten years, continuing as migrant laborers. Not everyone is able to cope with the hardships of labor migration. Some prefer to return to their home township to set up a family business such as contracting a pig farm from a leading agricultural corporation (for example, Guangdong Wens Foodstuff Group), but labor migration remains extremely popular. To cope with the challenges of integrating work with family, Lotus Flower's generation relies on the support provided by elders for domestic help and child care.

Lotus Flower's generation is very critical of the two-tiered household registration system that denies them full access to urban welfare benefits and job opportunities, but they are realistic about their possibilities. They like to live in the city, but they see themselves as sojourners living in the periurban margins. They are no longer as tied to their native village and township as is the generation of their parents, but they continue to participate in social and ritual activities back home, and while they enjoy the freedom of working in the city away from the prying eyes of other villagers, they also work hard to keep in touch with everyone back home via daily exchanges in WeChat groups for lineage village relatives and former school classmates.

This new generation of migrants is constructing a very different experience of love, marriage, and family life, in which money is important (see Constable 2009 on the commodification of intimacy). Old-style marriage ritual protocols like paying "corporeal body money" to the bride's family or hosting a banquet in the groom's village or at a restaurant in the market town continue to be practiced alongside official registration procedures, but the extent to which one can express "human feeling" (C: *yan-ching*) is dependent on money. A marriage banquet is very costly, and not everyone can afford to pay at the very least ¥10,000 (US$1,500) for brideprice, an amount that is about eight times higher than in the early 1980s.[10] Some youngsters manage to negotiate their way around some of these ritual procedures. For example, Lotus Flower's marriage involved a brideprice payment of ¥20,000 (US$3,000), but she and her husband refused to hold a marriage banquet in their home township because they thought it a waste of money. Lotus Flower and her husband are not alone in their willingness to simplify practices that were once based on complex ritual protocols. This trend toward ritual simplification has become more salient in the early 2010s, but many people look at this phenomenon as an indicator of low economic status and/or lack of refinement, so there is still strong pressure to conform to reconfigured "old-style" ritual expectations. However, as Bright Gold's second son, Buddha Cassia, put it during an informal conversation in March 2012, "Young people nowadays do not follow as many rules as in 'old times.' Contemporary rules are simpler and more flexible." Marriage for this younger generation remains to some extent a series of communally shared procedures that require a significant effort of coordination between ritual experts, family relatives, lineage communities, and official authorities, but there seems to be a generalized trend toward ritual individualization that allows for greater strategic flexibility.

A similar process of individualization is taking place at the level of matchmaking procedures and courtship practices (see also Y. Yan 1997, 2003, 2006, 2009b; Jankowiak 2016; Jankowiak and Li 2017). Arranged (nonforced) marriage is still common, and older women (including close relatives and matchmakers) continue to play a decisive role in many local matches, but young people have more freedom to have the initiative and to get to know their future partners before marriage. Most nowadays agree to marry only after a process of getting to know each other, not just after a ritual of meeting. This process of "dating" (C: *paak-to*) involves both face-to-face contact and intense online contact. Most young people today have mobile phones, and these gadgets have already become an important tool of romantic attachment. Premarital sexual contact is also not uncommon in the context of dating, but this issue is usually not openly discussed, not even with members of one's close network. Getting the agreement of one's parents and relatives is still very important when it comes to the choice of marriage partner, but marriage is increasingly depicted—as in urban contexts—as a voluntary relationship grounded in individual emotional satisfaction (Davis 2014a, 2014b). Love is an important component of this sense of emotional satisfaction (Jankowiak 1995; Y. Yan 2003; Farrer 2014), but one should bear in mind that there are different kinds of love. Lotus Flower made this same point in a conversation in March 2012:

> My father [Bright Gold] never gave a gift to my mother [Full Elder Sister], and I never heard him say "I love you." I think he loves my mother, but his way of expressing love is not very contemporary. For his generation, showing emotional connectedness was not important to build marital relationships. For his generation, love was primarily a matter of commitment, work, and duty. My parents did not know each other before they got married, and after marriage, they only talked about matters related to livelihood, family, and work. They never really learned how to discuss passion and talk of love. Love nowadays is also about showing and expressing emotional support. It is not enough to encourage one's wife to go see a doctor when she feels sick; one needs to take her to the clinic, comfort her and tell her not to worry, and do many other things to help her recover and show that one cares for her wholeheartedly.

Recombining Patriarchal and State-Driven Forms of Family Planning

The Birth Planning Policy remains a central component of the local shift toward a more sentimentalized and individualized regime of love, marriage, and family life, and the latest revision of the Second Marriage Law of 1980—the Revised Marriage Law of 2001—continues to refer to birth planning as a national duty (Davis 2014a, 54; Palmer 2007, 686). To be sure, the main goal of the 2001 revision was not to reinstate the notion of birth planning. Building on the previous law, its main concern was to define marriage as a voluntary contractual relationship based on individual emotional satisfaction and to promote a legal-administrative framework that favors a deferral to individual preferences when regulating marital sexuality and conjugal property. This legal emphasis on emotional satisfaction and individual preference is symptomatic of a larger political shift away from close surveillance of marital and sexual practices, but there was no comparable move away from close surveillance of reproduction. The Revised Marriage Law of 2001—together with the Population and Family Planning Law of 2001—continue to support the monitoring of reproductive practices (Davis 2014a; Palmer 2007, 686), while still maintaining that the only legitimate arena for reproduction is free monogamous heteronormative marriage (J. Zhang and Sun 2014).[11]

When the Birth Planning Policy was launched in the late 1970s, it was meant to encourage late marriage and late childbearing and it advocated one child per couple, even though it allowed many exemptions. The policy was a key component of nation-building governmentality in the early Reform period, and the strict enforcement of a "one-child" family model in most major cities by the end of the 1990s helped reinforce state power. The policy was supposed to expire twenty years after its official implementation, but this never happened. In 2001 the government decided to turn the Birth Planning Policy into a national law, and the state continued to approach reproduction and marital fertility as "a demographic problem to be dealt with by bureaucratic regulation, rather than an issue of reproductive rights" (Palmer 2007, 686; Davis 2014a, 54). In the last two decades, there has been a significant decrease in the ferocity with which the policy is enforced, and in 2015–16, the government put an end to the thirty-five-year old "One-Child Policy," encouraging all couples to give birth to more than one child: first to two children and since 2021 to three children.

This change in policy orientation was undoubtedly motivated by increasing worries about stagnant population growth and accelerated population aging under the One-Child Policy (Zeng and Hesketh 2016). The main goal of the government is to counter this growing demographic crisis and related economic side effects such as the challenge of rising labor costs caused by a shrinking workforce and the challenge of declining economic productivity. Beyond these larger issues of macro-structural governance, the new policy framework introduces important changes in existing technocratic procedures of family planning governance. After 2015–16, couples officially registered in major cities are no longer required to seek approval to have a child, whether the first, second, or (since 2021) third, but only to register the birth afterward. Some commentators have celebrated these changes as a step toward greater reproductive freedom, but the new multiple-child policy framework still contains a strong rhetoric of state surveillance, and the state continues to use the language of bureaucratic regulation to promote its birth-planning civilizing agenda. This suggests that the changes occurred since 2015–16 should be placed in the context of a larger shift—consolidated in the twenty-first century—toward a mixed regime of family planning governance based on both "harder" approaches of direct bureaucratic control and "softer" approaches of indirect governance through market forces, social values, and state propaganda (Greenhalgh 2008; Greenhalgh and Winckler 2005).

Direct bureaucratic control remains visible in Yellow Flower township because there is still a mismatch between local patriarchal expectations of family planning and official policy stipulations. This was true for the generation of Bright Gold and Full Elder Sister, and it is still true for their children, Lotus Flower and Buddha Cassia, even though they tend to represent themselves as less antagonistic to the Birth Planning Policy. For the generation of Lotus Flower and Buddha Cassia (born in the 1980s and 1990s), the obligation to beget children and male heirs in the context of a regime of "free monogamous heteronormative marriage" remains a central value, but they no longer want to have as many children as did their parents. For the generation born in the 1960s or before, the minimal acceptable offspring set was two sons and one daughter. Most couples wanted to have three or four children with at least two sons, and this often resulted in five or six children, if not more. These reproductive ideals are no longer popular.

Today, most young couples want to have no more than two children, sometimes three, but most still hold on to the idea of having at least one son, and because fetal sex screening and sex-selective abortion are illegal, this sometimes leads to four or five children, if not more, until they have a son.[12] This desire for a male child suggests important continuities with earlier forms of patriarchal family planning (Greenhalgh 2013; Harrell and Santos 2017), but the cultural shift toward a smaller "two- to three-children" family ideal reflects an important transformation in local reproductive practices from the mid-1990s onward under the influence of the Birth Planning Policy and its harsh regulations.

In Harmony Cave in 1993, the birth of a third and fourth child cost ¥3,000 (US$520) and ¥4,000 (US$690), respectively, but in 1999 these penalties would reach ¥6,000 (US$725) and ¥10,000 (US$1,200), respectively, an amount that few could afford. In the mid-1990s, the local authorities introduced a new birth-planning fine—the "birth-spacing fine" (C: *gaan-gaak-fai*)—for transgressors of the mandatory four-year birth-spacing interval. To promote higher levels of compliance with this birth-spacing requirement, the official authorities introduced a mandatory system of gynecological checkups: All mothers were asked to go to the local clinic soon after the birth of a planned child to have a stainless steel ring IUD inserted in their uterus, which would remain four years, after which they could get a new birth permit. After the birth of their second child, one of the spouses was expected to undergo sterilization. The only exception was couples who still had not managed to have a son after two attempts.

These policy stipulations were significantly less permissive than in the late 1980s and the early 1990s, but their enforcement was uneven because the practice of not reporting births or giving birth in secret locations was widespread. To improve enforcement, the local government increased the number of staff working on this issue and tried to showcase its power locally by means of surprise visits to selected villages to recruit couples for compulsory sterilization or to destroy the property of transgressive families. At the same time, the government introduced a system of monetary rewards for "village snitches" (C: *yi-ng-jai*), and soon every village—including Harmony Cave—had one or several snitches shamelessly denouncing the misconduct of fellow villagers to get a monetary reward. This climate of snitching and persecution led villagers to become increasingly secretive about their birthing practices, and a significant portion of births that occurred from the mid-1990s onward took place in secret locations outside the township, usually in the vegetable gardens of migrant villagers in the

Pearl River Delta region. These strategies of resistance were an attempt not just to have more children than stipulated by the policy, but to escape or at least delay the various punitive measures (including mandatory unplanned-birth fines and mandatory practices of IUD insertion and sterilization) used by local officials to enforce birth-planning regulations. By the late 1990s, there was growing popular discontent with the highly inflated birth-planning fines requested by officials, and a number of public protests denounced the corruption of local birth-planning officials.

Starting from the early 2000s, policy enforcement was almost completely transferred from lower-level "village or brigade" officials to higher-level township officials based in a completely independent unit: the Birth Planning Office under the National Population and Birth Planning Commission, formerly National Family Planning Commission. This was an important turning point. Instead of relying primarily on pecuniary fines aimed at penalizing transgressors and discouraging infraction, the Birth Planning Office started regulating reproductive practices by means of a compulsory system of birth registration and gynecological examinations involving the issuing of various kinds of permits and certificates including "birth planning permit," "planned birth certificate," "sterilization certificate," and "IUD insertion certificate." Some of these were already in use, but they were not very effective. This started to change only when the local township government started to require the presentation of these permits and certificates for undertaking basic administrative procedures such as registering children in a local school.

Affiliated with these permits and certificates was a system of compulsory gynecological examinations locally known as "three yearly examinations" (C: *yat-nin saam-cha*), which has since been transformed into a system of one yearly examination. Every local married woman of reproductive age is required to keep an examination booklet in which the results of every gynecological examination is recorded. The local Birth Planning Office has spent a significant amount of resources to get most local married women onto their radar. When this system was launched in the early 2000s, important changes were introduced in local birth-planning regulations, which still stipulated a birth quota of two children but no longer allowed couples to have additional unplanned children simply by paying fines. The idea that people could pay to have more children was a major source of popular discontent because it was seen to favor the rich and well connected. The new regulations relied instead on a system of reproductive monitoring that promised to be equally tough on everyone. If a second child were born within four years of the first child, the parents would have to pay a birth-spacing fine. When sterilization after a second child was not effective and a third child was conceived, an abortion was required. If such a mother managed to hide her pregnancy and give birth to a third child, the parents would have to pay a very high fine or give the child away for adoption. After this third child, *both* parents would have to undergo sterilization. These birth planning regulations remained largely unchanged until the mid-2010s.

The Increasing Costs of Raising Multiple Children

In 2015–16, following the launching of the Two-Child Policy (a Three-Child Policy since 2021), the township government introduced important changes in local regulations. Local authorities continue to be committed to promoting a birth quota of two children, except for couples that still do not have a son after two attempts, but they no longer are so strictly enforcing gynecological examinations, IUD insertions, compulsory sterilizations, and birth planning fines. There is still a distinction between "planned children" and "unplanned children," but it is no longer necessary to request a "birth planning permit" before giving birth to a baby, and the government has temporarily waived all the fees associated with the registration of "unplanned children"—the term used by state media is "black children" (SC: *hei haizi*)—in parental household booklets. This last measure was particularly welcomed by families who postponed the registration of their unplanned children due to the high cost of registration penalties, and the measure will prove vital for the children in question because it will give them a legal existence and grant them access to basic welfare benefits such as education and health care. These changes reflect a decline of "harder" approaches of direct control in line with larger nationwide trends in policy implementation.

The generation of Lotus Flower and Buddha Cassia continues to cherish the importance of having at least one male child to carry on the patriline, and even those who do not strongly support this ideal often end up yielding to pressure from parents, peers, and close village relatives. This continuing attachment to sons suggests that there is still a mismatch between local patriarchal family planning expectations and official neo-Malthusian policy stipulations, but this mismatch has been significantly reduced. Most young couples nowadays do not want to have as many children as the generation of their parents, in large part because having children has become increasingly unaffordable due to the rising cost of living and increasing expectations and expenses for child care, health care, and education (cf. L. Shi 2017a, 2017b). These new challenges are likely to grow in significance in the coming years as villagers navigate their way through a regime of family planning that continues to stipulate through bureaucratic regulation that procreation can take place only within the framework of heteronormative marriage but is increasingly based on "softer" disciplinary approaches based on more indirect governance.

Consider the example of Buddha Cassia. His wife, Sister Spring, gave birth to their first son in 2012, only two years after the birth of their first daughter, so they had to pay a birth-spacing fine. This infraction was largely motivated by anxieties surrounding son preference. Sister Spring and her husband were happy with the birth of their daughter, but they wanted to secure the birth of a male heir as quickly as possible, so they decided to hire an underground doctor to remove the IUD from Spring Sister's uterus. After the birth of their son, they had to pay a birth-spacing fine. Moreover, it soon became clear that Buddha Cassia's parents wanted another grandson. Buddha Cassia himself was very keen on this idea, although he and his wife were struggling to make ends meet. They had already used up their birth quota, so if they had a third child, one of them would have to be sterilized. Buddha Cassia told me in 2012 that he and his wife had already decided that she should bear the burden of sterilization if they had a third child. Sister Spring told me that she would not mind undergoing a tubal ligation because she did not want to become pregnant again. Her reasoning evoked a calculus that fits the model of family planning promoted by the Birth Planning Policy: she did not want a third child, because costs of living were getting higher and higher, and she thought that having another child would only bring more poverty to the family.

I met again with Buddha Cassia and Sister Spring in February 2016, not long after the township authorities in Yellow Flower announced major changes in local birth-planning regulations. Sister Spring had just given birth to their third child, a second son. This birth did not come as a surprise. Back in 2012, soon after giving birth to their second child, the first son, in Guangzhou, Sister Spring was supposed to return to Yellow Flower to undergo a medically assisted IUD insertion, but she failed to do this and the

Birth Planning Office did not follow up. She had a miscarriage in 2014, and Buddha Cassia told me that they were not using any birth control when his wife got pregnant once again. Sister Spring delivered this third child in a public hospital in Guangzhou in January 2016, and in late 2016 she and Buddha Cassia returned to Yellow Flower to report to the local Birth Planning Office.

They told me that the local Birth Planning Office did not ask them to pay any fine for this third child. Under normal circumstances, they would have had to pay a "birth-spacing fine" for having an interval of fewer than four years between children, and additionally they would have had to also pay an "unplanned-birth fine" for having a third child when they already had a son. They were even more surprised when they did not have to pay any penalty to register their third "unplanned" child. Furthermore, officials told them that it was *not* necessary to undergo sterilization. Buddha Cassia summarized these changes in the following manner:

> The policy is more relaxed, but we do not know how long this trend will last. Official authorities are not monitoring so closely the number of children, but . . . no one can really afford to have many children nowadays. We have decided that we will not have another child. It is too expensive. We cannot afford it. We only had this third child because of my parents. Official authorities are not investing so much effort on chasing people to impose birth-planning penalties. The punishment nowadays is the economic hardship of raising children. Raising children has become too expensive. Health expenses, formula, clothes, nappies, and whatnot . . . Everything is about money. Sons are especially expensive. In Yellow Flower, everyone wants sons, but raising sons is too expensive, and they may not be able to get married. Look at my brothers. My eldest brother is thirty-four and is still unmarried, and my youngest brother is already twenty-eight and is still unmarried. It's all about money. No money, no wife!

A Bottom-Up Approach to the Birth Planning Project

The transformation of intimacy and the rise of a more individualized, affection-focused model of marriage and family life in village China is the subject of a large body of literature (Y. Yan 1997, 2003, 2006, 2009b, 2015b, 2016). This individualization thesis is very useful to make sense of recent changes such as the increasing unwillingness of young villagers like Lotus Flower and Buddha Cassia to stick to the elaborate etiquette of traditional marriage rituals, but this thesis overstates the extent to which Reform-era transformations have allowed individuals to "break free" from the binding power of larger moral and normative frameworks (Harrell and Santos 2017; Santos 2017a, 2017b; J. Zhang 2017a). Alternatively, attention to the technocratic governance of everyday practices of love, marriage, and family planning illuminates the important role played by social institutions like the Birth Planning Policy in re-embedding individuals in larger moral collectives and normative frameworks by means of both top-down disciplinary procedures and bottom-up processes of self-formation.

At the global level, the Birth Planning Policy is linked to a larger transnational neo-Malthusian enterprise that is concerned with restricting global fertility levels and controlling the growth of world population. Many states in the global South have employed neo-Malthusian technocratic family planning policies as a project for building the nation-state, and China offers a particularly extreme example of this attitude of social engineering. As anthropologist Susan Greenhalgh (2010, 88) notes, the estimated 825 million IUD insertions, IUD removals, abortions, and sterilizations that by the early 2000s had been conducted on women's bodies are treated as matters of contraceptive prevalence and reproductive health in the medical literature on China's birth control program, but the larger political significance of this surgical effort should not go unremarked. Each of these state-mandated surgeries is a serious political act that has extended the reach of the state to a place it had never gone before. With the Birth Planning Policy, the state was able to reach not only into the bedroom, intruding on sexual negotiations and reproductive deliberations that had long belonged to the sphere of the patriarchal family and community. It also reached into the biological bodies of individual citizens, especially women, whose wombs are deemed the wellspring of generativity for families, lineages, and whole communities. The state has penetrated to the biological and symbolic core of Chinese society, taking unto itself fearsome new powers that go beyond the remaking of the family to the making of life itself.

Up until quite recently, the theme of state coercion dominated international discussions of the Birth Planning Policy. However, fertility began to decline in China in the 1960s, well before the launching of the Birth Planning Policy and the mass availability of modern technologies of contraception and birth control. The state coercion narrative also does not take into account the fact that there is no single unified Birth Planning Policy and that the policy's history in a city like Guangzhou differs radically from the experience of rural townships like Yellow Flower (Harrell et al. 2011). Instead of viewing the state as a unified entity or agent that exists above society, dictating its every move, it is more useful to consider the state as a spatially differentiated multiple set of normalizing practices oriented toward the production of particular kinds of political subjects. This approach, associated with Michel Foucault's work on governmentality (see especially Foucault 1991, 2009), traces the emergence of a distinct form of power that is still repressive and concerned with questions of sovereignty and discipline but that increasingly operates through indirect techniques of governance that seek to regulate and optimize the vital characteristics of the larger national population. This work of governing the larger population is not just in the hands of state organizations but involves a widening range of quasi-state and nonstate actors, technologies, and institutions including ordinary individuals, families, and communities.

Building on this Foucaultian approach, Susan Greenhalgh (2003, 2008, 2010; Greenhalgh and Winckler 2005) has questioned the scholarly tendency to attribute too much agency to the Chinese state and its authoritarian methods when talking about the Birth Planning Policy. Greenhalgh does not deny the importance of state coercion in policy implementation, but she notes that the launching of the Birth Planning Policy marked an important turning point in Chinese politics toward a more pluralistic technocratic framework of population governance based on the authority of modern science and technology. Acknowledging this transformation is important to bring into focus the role of a whole ensemble of nonstate actors, institutions, and organizations. Greenhalgh's research played a pioneering role in unpacking the complex negotiations between party officials, high-profile population experts, and other elite actors in Chinese society in the period leading to the launching of the Birth Planning Policy in the late 1970s. Her account documents the increasing influence of the science of population cybernetics in the process of policy making, and it clarifies the impact of this form of technocratic expertise in the way the Birth Planning Policy was formulated and how it came to create sharp distortions in the social structure that planners are still struggling to correct. This perspective is important, but it says little about the views of ordinary citizens and communities, especially those situated in the margins of Chinese society.

Intimate Choices Beyond the Romance of Resistance

Yellow Flower township's relative isolation helps explain why the Birth Planning Policy was not locally implemented in any vigorous manner until the late 1980s, but this does not explain why locally a flexible two- to three-children policy evolved that allowed many exceptions. These exceptions were meant to reassure local communities that embracing the new policy would still allow young couples to meet local expectations in terms of family size and offspring configuration, but this was not enough to appease local aspirations. The local population resorted to various strategies to escape the control of birth-planning officials and regulations. Local strategies of resistance often involved significant personal sacrifice and included practices such as bribing officials, failing to report unplanned births, and reversing compulsory disciplinary punishments such as IUD insertion.

These rural strategies of resistance have been amply documented in different parts of rural China, including Guangdong (see, for example, Ku 2003, chap. 7). Villagers in northern Guangdong engaged with the Birth Planning Policy, domesticated it, moralized it, and turned it into a set of inhabitable discourses and procedures that are compatible with local projects of family and population governance. The policy's implementation in Yellow Flower involved a high degree of coercion, but these coercive techniques of policy implementation went hand in hand with significant popular resistance aimed at challenging policy regulations in terms of number of births, spacing of births, and gender of births. This resistance never really took the form of an organized collective insurgency aimed at reasserting the power of local reproductive freedoms, but it was significant enough to suggest that local families and communities retained some degree of moral autonomy. It was this moral autonomy that allowed villagers to construct a local subculture of family planning that is not entirely controlled by dominant state values.

It is tempting to analyze local strategies of resistance as evidence of the resilience and creativity of the human spirit in its refusal to be dominated by powerful civilizing technocratic forces (Scott 1985, 1990, 2009), but this would be an overstatement. If it is true that "where there is power, there is resistance"—as Michel Foucault (1978, 95–96) famously put it—it is also true that "resistance is never in a position of exteriority in relation to power" (ibid.). Local strategies of resistance can be read as signs of the human refusal to be dominated, but this resistance was accompanied by increasing acceptance of official ideologies. Local resistance to the Birth Planning Policy was strong enough to suggest that "peasant" populations in Guangdong have sufficient symbolic and material resources to defy official stipulations and engage in the creation of partly autonomous and resistant subcultures, but this creative process of resistance was highly fragmented and proved powerless in the face of larger institutional forces. To cope with these powerful forces, local villagers and communities engaged in a process of cultural hybridization whereby official discourses were recombined with local patriarchal ideals. This work of cultural hybridization resulted in dramatic changes in local reproductive ideals and practices, and these changes were shaped by the increasing medicalization of local family planning practices, as documented by the high rates of IUD insertions and sterilizations performed mostly on the bodies of local women.

These local dynamics challenge what the anthropologist Lila Abu-Lughod (1990) has called the "romance of resistance." Studies of everyday forms of resistance in anthropology and other disciplines tend to focus on the relationship between the dominant and the subordinate, while paying very little attention to forms of internal conflict between chiefs and commoners, landlords and peasants, men and women, parents and children, and seniors and juniors, as well as inheritance conflicts among brothers, conflicts between lineage factions, and on and on. As Sherry Ortner (1995, 176) notes, "It is the absence of any analysis of these forms of internal conflict that gives studies of resistance an air of romanticism." Instead of drawing on simplistic dichotomies opposing local views and official discourses, dominant discourses and subordinate transcripts, a more productive starting point is the idea that strategies of resistance are not the product of a unified framework of cultural values but are themselves the product of internal tensions (see also Ortner 2006). These internal tensions play an important role in local processes of engagement with global transformations, but they tend to be neglected because of a bias toward macro-level explanations.

Examination of intimate choices represents a combined micro-macro alternative to macro-level explanations, which start with state policies and global forces and then show how these macro-level developments impose themselves on local realities, sometimes with coercive force, sometimes involving strong resistance. Intimate choices encompass individual experiences and micro-level tensions, which intersect with macro-level forces. Micro-level realities and macro-level forces thus coproduce each other through frictions of various kinds.

Friction makes macro-level forces powerful (as when the interests of Full Elder Sister clashed with those of Bright Gold but supported the interests of birth planning officials committed to enforcing sterilization) and also gets in the way of the smooth operation of macro-level forces (as when Full Elder Sister agreed to have a third and a fourth child at a time when official birth planning regulations stipulated a birth quota of two children). Friction disrupts the motion of power (as when local women illegally remove IUDs from their bodies in order to give birth to unplanned children) and also keeps power in motion (as when local women agree to use an IUD or agree to be sterilized in order to prevent pregnancy and reduce the number of children). Friction generates difference, but it is not a synonym for resistance. When Buddha Cassia and Sister Spring gave birth to their third child, they were resisting the Birth Planning Policy, but they now fear that this behavior of resistance may have placed them in a more vulnerable position, given the growing costs of living and the lack of public welfare support. Friction does not necessarily imply resistance, but it is always what makes "translation"[13] possible, what allows the construction of a network of local-national-global interactions. Much has been written about the impact of macro-level forces on local intimate practices, but the idea that such macro-level forces—including globally shaped forms of state power—are themselves "translations" of micro-level negotiations is more provocative. This view can be productively used to explore ongoing processes of scientization and technologization affecting intimate practices such as childbirth and child rearing.

CHAPTER 3

Women and Childbirth

The Ambiguities of High-Tech Medicalization

IN THE LATE MORNING OF CHINESE NEW YEAR'S EVE IN 2008, Candy (first mentioned in the introduction), who was staying at her husband's family home in the market town of Yellow Flower, started to have contractions. She and her husband, who had met in Shenzhen in 2005 and married in 2007, now lived and worked in Guangzhou but returned regularly to Yellow Flower for short visits. Candy, born in the mid-1980s in Sichuan, got along well with her in-laws, but she would have preferred to stay in Guangzhou for the birth of her first child. She was not confident about the quality of the township clinic, but her mother-in-law and her husband reassured her, and Candy's mother agreed to come to offer additional support.

Candy had prepared herself for a vaginal birth as advised by her family doctor in Guangzhou, but her plan was derailed. She arrived at the local health center around 5:00 p.m. accompanied by her husband, mother, and mother-in-law. At 5:30 p.m., she was taken to a small room to be checked by the young female doctor on duty. Everything seemed to be fine, and the fetus was in the right position, but the doctor said that the fetal heartbeat was a bit slower than normal and thus recommended a cesarean section to avoid subjecting the fetus to the stress of vaginal birth. This exchange with Candy was very brief, and the doctor soon left the ward to get Candy's husband and mother-in-law to sign the C-section consent form on behalf of Candy.

In China, doctors are required to also seek the approval of close family members before performing a cesarean surgery (Y. Cong 2004). This is not just a bureaucratic requirement; it is a matter of professional ethics that is based on a culturally distributed model of what counts as appropriate good care—a model that also applies to the pregnant woman and her family members. For family members, leaving a pregnant woman alone to make decisions by herself in a situation of vulnerability would be a form of neglect. For the pregnant woman, childbirth is too important to be pondered in isolation without taking into consideration the views of family. Candy was certainly not alone on that day, and while her mother-in-law and her husband were not convinced about the necessity of a cesarean, they responded positively to the doctor's recommendation. It all happened very quickly, and the rapidity of the whole process reflects a crucial shift from earlier decades when hospital births were still not normative and most rural clinics were not even equipped to perform cesarean deliveries. Candy underwent a C-section half an hour after her husband and mother-law signed the consent form, giving birth to a healthy baby girl.

In rural townships like Yellow Flower, the shift from home births to hospital births rapidly accelerated during the first decade of the twenty-first century. For women of Candy's generation (born in the 1980s or later), the main question is no longer whether to give birth at home or in the hospital—hospital births have become the norm for this generation—but, along with increasing medical supervision, there has been a dramatic increase in the total number of biomedical interventions, including cesarean sections. This means that the main question nowadays for women of Candy's generation is whether they will have a cesarean section or not—that is, whether they will have a medically assisted "smooth birth" (C: *seun-chaan*), meaning a vaginal delivery, or a medically assisted "difficult birth" (C: *naan-chaan*), meaning a "cesarean birth." This new "framework of choice" (Sleeboom-Faulkner 2010) poses a whole new series of techno-moral dilemmas for rural women when it comes to coping with the uncertainties of childbirth.

These developments are not circumscribed to rural townships like Yellow Flower but reflect larger developments in Chinese society. In the last four decades, China has moved from a low-tech birth system with high rates of home births to a high-tech birth system with universal hospital births and high rates of cesareans. To be sure, Chinese women started to give birth in hospital settings under medical supervision as early as the last decades of the nineteenth century, and the country launched a national program of childbirth modernization as early as the first decades of the twentieth century, but these developments affected only a limited percentage of women. The shift to hospital births was accelerated after the establishment of the People's Republic of China in 1949, and again after the launching of the Birth Planning Policy in 1979, but the average rate of hospital births nationwide was still below 50 percent in 1988 (X. Feng et al. 2011, 433). In the 1990s and the 2000s, the country's hospital infrastructure was significantly expanded and improved, and the government enforced a policy of mandatory hospital births that put an end to the rural practice of home births.

It was only after the turn of the millennium that China started to move closer to a regime of universal hospital births, but this "hospital birth revolution" was accompanied by a few unintended effects, including a dramatic increase in cesarean rates, rising from a mere 4.9 percent in 1993 (Sufang et al. 2007) to about 32.7 percent between 2008 and 2014 (H. Li, Luo, and Trasande, et al. 2017), well above the 10 to 15 percent threshold recommended by the World Health Organization (WHO 1985, 2016; WHO and HRP 2015). The alarm was first launched in 2010 with a publication from the WHO Global Survey on Maternal and Perinatal Health Research Group reporting a 2008 cesarean rate of 46 percent in three regions of China (see Lumbiganon et al. 2010). The Chinese government was quick to respond to this WHO report with a number of measures and initiatives coordinated by the National Health and Family Planning Commission (NHFPC) and developed in coordination with WHO and the United Nations Children's Fund (UNICEF)–guided Baby-Friendly Hospital Initiative.[1] These changes were meant to curb cesarean rates and improve the quality of obstetric services and maternal health care, but the latest available figures suggest that national C-section rates remain high (well above 30 percent), and there is even some evidence suggesting that while there was a plateau period of no growth between 2012 and 2016, this slowdown was followed by a period of renewed growth between 2016 and 2018 (H. Li, Hellerstein, Zhou, et al. 2020).[2]

At a very basic level, the dramatic rise in cesarean rates from the 1990s onward was a by-product of the increasing *technocratic medicalization* of the process of childbirth management.[3] Childbirth in twenty-first-century China has become a highly medicalized and technologized process that takes place in the hospital and is managed by obstetric professionals. Under this new paradigm of childbirth management, childbirth is conceptualized as a dangerous process that must be managed as a "cascade of obstetric interventions" (Brackbill et al. 1984) designed to minimize the risks and the dangers of "natural" physiological processes.[4] A large body of literature documenting the rise of a "technocratic model of birth" (Davis-Floyd 1992, 1994) in North America and western Europe from the 1960s onward shows how this model of birth spread to other parts of the world from the 1980s onward under the influence of transnational developments in obstetric medicine, medical technologies, and public health policies.[5] This technocratic approach to birth has many virtues, but it has also increased the number of technological and medical interventions during the process of birth, opening the way for the routinization of nonemergency cesarean deliveries (Oakley and Houd 2013; S. Miller et al. 2016). This trend toward rising cesarean rates is particularly strong in middle- to high-income countries (Odent 2004; Betrán et al. 2016), and it usually goes hand in hand with the emergence of increasing moral divisions in society, with some women favoring the routine use of cesareans and others insisting on the virtues of natural labor and vaginal delivery.

This chapter offers a Chinese perspective on these larger global moral debates on rising rates of cesarean deliveries. China is an interesting case because, like the United States, it has very high rates of cesarean births, higher than 30 percent, among the highest in the world, but China and the United States have very different trajectories of technocratic medicalization. In the United States, the rise in cesarean deliveries started in the 1960s and the routinization of cesarean procedures was initiated in the 1970s and 1980s (J. Wolf 2018). In China, the rise in cesarean deliveries started only in the 1990s, first in urban areas and then also in rural areas, but the increase was significantly sharper than in the United States, reflecting the rapid upgrading and expansion of China's modern hospital infrastruture. In the United States, the increase in cesarean rates was accompanied by a countermovement that questioned the power of the medical establishment and called for a return to more "natural births" at home or in the hospital with limited medical intervention. These "birth wars" created profound moral divisions in society, with some women embracing medicalization, others seeking a return to more natural arrangements. Both visions of childbirth care have become acceptable, and the choice between the two is framed as a question of informed individual choice. In China, the rise in cesarean rates also led to significant moral frictions in society, but these divisions take different contours. Most women in China do not question the necessity of giving birth in the hospital under medical guidance, but there are increasing public concerns over rising cesarean deliveries. These concerns do not involve a radical critique of the authority of the medical establishment, and there is no call for a return to a more "natural" model of childbirth free from medical supervision (Harvey and Buckley 2009; Cheung and Mander 2018).

Here I adopt a woman-centered approach to Chinese moral debates on rising cesarean rates and the limits of childbirth medicalization. My account focuses on the moral views of ordinary village women in rural areas, and I propose a gendered, generational approach that situates the views of younger mothers in the context of larger intergenerational conversations regarding changing childbirth practices. I draw on two decades of ethnographic interviews with village women in the township of Yellow Flower to show how different generations of mothers have developed highly contrasting and conflicting positions on the recent trend toward high rates of cesareans. I build on historian Gail Hershatter's argument that a fully historicized understanding of ongoing processes of childbirth medicalization in rural China must entail "an investigation of women's memories, or at least the memories they are willing and able to narrate" (2007a, 358) to call for an intersectional approach that combines the study of women's mundane evaluations of technological change with the study of generational time.

Focusing on generational time adds significant complexity to existing woman-centered accounts of processes of techno-moral change. There is a vast body of feminist scholarship in the field of science, technology, and society (STS) studies that highlights the linkages between technology, gender, and morality.[6] Writing about women's work and technological change in late imperial China, from the fourteenth century onward, historian Francesca Bray (1997) masterfully argues that technology, gender, and morality are mutually constitutive and that this relation of mutual constitution is shaped by history and culture. I draw on Bray's pioneering analysis of Chinese gyno-technical assemblages to propose a multilayered, woman-centered account of Reform-era processes of technocratic medicalization of birth in rural China. I contrast the views of two very different living generations of rural mothers: women of the older generation grew up in the Mao era (1949–78), had four or more children, and were the last to experience low-tech births at home; women of the younger generation grew up in the Reform era (after 1978), had two or three children, and were the first to experience the transition to a regime of universal hospital births within an increasingly medicalized and technologized framework.

I argue that in addition to their very different experiences of childbirth, these two groups of rural mothers have developed very different generational frameworks of techno-moral evaluation of the recent trend toward high rates of cesarean deliveries. The older generation believes that scientific medicine helps women give birth more safely but is critical of the contemporary trend toward excessive medical supervision and excessive medical interventions. The younger generation is more open to high-tech medical procedures because they share a more interventionist vision of childbirth management. That these generational differences are so salient in rural townships like Yellow Flower probably has to do with the pace of change. As Hungarian-German sociologist Karl Mannheim (1952) famously argued, whether a generation succeeds in developing a completely distinctive set of values is significantly dependent on the pace of change, and rural China has witnessed particularly dramatic changes in childbirth practices since the beginning of the Reform period in the late 1970s (Harvey and Buckley 2009, 57–58).

Understanding the extent of the generational differences between the moral views of rural women is important because—as I show in this chapter—the most reliable source of nonprofessional childbirth support for young rural mothers like Candy are senior female relatives like mothers-in-law, and the views of these older women play an important role in shaping women's childbirth experiences. Most accounts of rising cesarean deliveries in China focus on the actions of medical doctors or on the individual preferences of pregnant women as reproductive consumers. Here I focus on childbirth neither as a medical imposition nor as an individual consumer choice but as a complex process of negotiation that involves not only the recommendations of medical professionals but also the views of pregnant women and their gendered multigenerational family networks of childbirth support. Understanding the complex moral exchanges taking place within these gynocentric multigenerational family networks is crucial to understanding how young rural women like Candy are engaging with larger forces of technocratic medicalization of birth pushing for the routinization of cesarean procedures.

Technocratic Birth and the Rise of Cesarean Deliveries in Rural China

China is a massive country with its own medical traditions and a history of more than a hundred years of childbirth medicalization. Starting from the late nineteenth century, Chinese intellectuals and reformers began to question the "backwardness" of indigenous medical practices and conceptualizations of childbirth, including the idea that childbirth is a "natural" process that requires little intervention and the idea that only women like midwives and grannies can attend the process of childbirth. These intellectuals and reformers called for the need to modernize childbirth on the basis of techniques and forms of knowledge derived from "Western" scientific medicine (T. Johnson 2011; Nedostup 2010). These debates on childbirth and reproductive modernity intensified during the first decades of the twentieth century when May Fourth Movement reformers and intellectuals identified the figure of the "traditional" midwife (SC: jieshengpo) as a symbol of "backwardness" and "feudal superstitions"[7] and started to imagine a world in which Chinese women would deliver their children in modern medical settings under the supervision of medical professionals (Nedostup 2010).

This narrative of emancipatory transformation opened the way for the beginning of a large-scale project of medical modernization of childbirth that would go through different phases and periods during the twentieth century, resulting in significant social and spatial variations. One way to look at these variations is to focus on historical processes that American sociologist Adele Clarke (2010) has called "stratified medicalization" (unequal development, distribution, and access to scientific medicine) and "stratified biomedicalization" (unequal distribution and access to high-tech biomedicine). These processes of stratification have resulted in significant differentiations of "reproductive governance" (Morgan and Roberts 2012), creating profound cleavages between Han Chinese and ethnic minorities, between coastal areas and inland areas, and between urban and rural areas. The rural-urban axis of variation is particularly important because the Chinese system of maternal and infant health care has a long history of differentiations between rural and urban areas.

These rural-urban differentiations were first instituted in the 1920s by the Nationalist government (1925–48) with the drafting of the first national program of maternal and infant health care, based on May Fourth Movement reformist ideas and globally circulating models of medical modernization (Lucas 1982; T. Johnson 2011; Andrews and Bullock 2014). Nationalist reformers were concerned with the country's high rates of maternal and infant mortality in childbirth, so they called for a "scientific" project of medical modernization of childbirth that sought to reduce mortality rates and strengthen the Chinese nation. Due to limits of medical personnel and hospital infrastructure, the reforms focused on upgrading the knowledge of "traditional" midwives, creating instead a professional class of midwives and professional schools of midwifery and introducing new regulatory frameworks for the practice of midwifery, with different requirements for urban areas versus rural areas. In major cities like Beijing, there emerged a generation of "new-style midwives" trained in scientific childbirth methods and the practice of antisepsis. A growing number of births were attended by these new-style midwives, sometimes in the hospital.[8] In rural areas, the reforms focused on retraining "traditional" midwives and improving the quality of home births, but there was significant resistance to change. Some new-style midwives tried to overcome rural resistance by means of more radical campaigns such as Yan Yangchu's Mass Education Movement, but even these efforts had limited results, and the country soon entered a period of warfare and political instability that lasted several decades.[9]

After the establishment of the People's Republic of China in 1949, the Communists followed their Nationalist predecessors in pushing for the development of an upgraded system of midwife-led maternity care with clear-cut rural-urban differentiations (Lucas 1982; T. Johnson and Wu 2014). Gradually during the Mao era (1949–78), they worked to expand hospital infrastructures and to replace the "superstitious" practices of "traditional midwives" with more "scientific" childbirth methods sanctioned by newly established socialist health authorities. In urban areas, hospital infrastructures and training programs expanded, and more women gave birth in the hospital under the guidance of a new generation of professionally trained midwives.[10] In rural areas, women continued to give birth under the guidance of local midwives, but new government-certified lay midwives emerged who were required to do a short-term course on modern socialist techniques of accouchement—the so-called new birth methods.[11]

This reliance on community health workers was part of a larger rural health-care revolution that resulted in the development of a grassroots system of primary heath care based on paramedics, barefoot doctors,[12] and lay midwives. This system reflected the spirit of transnational models of medical modernization that recognized the value of low-tech models of childbirth management in the absence of adequate medical and hospital infrastructures (Sidel 1973; Lucas 1982). By the late 1970s, most rural areas in China had a highly sophisticated infrastructure of low-tech childbirth management based on local teams of certified lay midwives working in cooperation with barefoot doctors, and there is some evidence suggesting that this was effective in curbing infant and maternal mortality rates, even though most rural births were still taking place at home (Babiarz et al. 2015). In urban areas, the period between the 1950s and the late 1970s saw a significant increase in rates of hospital birth, but the national rates remained below 50 percent in the early 1980s (X. Feng et al. 2011), with most home births taking place in rural areas.

The launching of the Birth Planning Policy in the late 1970s marked the beginning of a more radical project of technocratic medicalization that sought to fully institutionalize birth and place it under the control of obstetric professionals. The Birth Planning Policy expected women to give birth in the hospital under obstetric monitoring for reasons of birth control and population planning, thus increasing medical and political control over the process of birth (Harvey and Buckley 2009).[13] In urban areas, this technocratic model of birth management led to a dramatic increase in the numbers of hospital births.[14] In rural areas, however, many women continued to give birth at home under the guidance of local midwives.[15] In the 1980s, most rural brigades (now called rural administrative areas) still had their own certified lay midwife. These midwives were still treated as community health workers in the employment of the government, but they no longer received a monthly salary, relying instead on monetary payments from villagers. Also in the 1980s, official regulations still recognized the necessity of home births in rural townships due to lack of hospitals and biomedical equipment, but this started to change during the 1990s under the influence of major global public health campaigns such as the Safe Motherhood Initiative (launched by the United Nations in 1987) and the Millennium Development Goals Program (launched by the United Nations in 2000).[16]

This was a major turning point. During the 1990s, the Chinese government received significant international financial aid to expand and upgrade existing infrastructures of maternal and infant health care, and public hospitals were allowed to finance their technological upgrading by charging patients increasingly high fees for medical services. At the same time, the government made hospital births compulsory, strengthened the authority of obstetric doctors and obstetric nurses, and marginalized the expertise of midwives.[17] After the UN's Millennium Summit, the Chinese government increased its technocratic commitment to increasing maternal access to hospitals and obstetric professionals in order to meet millennium development goals for maternal and infant mortality rates. In urban areas, most midwife training programs were discontinued and more hospitals started using obstetric doctors and nurses in the delivery room.[18] In rural areas, the government started subsidizing hospital deliveries and banned rural midwives from practicing midwifery, ending home births by the 2010s.[19]

It was in this context of increasing technocratic medicalization of birth that there emerged a nationwide trend toward rising cesarean deliveries, again with significant differences between rural and urban areas. In urban areas, the surge in cesarean deliveries started in the 1990s during the second decade of the Birth Planning Policy, when most urban women were already giving birth in the hospital under the care of obstetric professionals and birth control officials. In rural areas, the surge in cesarean deliveries started only after the turn of the millennium and was significantly accelerated toward the end of the 2000s in a context of increasing commercialization of the public health-care system.

I had the opportunity to witness from close range the surge in cesarean rates in rural areas in the course of two decades of longitudinal fieldwork research following the movements of Harmony Cave households. When I first arrived in Harmony Cave in the late 1990s, most village women still gave birth at home under the guidance of local lay midwives (C: *jip-saang-po*), but were increasingly pressured to deliver in the hospital. By the mid-2000s, most village women were giving birth either in a rural clinic or in a city hospital and some, like Candy, started to have cesarean deliveries. This trend was significantly intensified in the years that followed; my ethnography has documented the techno-moral conversations between different generations of local women regarding the merits of this cesarean surge.

A Woman-Centered Perspective on Techno-Moral Change

In China, as in other parts of the world, the rise in cesarean rates was shaped by several macro-level factors, including technological, institutional, and politico-economic factors. Here I develop an approach that takes into consideration the perspectives of women as birthing subjects and reproductive consumers. Most studies of the situation in China focus on supply-side factors such as the implementation of health-care policies that strengthen the power of obstetric doctors and nurses and that give hospitals and doctors strong economic incentives to favor the performance of cesareans. Although the official position of governmental health-care agencies is that vaginal delivery is the best option for the well-being of mothers and infants, medical professionals often recommend cesarean surgery because cesareans are more expensive than vaginal births, and there is also the fact that pharmaceutical and biomedical equipment companies provide additional monetary rewards for doctors to undertake cesareans (see Blumenthal and Hsiao 2005, 2015 on the commercialization of the public health-care system). Another factor prompting Chinese obstetricians to favor cesareans is that many doctors think that cesarean techniques are superior and safer than vaginal delivery, as well as that cesareans are easier to manage in terms of time, equipment, and human resources—which is important, because most public hospitals in China are burdened with very high patient-doctor ratios (Hellerstein et al. 2016; WHO and APOHSP 2015).

Some studies take into consideration the perspective of women as reproductive consumers and their increasingly active role in requesting cesareans, either before their due dates or during the process of labor. Some surveys suggest that the proportion of cesareans requested by mothers nationwide rose from 2 percent in 1994 to 28 percent in 2011 (J. Zhang et al. 2008; K. Liu et al. 2012). Demand started in urban areas (J. Zhang et al. 2008; Tang, Li, and Wu 2006), but women from rural areas were quick to catch up during the 2000s and the 2010s, making use of expanded rural social insurance schemes to get a partial reimbursement of their cesarean expenses (W. Cai et al. 1998; Bogg et al. 2010).

One problem with the literature on women's rising demand of elective cesareans is that it assumes that the decision to have a cesarean is a matter of individual choice. This view does not fit the institutionalized framework of choice shaping the process of childbirth in China. As shown by this chapter's opening story of Candy's experience, medical doctors in China are also required to get formal consent from close family members before performing a cesaren surgery. This framework of choice is very different from Euro-American legal and ethical traditions approaching the decisions of childbirth primarily as a matter of informed individual choice of the pregnant woman (Gammeltoft 2014; McCourt 2009; Morgan and Wilson 1999). In this chapter, I move away from this normative framework of informed individual choice to approach childbirth as a complex process of negotiation that involves not only medical professionals and nurses but also the pregnant woman and her family members. My account here of village women's childbirth experiences draws particular attention to the negotiations taking place between pregnant women and their families and personal networks of childbirth support.

The shift to hospital births in rural townships like Yellow Flower was meant to increase the power of conjugal ties and weaken the power of gendered generational hierarchies within the patrilineal joint family, but as shown by Candy's first cesarean in 2008, these gendered generational hierarchies were not dissolved, and the multigenerational family continues to be a major source of childbirth support (Santos and Harrell 2017; J. Zhang 2017a). Husbands are increasingly expected to be present in the hospital during the birth of their children, but in rural townships like Yellow Flower, the mother-in-law remains the most important source of childbirth support for pregnant women due to the strongly patricentric orientation of local families.[20]

This continuing reliance on mothers-in-law for childbirth support raises the question of what kinds of gendered intergenerational conversations are taking place within the larger patrilineal family and how these conversations are shaping women's childbirth decisions and their engagement with new birthing technologies. During my ethnographic research in the township of Yellow Flower, the question of moral change arose frequently in both individual interviews and focus group discussions. Although each woman had her own individualized vision of the benefits and limitations of new cesarean technologies, there were also clear generational differences in their attitudes toward cesarean technologies and in their normative understandings of childbirth. These generational differences sometimes led to moral clashes between younger and older mothers and were particularly strong when we discussed stories of cesarean deliveries that were performed without strong medical indication.

Let me give an idea of these generational frictions. When I last met Candy in September 2015, she was celebrating the "full-month banquet" of their second child, a baby boy.[21] This birth too was a C-section, but the baby was born in a major public hospital in Guangzhou at twice the cost (¥8,000, roughly US$1,100). Candy had prepared once again for natural birth, but upon arriving at the hospital, the doctors told her they had to do surgery because the stitches of her previous C-section were showing signs of tear. She blames the low quality of the health center in the market town of Yellow

Flower for this second C-section. Looking back at her first birthing experience in 2008, she told me that the surgical skills of the doctor on duty were very poor and that the doctor's cesarean recommendation had less to do with medical issues than with the doctor's monetary interests (cesarean sections are more expensive than vaginal deliveries) and desire to wrap up things quickly in order to go home in time to celebrate Lunar New Year's Eve.

A few days after the full-month banquet, I joined Candy and five other young village mothers of her generation (born in the 1980s and 1990s) for a group discussion on their birthing experiences.[22] I usually interviewed mothers from the same generation in small groups of five or six, but I also organized group interviews with mothers from different generations. It is not enough to interview mothers once, as the point of this focus group methodology is to get mothers to compare accounts for inconsistencies in their own individual stories. The discussion group that afternoon included only village mothers from Candy's generation, and we talked at length about Candy's first cesarean birth in 2008. Everyone agreed that many things have changed for the better since 2008.[23] The quality of the local medical staff and equipment has improved, and local women now have access to an increasing number of higher-quality hospitals in neighboring cities like Guangzhou. At the same time, the number of cesarean births has increased dramatically since 2008, and they noted that this increase is not just linked to questions of medical necessity. Two important nonmedical factors are the monetary interests of medical actors, like the one encountered by Candy in 2008, and the fact that more and more women are themselves choosing to have a cesarean, quite often only after labor starts. They all agreed that it was better to have a vaginal delivery under normal circumstances, but this is not always possible because of the risks of vaginal delivery to the mother and baby. Talking about the benefits of C-sections, Candy and the other five village mothers drew a clear-cut line between their generation, who are giving birth during a time when they can benefit from the assurances of medical science and hospital technologies, and mothers in previous generations, who had to face the hardships of extreme poverty and dangerous home births.

This strong belief in the assurances of modern obstetrics and its advanced hospital technologies is not so salient among older village mothers. A few days after meeting Candy and her village mates, I met a group of older village mothers (born in the 1940s and 1950s), whose birthing experiences went back to the high socialist period (1960s and 1970s) and the first decade of the Reform period (1980s).[24] These mothers also described recent improvements in biomedical infrastructures as a progressive development, but they expressed strong concerns about the recent increase in cesarean rates. Mou-dai, a charismatic sixty-eight-year-old grandmother and former village midwife, led the discussion that afternoon. She said that her generational cohort did not have access to hospitals, but the rates of "smooth births" were high, and there were very few "difficult births" requiring cesarean delivery. Giving birth at home was not always easy, but women were encouraged to be strong and patient, and they benefited from the practical advice of women with multiple birthing experiences of their own. Mou-dai was convinced that very few local women ever died during childbirth under this low-tech system, and my survey data on village reproductive behavior suggests that there were indeed low rates of maternal mortality in the 1970s and 1980s.[25] Mou-dai went on to ask questions that perplexed most women of her generation: What is the reason for the increase in "difficult births" requiring cesarean surgery? How did women ever manage to deliver babies without having access to doctors and C-sections? Are young women nowadays becoming too soft?

As I moved from one group discussion to another, it became increasingly clear that there were significant gaps between the views of Candy's generation and those of Mou-dai's. These gaps pointed to significant generational differences in women's normative evaluations of new cesarean technologies, generational differences that suggested conflicting moral understandings of technological change. As technology historian Ruth Schwarz Cowan (1987) has long argued, technological change can also be approached from the perspective of what she called the "consumption junction." By this, she means the actual situations and sociocultural environments in which ordinary consumers (in this case, laboring women) come to favor specific technological choices.[26] But if focusing on the perspective of consumers is particularly important in this case because of the direct consequences that childbirth choices have on the bodies and well-being of women, one should not assume that the category "women" forms a homogeneous whole. There are significant variations in women's moral understandings of changing childbirth technologies, and these differences contain an important generational component.

Younger Mothers and the Ambiguities of High-Tech Medicalized Visions of Childbirth

Informal conversations and interviews with mothers of Candy's generation reveal the extent to which they endorse Reform-era narratives of technocratic medical modernization. These endorsements in turn show the emergence of new techno-moral subjectivities and new high-tech medicalized visions of childbirth.

Young mothers think that childbirth is too dangerous to be left to low-tech procedures of management. They say that the practice of home births is a "backward" custom, and they praise the government's decision to restrict the activities of village midwives. Young mothers do not trust "old-style" village midwives because, as a thirty-three-year-old mother of two sons put it, "The methods of village midwives are not safe, and if something happens to the baby during childbirth, everyone will blame the mother."[27] These mothers also narrate stories about home births attended by midwives and grannies that resulted in the death of either the baby or the mother. It is notable that such stories are rarely based on actual events.[28] Mothers like Candy are aware that the local shift to hospital births from the 1990s onward under the framework of the Birth Planning Policy had some negative dimensions (for example, many local mothers were subject to coercive sterilization procedures after giving birth to "unplanned children" in the hospital), but they agree that the move away from a low-tech birth system based on home births and village midwives was important for moving toward higher standards of safety, scientific advancement, and civilizational progress.[29]

For women of Candy's generation, childbirth is dangerous, and pregnant women must be protected from its dangers through life-saving medical and technological interventions. This highly technocratic vision of childbirth management is shaped by a number of tensions and ambiguities. Younger mothers place a strong emphasis on the life-saving benefits of new frameworks of childbirth management based on obstetric supervision and technological intervention, but they also continue to emphasize the importance of "traditional" ideologies celebrating the virtues of vaginal delivery and the moral duty of mothers to endure the pain of labor. Most young mothers I spoke with say that the ideal birthing experience—the one that is recommended by public health authorities, medical doctors, and childbirth guidebooks—is to have a "smooth birth" with vaginal delivery. This notion of "smooth birth" is shaped by the imperative of giving birth in the hospital under close obstetric supervision, and it actually involves a significant amount of medical intervention. It comes across as "natural" because it is opposed to a cesarean delivery.

The "smooth birth" is sometimes referred to as "natural birth" (C: *ji-yin chaan*), but this latter term has little to do with alternative notions of "natural childbirth" that started to become popular in the United States and western Europe in the 1960s and 1970s.[30] China did engage with alternative childbirth methods such as the Lamaze method from as early as the 1950s (as is discussed later in this chapter), but this engagement did not entail a radical rejection of medical supervision as it often did in the Euro-American context. Most Euro-American models of "natural childbirth" (including the Lamaze method) were developed in the context of social movements of reproductive rights and reproductive justice aimed at freeing women and humanity from medical supervision and from the oppressive effects of excessive medicalization. Calling for the legalization of home births free from medical and pharmacological interventions, birth activists also pushed for the development of a more "natural" model of hospital birth that privileged low-tech care procedures over high-tech medical and pharmacological interference.

This vision of "natural birth" is now starting to circulate within cosmopolitan urban circles in China, but its reach remains limited because the law still makes it compulsory for women to give birth in the hospital under obstetric supervision. It is not surprising, therefore, to find that none of the mothers of Candy's generation ever expressed a desire to give birth at home or without medical supervision. These mothers share a strong belief in the power of science and technology to improve ordinary lives, consonant with official policy. For example, Saam-dai, a mother of two sons, both born during the 2000s, told me in September 2017 that she cannot really imagine the horrors of giving birth outside the hospital. Although she experienced a lot of pain during the birth of her first child, especially when the doctor started to stitch the surgical incision of the episiotomy, the fact that she was in a hospital assisted by doctors and advanced technologies made her feel both safe and modern.[31]

The stories of medically assisted "smooth births" told by mothers of Candy's generation are not just from mothers who fervently believe in the benefits of childbirth modernization and technocratic supervision; they also come from mothers who are convinced that vaginal delivery is the best way to deliver a child, making it a mother's moral duty to endure the pain of labor. This emphasis on vaginal delivery is popular and has the support of national public health authorities, but it also resonates with historical traditions of childbirth management. As shown by the historian Yi-Li Wu (2010), Chinese medical traditions in the seventeenth through the nineteenth centuries recommended little or no intervention (manual or pharmacological) in the process of childbirth (see also Furth 1987, 1999). Chinese (male) medical doctors viewed childbirth as a natural process that was not pain-free but was intrinsically routine and easy, as opposed to polluting and dangerous. By claiming that childbirth was routine and that women were inherently prepared to endure the pain of labor, elite (male) Chinese doctors specialized in the field of medicine for women (SC: fuke) tried to restrict the interventions of healers and midwives at a time when childbirth remained largely in the hands of female experts due to strict rules of sexual segregation that followed from a very rigid gendered division of social space, with men being associated with the "outside" (SC: *wai*) and women with the "inside" (SC: *nei*) (Hershatter 2007b).

These conceptualizations of childbirth were by no means universally shared, but they were influential (and to some extent they still remain influential at present) in the first decades of the twentieth century in a context of increasing engagement with scientific medicine.[32] After the Communists rose to power in 1949, childbirth was subject to increasing forces of medicalization, but local midwives in rural areas mixed new idioms of medicalization with earlier noninterventionist conceptualizations of childbirth. At the same time, the government started to promote a more "scientific," noninterventionist approach to birth: the psychoprophylactic method of painless natural delivery used in the Soviet Union. This would later become known as the Lamaze method after the French physician Fernand Lamaze, who visited the Soviet Union in the 1950s. In China, it is referred to as the "painless labor breathing method" (SC: *wutong fenmian huxi fa*), and its basic principles echo earlier Chinese medical notions of childbirth as a natural process that requires little or no medical intervention.[33] Investing in the dissemination of this noninterventionist, low-tech method of childbirth management suited the needs of a country that between the 1950s and 1970s had at its disposal a very limited amount of material resources, medical staff, and medical infrastructures (Lucas 1982).

The stories of medically assisted "smooth births" told by mothers of Candy's generation retain some traces of noninterventionist childbirth cultures. Mothers are proud of their capacity to endure the pain of labor, a pride enhanced by the fact that most public hospitals in China do not routinely provide pain relief during natural delivery.[34] The official explanation for this is a lack of anesthesiologists, but the stories told by mothers of Candy's generation suggest an alternative scenario. Their descriptions of a "smooth birth" typically involve a mother arriving at the hospital with her husband or mother-in-law but being taken alone to the delivery room to give birth under the supervision of a medical doctor and one or two nurses. Some mothers found the experience of giving birth alone in the company of strangers terrifying, making it even more difficult to endure the process of labor without pain relief. Some mothers suggested that the absence of pain relief was to make cesarean procedures (with anesthesia) more appealing to mothers and thereby to maximize the earnings of doctors and hospitals, as cesareans are three times more expensive than vaginal deliveries. These comments suggest that young mothers are aware that medical technologies are not necessarily used to facilitate women's birthing experiences, but they are still deferent to medical authorities and do not seem to question the desirability of giving birth in the hospital under medical supervision.

Mothers of Candy's generation constructed a high-tech medicalized vision of birth based on two mutually conflicting messages. They accept that childbirth taking place in the hospital under medicalized and technologized conditions is a step forward from a "backward" past of home-birth horrors. Yet they continue to insist on the importance of having a vaginal delivery because it is their moral duty as mothers to endure the pain of labor and give birth the way that is best for the child. This tension between the "goodness" of technocratic visions of childbirth and the "goodness" of "traditional" visions of childbirth creates dilemmas in terms of risk management.

Cesarean Deliveries, Risk Management, and New Ideals of Feminine Beauty

Young mothers' insistence on the moral duty of women as mothers to endure the pain of labor creates important challenges. Mothers like Candy are not just afraid of the pain associated with normal physiological processes; they are also afraid of the pain associated with medical interventions regulating the process of vaginal delivery, such as the episiotomy mentioned above, a surgery performed without anaesthesia.[35] For some mothers, the pain during the process of stitching prompts them to consider choosing a cesarean with anesthesia in later pregnancies.[36] Others continue to insist on medically assisted vaginal delivery in later pregnancies because they support "traditional" ideologies of childbirth celebrating the virtues of mothers who are capable of enduring the pain of labor.

All mothers of this generation agree that childbirth is dangerous and must be managed by obstetric professionals, but they disagree in their assessments of the relative risks of having a vaginal delivery and having a cesarean delivery. At least 40 percent of all young mothers interviewed (about twenty in total) had a cesarean delivery. None of these cesareans was prescheduled; they were all decided on after the onset of labor, for significantly varied reasons.[37] Not all mothers were "tricked" like Candy was. At least half of the sample of cesarean-section mothers admitted that they requested the procedure. Inability to cope with the pain and/or the physical toil associated with vaginal delivery was the most commonly cited reason. Another important reason was the perception that vaginal deliveries involved significant risks for newborns. Many mothers stated that vaginal deliveries are dangerous for newborns because fetuses are becoming too big to fit through the pelvis, and Asian women have especially small pelvises. Mothers also risk disfigurement of their bodily shape, including the shape of the pelvis and the uterus. Some women also mentioned that having a cesarean birth is better because it allows mothers to have a longer period of postpartum recovery with time off from family duties and income-earning labor. The longer recovery time of cesareans compared to vaginal deliveries is an important issue of moral contention within rural families, as is the high price of cesareans compared to vaginal deliveries.[38] In 2017 the basic price of a cesarean in a major public hospital in Guangzhou was about ¥10,000 (roughly US$1,450). This is about three times the price of a vaginal delivery and would be largely unaffordable for many rural families if not for the fact that cesarean births are partially covered by medical insurance schemes such as the New Rural Cooperative Medical Insurance (SC: *xinxing nongcun hezuo yiliao*) established in 2003. This scheme of subsidies is an important factor behind the cesarean surge in rural areas.[39]

Young mothers who are critical of elective cesareans often point out the high economic costs of cesareans. They say that it is acceptable to have a cesarean for emergency reasons, but having a cesarean simply because of fear of pain is selfish and amounts to reckless spending of family resources. Moreover, they say that cesarean deliveries are not free of pain, as pro-cesarean mothers argue, and they add that having a cesarean is riskier and more dangerous than having a vaginal delivery, because it involves a major surgical intervention with anesthesia. There is also the fact that cesareans leave a big scar on the abdomen that is not very pleasing aesthetically.

Given this long list of negatives, why did anti-elective cesarean mothers believe that more women of their generation favor a cesarean delivery? The first reason offered was the role played by contemporary medical discourses and idioms of risk assessment in cultivating a negative perception of vaginal birth as something that is intrinsically difficult and dangerous. The second reason pointed to changing notions of femininity and the female body. Young women nowadays, they said, are "too delicate" (C: *taai giu-ching*) to handle the hardships of a vaginal delivery because their mode of livelihood no longer requires them to do physical labor in the fields or elsewhere. This "delicateness" is not just a matter of changes in mode of livelihood; it is also a matter of changes in feminine body culture. Many young women nowadays are not interested in cultivating a strong physical body and a strong sense of physical competence and endurance; they are more interested in cultivating a delicate figure and a sense of feminine beauty that is shaped by mainstream urban ideologies, which promote a model of the body that is pale and ultrathin. These urban ideals of feminine beauty are powerful and may be encouraging young women to construct themselves as fragile subjects who require medical and technological mediation to overcome the uncertainties of childbirth.

Older Mothers and Their Low-Tech Medicalized Visions of Childbirth

Older mothers like Mou-dai provided similar explanations, but they viewed the shift to "bodily fragility" negatively. Mou-dai recounted a situation that illustrates this point.[40] A few years ago in the early 2010s, Mou-dai was asked by a close female elder relative to accompany her young daughter-in-law to the local health center to offer guidance during labor. This kind of request is quite common in the context of local gynocentric networks of maternity care and childbirth support. The doctor on duty at the local health clinic that afternoon did not take much time in concluding that, because the cervix was not sufficiently dilated and the girl was shouting with pain, it was better to perform a cesarean section. The mother-in-law did not agree with this decision, and Mou-dai—locally known for her outspoken personality—challenged the doctor: "Doctor, I'm sixty-two years old. I have six children myself and I have assisted the delivery of many babies. I never met a woman capable of giving birth without pain. This girl is young, well built, and eats well; the fetus is in the right position; and everything else seems fine. Why does she need to be cut open?"

The doctor warned the girl and her mother-in-law that the health center would not take any responsibility if they refused to do a cesarean section. The girl did not want to challenge the doctor because she was afraid of being held responsible for whatever went wrong during the birth, but her mother-in-law insisted on a vaginal delivery, in part for economic reasons. In the end, the girl was taken to the delivery room, where she delivered vaginally under medical supervision in less than forty minutes.

Mou-dai did not question the benefits of advanced medical technologies and hospital infrastructures, but she argued that young women had become too soft when it comes to childbirth. In her view, most young women do not want to have many children and many are afraid of having a vaginal birth, so they prefer to spend the money and have a cesarean. Some women—including the daughter-in-law mentioned above—are not afraid of having a vaginal birth but the moment they begin experiencing labor pain, they consider requesting a cesarean because they want to get anesthesia in order to stop feeling the pain. Older mothers do not understand this fear of labor pain, and they find it strange that young women are so willing to blindly trust the advice of medical doctors, many of whom lack practical experience or make decisions on the basis of their own interests. Significant disagreements exist among older mothers on many of these issues, but there is sufficient convergence to point to a shared generational framework of ethical imagination. The life history of Mou-dai offers a good entry point into this system of shared values and its emphasis on the importance of self-reliance, practical wisdom, and accepting that not everything can be controlled.

Mou-dai was born in 1946 and married into her husband's village at the age of sixteen. Women of Mou-dai's generation experienced childbearing in the high socialist period under a low-tech, midwife-led birth system. Mou-dai never went to a hospital for a pregnancy checkup, let alone to deliver a baby. Each of her six children was delivered at home between 1966 and 1982. Three of these children were delivered at home with the help of her mother-in-law and the local village midwife. This was the "normal" way of giving birth for much of the 1960s, 1970s, and 1980s. "Difficult births" requiring special interventions were rare, especially in the 1970s and 1980s, but when they happened—and they did happen—assistance from midwives and barefoot doctors was not always sufficient, and the nearest hospital was too far away to offer any help, given the poor conditions of transportation.[41] Because there were a limited number of certified midwives (C: *daai-deui jip-saang-po*) in northern Guangdong (usually no more than one per brigade), laboring women often had to rely on noncertified experienced midwives, quite often female relatives or other female members in their networks of support.

Mou-dai is one such noncertified lay midwife. Under the guidance of a close female relative who happened to be the first certified midwife of their village brigade, Mou-dai was introduced to basic medical knowledge and the new socialist methods of midwifery, including techniques of sterilization, cutting the umbilical cord, and suctioning the mouth and nose of the newborn to facilitate breathing. She also acquired significant practical knowledge through her own birthing experiences, some of them unassisted. Her second daughter (born in 1972) was her first experience of unassisted childbirth, and it turned out to be the most complicated because it was a breech birth. Her mother-in-law had gone out to harvest taro, and her husband was out in the fields. She had just returned home from herding the cow, and there was no one to help. She went to her bedroom but instead of lying down on the bed, the way she had delivered her two previous babies, she decided to kneel on the ground next to the bed. As the contractions got more intense and frequent and her cervix dilated, she tried to feel the baby's head with her hand but could find only the baby's feet. She got very scared because she knew the fetus could very easily die coming out in this position, but she continued pushing while using her right hand to gently pull the baby out. After the feet came out, it was the buttock, and by the time the head came out, Mou-dai was exhausted and her lower back was in pain. She placed the baby in a bamboo basket underneath her body, and she lay down for a while next to the baby before cutting the umbilical cord.

This was not Mou-dai's only experience of "self-delivery." Her second son (born in 1975) and youngest daughter (born in 1982) were also delivered at home without any assistance, but in both cases, the delivery was uneventful.

There is something truly out of the ordinary about the way Mou-dai talks about these birthing experiences, but one should not think that delivering babies without assistance was entirely uncommon in this period.[42] Most women of Mou-dai's generation have heard personal accounts of unassisted childbirth from female relatives or other members of their own gynocentric support networks. One of the characteristics of these "do-it-all-alone" birthing dramas—especially when told by eloquent storytellers like Mou-dai—is the strong emphasis on the power of women to be self-reliant, take responsibility, and show ability to cope with the hardships and uncertainties of birth, a system of values that clearly builds on earlier cultural traditions of childbirth management and their emphasis on reduced medical intervention and the moral duty of mothers to endure the pain of labor. When talking in general terms about the female experience of labor pain, women of Mou-dai's generation differentiate themselves from younger women by saying that childbearing today is not as hard and dangerous as it was back in the days when giving birth, to use one of Mou-dai's favorite animal metaphors, resembled "cockroaches going right and left on the surface of a kitchen wok, struggling to avoid the fate of death."[43]

In one particularly vivid illustration of the hardships of earlier birthing practices, one of Mou-dai's friends recalled the painful experience of giving birth to her second son in 1972.[44] She bled heavily during the birth (a home birth attended by her mother-in-law), and one or two hours later, when the bleeding finally stopped, she wanted to put on some clean clothes, but there were none available. She felt very weak due to the bleeding, so she asked her mother-in-law for help. Her mother-in-law refused to help on the grounds that washing the clothes was not her task in the family, so the bleeding mother had to stay in bed with dirty clothes for many hours until she was able to get up in pain to go to the local fountain to wash some clothes and get them to dry. The attitude of this mother-in-law may seem very insensitive and uncaring by today's standards, but these experiences of familial hierarchy and physical hardship were common in earlier generations. These are the kind of experiences that help explain Mou-dai's puzzlement when she was confronted with a medical doctor wanting to perform a C-section with anesthesia on a healthy young woman simply because she was complaining about labor pain. More generally, these experiences help explain why women of Mou-dai's generation find it so difficult to understand why younger mothers embrace the recent shift to a highly interventionist model of birth that treats women as vulnerable beings who are largely incapable of handling the hardships of childbirth without the support of doctors and their life-saving technologies. In this new model of birth, the moral emphasis shifts from the mother as one who bears pain as a responsibility to her children and family to the doctor and hospital technologies as essential protectors of women's lives.

Enduring the Pain for Family and Lineage

An important aspect of the moral frictions between the low-tech medicalized vision of childbirth shared by mothers of Mou-dai's generation and the high-tech medicalized values of mothers of Candy's generation has to do with the tension between family and lineage interests and national state interests. For women of Mou-dai's generation, the "bloody" work of begetting children represented an ethical duty framed primarily as a matter of private interest—that of the patrilineal family and lineage. It was only when the rates of hospital births began to increase quite significantly from the 1990s onward that childbirth started to become defined primarily as a matter of national interest. This shift contributed to an important ethical transformation that resonated with broader state efforts to take control of people's reproductive freedoms for the sake of economic development and modernization. Mou-dai's work as a lay midwife offers insights into the extent to which her generation resisted state appropriation of local reproductive practices.

In response to requests from close relatives, neighbors, and friends, Mou-dai started practicing as a lay midwife in the late 1970s at around the same period when the Birth Planning Policy was launched nationwide. This policy was very tightly enforced in urban areas but had limited effects in impoverished rural areas like Yellow Flower township.[45] In these areas, home births and high fertility rates remained the norm, and the total number of births per year was still so high that the work of certified village midwives had to be complemented by the services of lay village midwives.[46] In the 1990s, as local birth planning regulations became stricter, demand for lay midwives like Mou-dai increased because there were still many women having "unplanned children," and some certified midwives started refusing to attend "unplanned births" out of fear of political punishment. In those days, having a secret home birth attended by a lay midwife was better than going to the local clinic, because women wanted to minimize the risk of being caught by government officials seeking to collect unplanned-birth fines and/or to implement procedures of forced sterilization.

Many secret home births took place across regional borders. In the 1990s, temporary labor migration to major cities like Guangzhou became a way of life for many families in the township. The most popular mode of livelihood for migrant couples was to set up a family-run vegetable gardening enterprise in peripheral urban areas, where people could build their own hut, save money on rent, and have more autonomy. These vegetable gardens also offered Yellow Flower women a safe refuge to give birth to "unplanned children," and the services of lay midwives like Mou-dai were in heavy demand in these instances.

Between 1988 and 2005—according to her own estimates—Mou-dai assisted more than 400 vaginal births in Guangzhou and Foshan.[47] State media often refers to these midwifery activities as dangerous and criminal, but this is not the view of most Yellow Flower women of Mou-dai's generation, because they were doing all they could to help their daughters-in-law fulfill their reproductive duties as members of a local family and lineage. For women of this older generation, the local shift to a regime of hospital births with high cesarean rates represents increasing medical and governmental control over the reproductive practices of local communities. These women find it very hard to understand why young mothers are so willing to trust the advice of medical doctors and their high-end hospital technologies. Women of Mou-dai's generation view the advice of doctors as far from neutral and certainly exploitative. From their perspective, when doctors today recommend cesarean sections, they are not really thinking about the well-being of women; they want to make money by charging high fees for the procedure. Even during periods of strong enforcement of the Birth Planning Policy in the 1990s, doctors would advise local women to give birth to unplanned children in the hospital. Yet they were not making these recommendations in the interests of women's health; rather, they wanted to garner the financial rewards offered by the state to help the local government implement draconian birth planning regulations by means of surgical procedures such as IUD insertion and sterilization.

Technocratic Medicalization and Techno-Moral Change Across Generations

This chapter draws on a well-established feminist tradition of historical and sociological studies of reproductive technologies to bring into focus the techno-moral conversations taking place among ordinary women in village China regarding ongoing processes of routinization of cesarean deliveries. Existing woman-centered research on the rise of cesarean deliveries in China from the 1990s onward has linked the increase in maternal requests for cesareans to changes in women's normative understandings of childbirth, but these studies focus mainly on the young mothers at the heart of the cesarean surge. By instead situating the views of young rural mothers in the context of larger intergenerational conversations regarding the merits of recent changes in childbirth practices, this chapter offers a more nuanced and multilayered woman-centered narrative of high-tech medicalization in rural China.

My analysis focuses on the contrasting techno-moral visions of childbirth of two very different generations of village mothers. Older mothers like Mou-dai are supportive of hospital births but are critical of excessive medical interventions. This older generation approaches childbirth as something that is both routine and natural, and they believe in the capacity of women to use self-reliance and strength to overcome the hardships of vaginal birth. They think that the best way to give birth under normal circumstances is to have a vaginal delivery with little external interference, and they feel that a good mother must strive to fulfill this moral duty. This older generation has developed a low-tech medicalized vision of childbirth that embraces the benefits of increased medical supervision without rejecting the value of earlier noninterventionist models of childbirth. For this older generation, cesarean deliveries must be performed only very rarely and in cases of extreme emergency.

The younger generation no longer considers cesarean surgery to be a rare medical intervention, but views are mixed. Some mothers insist that cesarean interventions are major surgeries that should be performed only when there is a strong medical indication, while others consider that it is acceptable to request a cesarean to alleviate the pain of labor or other perceived negative side effects of a vaginal delivery. These disagreements hide significant generational continuities and a shared generational framework of ethical imagination that is very different from the one shared by older mothers. In contrast to the low-tech views of older mothers, the younger generation has constructed a high-tech medicalized vision of childbirth that places a strong emphasis on the life-saving importance of obstetric supervision and increasing medical and technological intervention. This younger generation of mothers approaches childbirth as dangerous and sees women as delicate creatures in need of protection and care. They continue to be strongly influenced by "traditional" ideologies celebrating the virtues of vaginal labor, but their vision of vaginal birth is very different from the older generation's low-tech model of vaginal birth. Their model of vaginal birth entails significant obstetric supervision and intervention, and they no longer feel that they have to do whatever it takes to fulfill the moral duty of having a vaginal delivery. Childbirth for them has become a process of risk management, and they feel that it is better for pregnant women to place themselves in the hands of medical doctors and their high-tech procedures instead of insisting on low-tech practices of virtuous sacrifice and self-reliance. As techno-moral agents, young mothers prioritize the minimization of risk over cultivation of virtues.

These generational differences in women's normative understandings of childbirth often lead to techno-moral clashes between younger and older mothers. These clashes are important because they help shape the views of younger mothers as they gather information about childbirth and prepare for their birthing experiences. Younger mothers like Candy have access to a large amount of information on childbirth via books, doctors, or the Internet, but this information still has to be processed and domesticated in order to be useful, and this work of information processing and domestication often takes place in the context of intergenerational interactions within families and larger gynocentric networks of support and reproductive care.

This is not to say that the choices of younger mothers are completely determined by the views of older mothers and the gynocentric hierarchies within their larger multigenerational family arrangements. There is a large body of literature on rural families in Reform China showing that younger rural mothers like Candy have gained significant bargaining power within the household and the larger patrilineal family since the beginning of China's Reform and Opening (Santos and Harrell 2017). This has given young mothers more decision-making power in childbirth matters, but one should not overstate this transformation. Young married women in village China may have more decision-making power, but they are not autonomous subjects and they continue to rely on the advice of older female relatives, especially their mothers-in-law, for childbirth support. Some younger mothers like Candy appear to be following the trend in urban China of seeking support from mothers and husbands, but most local women continue to benefit from the support of the mother-in-law and other patrilineal female relatives. This point is important because it suggests that the childbirth decisions of younger mothers continue to be made in the context of intense exchanges with older female relatives like Mou-dai, whose advice they may or may not take and whose views may or not be determinant in affecting the final choice of childbirth method.

The views of older mothers are particularly important in the current conjuncture of high national cesarean rates, because their personal experiences and practical knowledge of childbirth render them less supportive of cesarean deliveries. Older mothers like Mou-dai believe that giving birth in the hospital represents a step forward in terms of safety, but they are critical of too many medical interventions and they favor the reembedding of woman-centered networks of support in the maternity ward. When mothers of Mou-dai's generation gave birth to their children, they lacked infrastructural support from hospitals and medical doctors but benefited from the informal support provided by local midwives and experienced women in their circle of relatives and friends. These gynocentric networks of care relied on low-tech forms of practical knowledge or *mêtis* (wisdom, skill, or craft; Scott 1998) that were largely marginalized and dismissed as "backward" by Reform-era technocratic policies of childbirth medicalization, but this state of affairs may be changing.

This change is prompted in part by larger changes in transnational models of medical modernization. There is growing awareness within leading global public health organizations such as WHO that later twentieth-century and early twenty-first-century trends in childbirth governance have placed too much emphasis on obstetric supervision and that this has had negative effects on the quality of maternal health care—leading, for example, to rising rates of medically unnecessary cesarean deliveries (WHO 2016; see also Oakley and Houd 2013; S. Miller et al. 2016). In 2011, one year after the publication of a critical study by WHO reporting an alarming 46.2 percent rate of cesarean sections in China, the central government launched a series of measures aimed at curbing national C-section rates in line with the goals of WHO and the United Nations Children's Fund (UNICEF)–guided Baby-Friendly Hospital Initiative. For example, some public hospitals started to offer compulsory vaginal-birth classes for pregnant women, and the government initiated a system of C-section limits with heavy fines, including cutting state subsidies and revoking hospital licences, if those limits were exceeded.[48]

Judging from the latest statistics on C-section rates, including my own evaluations for the city of Guangzhou, these measures have had limited quantitative effects so far. They are, however, leading to growing public awareness of the problems associated with rising cesarean rates, as shown by the growing number of social movements, smart-phone apps, book publications, and websites promoting the practice of vaginal delivery. Pregnancy and childbirth manuals published since 2011 reflect the rise of an industry of scientific and medical expertise that is both independent of and aligned with official policy discourses.[49] At the same time, a growing number of WeChat public accounts and smart-phone apps promote public exchanges on the subject of childbirth.[50] One important factor shaping these exchanges is the rise of a wellness culture among the urban middle classes. Many Chinese mothers want to live healthier lives, and this desire drives them to actively seek information about childbirth. Most public hospitals do not allow mothers to have their own birth plan, and the birthing options available are still limited, but most mothers want to know what their options are and to compare these with the situation in other countries.

Having access to more information and processing this information with the help of one's informal networks of support does not necessarily lead to a strong preference for vaginal birth. Not all young mothers favor having a vaginal birth, and there are many situations in which C-sections are indeed the most appropriate course of action (not just for strictly medical reasons). One of the problems of the recent attempt to enforce a system of C-section quotas for public hospitals is that this system encourages doctors to take into consideration the C-section quotas of their hospitals before they attend to the needs and demands of pregnant women and their families. This is of course highly problematic, and judging from a number of recent scandals, it is already leading to situations of extreme distress in public hospitals. One example is the 2017 case of a young laboring woman in a hospital in the city of Yulin who committed suicide by jumping out of a fifth-floor hospital window after experiencing several hours of labor pain and having her repeated C-section requests ignored.[51] In 2018 an obstetrician in a major public hospital in Beijing was beaten up by relatives of a pregnant forty-four-year-old woman for refusing to perform a C-section delivery when she was past her due date (V. Zhou 2018).

Although unverifiable, such stories reported in the media are detailed enough to highlight the potential dangers of systems that are narrowly focused on achieving quantitative targets at the expense of attending to the needs and desires of pregnant women and their families. Instead of a rigid program of C-section quotas that does not give much space for ethical reflection, what is needed is a more flexible approach that focuses more on creating a more humanistic environment of childbirth care that is concerned not just with saving lives but also with improving the quality of maternity care and securing the well-being of women. The first step toward developing such a flexible approach is to understand that the history of childbirth medicalization in China and elsewhere is not just a history of changing institutions, technologies, and policies; it is also a history of changing techno-moral visions of birth that should be told from the perspective of women as birthing subjects. Focusing on this history of techno-moral change requires taking more seriously the views of ordinary mothers, but it also requires taking more seriously the generational frictions shaping the construction of women's techno-moral understandings of birth.

CHAPTER 4

Grandparents and Labor Migration

Technologies of Multiple Mothering

CHILD REARING, LIKE FAMILY PLANNING AND CHILDBIRTH, IS A key part of the process of "people making": the work that is involved in the biological, social, and material reproduction of human life. This chapter approaches the work of child rearing as a "sociotechnical ensemble" that involves multiple actors, artifacts, techniques, institutions, and ideals.[1] My account explores the transformation of Chinese rural sociotechnical systems of collective child rearing—what I call technologies of multiple mothering—in the context of larger nationwide shifts in public policies and moral values. But instead of assuming that macro-level changes are simply imposed on rural folks by powerful external forces, I analyze the intimate choices made by village families in the context of increasing engagement with labor migration. I also show how these choices reveal changing generational power dynamics within village families, as well as increasing moral tensions between customary arrangements of multigenerational parenting based on the traditional ideal of the patrilineal joint family and emerging ideologies of intensive parenting that place on parents (mothers in particular) the sole responsibility for an increasing number of duties and tasks associated with the education of their children.[2]

I got my first glimpses of these power struggles and moral tensions during my first long-term fieldwork in Harmony Cave, between 1999 and 2001. In January 2000, a few weeks before the Lunar New Year celebrations, a major festive occasion when most migrant villagers return home, a sixty-five-year-old grandfather whom I will call Bright Moral explained his anxieties as a primary caregiver of children whose parents left to work in the city:

> I can't go anywhere now. My daughters [who married into neighboring lineage communities] often complain that I never visit them, but I don't have time. My third daughter-in-law is away from the village running a small vegetable farm in Nanhai [near Guangzhou], and she asked me to take care of her kids [literally "little mosquitoes" (C: *sai-man-jai*), a local affectionate term for small children], so I can't leave the kids by themselves. I only have four now. In previous years, I also had to take care of my second daughter-in-law's four kids, but their father returned to the village last year. My wife is looking after the eight kids of our fourth and fifth daughters-in-law, including a few young babies. We live in separate houses: I stay at our third son's and she stays at our fourth's. . . . Taking care of children is hard work. . . . I feel more at ease when the mother of the kids is around [about three or four times a year].

At this time, a significant proportion of the population of Harmony Cave was engaged in temporary labor migration to the highly industrialized and urbanized areas in the Pearl River Delta region. This trend has since intensified in the whole of Yellow Flower township as the practice of temporary labor migration established itself as the main source of household income for the majority of the local population. This increasing engagement with labor migration has created new challenges for village families in terms of child rearing: When both parents have to leave the village to find work in the city, who steps up to take care of the children back home? Who takes responsibility whenever something goes wrong? And who has the power to call the shots regarding these child-rearing issues? These questions were clearly in the back of Bright Moral's mind when—also in January 2000—he told me of an episode that pointed to the existence of significant moral tensions in local multigenerational child-rearing arrangements designed to help village families cope with the hardships of labor migration:

> A few days ago, one of my grandsons' primary-school classmates injured himself quite severely. . . . On the day of the incident, the boy's grandmother [a fifty-eight-year-old illiterate village woman] left home early in the

> morning . . . to go up the mountain to get firewood for the cooking stove. The six-year-old boy fell out of a big tree and broke his leg quite badly. The boy would eventually recover, but the hospital bill—about ¥30,000 [approximately US$4,600 back in 2000]—bankrupted the family. The boy's parents returned to the village as soon as they received the bad news via pager. Upon their arrival, the boy's mother [a very outspoken thirty-one-year-old woman, also illiterate] scolded her mother-in-law in public for not taking proper care of the grandchildren. She said that they are working very hard away from the village to earn money and that it is not easy [as a mother] to be away from the children. . . . The boy's mother was not happy that her mother-in-law had gone up the mountain to fetch firewood when nowadays one can purchase dry firewood in the village. She said that going up the mountain to fetch firewood is a "backward" practice, and she repeatedly referred to her mother-in-law as a "stupid old woman."

Bright Moral noted that the boy's grandmother could not really be blamed because she was single-handedly taking care of as many as six grandchildren (three from each of her two sons) and because she was not given enough money to take proper care of the kids, but he said that this was not what most people were saying. "Most people who hear the story of this incident blame the old woman, and no one reproaches the daughter-in-law for not showing respect for her mother-in-law. . . . [This is why I prefer to] stay at home as much as possible. If something happens to my grandchildren in my absence, I will also be in trouble with my daughter-in-law. She is the boss, you know, and I prefer to be careful. Ancient people have a saying: one wrong step can cause a thousand regrets [C: *yat chi sat juk chin gu han*]."

Back in 2000, there were many village children like the boy above who were "left behind" by their migrant parents and placed under the care of patrilateral grandparents. At the time, most village couples were having at least three children, and it was common to see grandparents (especially grandmothers) taking care of six to nine grandchildren. This sociotechnical arrangement was not questioned by villagers and was seen to be a pragmatic solution that built on earlier customary practices of multigenerational parenting in order to allow village families to cope with the challenges of child rearing in the new economy of labor migration.

Since 2000, however, this vision of multigenerational collective child rearing—what I call "multiple mothering"—has come under significant attack in the wider society. The 2000s was the period when the term "left-behind children" (SC: *liushou ertong*) was coined and the plight of these children started to be discussed in the national public sphere as a major societal problem that needs to be eradicated (see, for example, Nie et al. 2008; Duan and Yang 2008). These discourses depict "left-behind children" as children who are abandoned by their parents and mothers and who are therefore exposed to various kinds of vulnerabilities. Incidents involving "left-behind children" often make headlines in the national media, and their situation has become a matter of significant public concern and online discussion. The plight of "the children of China's great migration" (Murphy 2020) is considered particularly worrying because of the scale of the phenomenon. An influential 2013 survey produced by the All China Women's Federation claims that there are at least 61 million "left-behind children" in the countryside (ACWF 2013), and a more recent 2018 UNICEF annual report puts that number at approximately 69 million—that is roughly a quarter of the nation's children and almost a third of its rural children. Some studies claim that about 15 percent of all such children are unable to see their parents even once a year.[3]

These discourses have become particularly popular in the last two decades under the influence of social policies, social movements, and media discussions. This growing public prominence of the plight of "left-behind children" goes hand in hand with important changes in Chinese mainstream conceptions of parenting and parent-child relations due to the Birth Planning Policy and the increasing popularity of globalized expert ideologies of intensive parenting built around the conjugal family.[4] The rise of intensive parenting discourses was the outcome of a major effort steered by the state and supported by many quasi-state and nonstate actors in civil society to set new scientific standards for how parenting and child rearing should be done in the new Chinese socialist civilization of the Reform period. According to this new paradigm of intensive parenting, parents (especially mothers) are expected to engage with expert discourses and to be directly involved in the upbringing and education of their children. Leaving children "behind" under the care of grandparents or other relatives is considered a form of neglect, and as such it is a pathological behavior that should be monitored more closely so as to be gradually eliminated. This new paradigm of intensive parenting started to become dominant in mainstream urban society in the 1990s, opening the way for a nationwide reconfiguration of customary practices of multigenerational child rearing.[5]

In the January 2000 incident described by Bright Moral above, the boy's mother was anxious about the well-being of her injured boy. Such anxiety is an important element of global intensive mothering and parenting ideologies (Hays 1996; Faircloth, Hoffman, and Layne 2013), but another important component highlighted by recent Chinese public discourses on "left-behind children" is the idea that mothers (and to some extent fathers) should be closely involved in the upbringing of their children as part of a nuclear family household. Anthropologists have long noted that there is often a gap between normative frameworks and actual practices of child-care provision and education. This point is particularly relevant to making sense of intensive parenting discourses in contemporary China. Evidence suggests that these discourses have become very popular in urban China (Kuan 2015; Choi and Peng 2016; Zhong 2019) and that much of the work involved in intensive parenting falls on the shoulders of mothers (Santos and Harrell 2017; Zhong 2019), but most existing ethnographies show that urban parents continue to benefit from the help of grandparents and other caregivers outside the conjugal unit, including domestic helpers and professional educators (Goh 2011; Kuan 2015; Zhong 2019). Analysis of the shift to intensive parenting in China must take into account the multiple actors, processes, and institutions that shape actual practices and sociotechnical ensembles of child-care provision. Child-rearing practices and sociotechnical ensembles worldwide are constantly being transformed, and these transformations involve complex power struggles and negotiations (Bourdieu 1977, 1980, 1992; Ortner 1995, 2006), sometimes leading to changes in ethical frameworks and regimes of value (Robbins 2007).

Gendered power struggles and negotiations have led to the transformation of rural practices and values of child rearing under conditions of increasing engagement with labor migration. In most rural areas in China, the Maoist attempt from the 1950s onward to put into practice the "Engels strategy" of pursuing gender equality by including women in the formal labor force was not aided—as was the case in urban areas—by the development of a public network of nurseries, day-care centers, and kindergartens (Stockman, Bonney, and Sheng 1995, 144–45). This means that rural working mothers had to rely on the support provided by mothers-in-law and other members of the patrilineal joint family in order to cope with the dual burden of child rearing and agricultural work. By the end of the Maoist period in the mid-1970s, the patrilineal joint family remained the most important safety net for the provision of child care in rural areas, and the work of child rearing remained strongly associated with women. More specifically, child rearing remained in the hands of a female-centered intergenerational parenting body supervised by the child's mother under the authoritative guidance of her mother-in-law (Santos 2004, 215–62). This multiple mothering formation (ibid., 224) could include more or fewer members depending on the size and circumstances of the family, but its function was everywhere similar: to help new mothers get on with their child-rearing duties without neglecting their productive responsibilities.[6]

The use of the term "help" here may be somewhat misleading (Brown 2017). Multiple mothering was not just an informal structure of collaboration and mutual aid; it was also a site of patriarchal exploitation. Although its very existence can be conceptualized as a celebration of female power, many of its structural features—including its normative emphasis on the authority of the senior generation and its conventional definition of the "inner" realm of the household as the proper place for women—play an important role in the reproduction of the broader system of intersecting generational and gender inequalities that anthropologists call patriarchy (Harrell and Santos 2017). This patriarchal multiple mothering formation was reconfigured from the 1980s onward so as to allow ordinary rural families and women to engage with a radically new mode of livelihood based on labor migration. This sociotechnical reconfiguration was possible only because of a broader intergenerational power shift within rural families that both challenged and reproduced existing patriarchal arrangements.

The incident that opens this chapter reflects a change in the balance of power between generations. Both before 1949 and under Mao, there were many instances of daily-life conflicts between daughters-in-law and mothers-in-law, but for old grandparents like Bright Moral, it was clear that a more fundamental process of power reconfiguration was initiated when their adult children started to leave the village to work in the city. As in other parts of rural China, restructuring of the "classic" patriarchal order was initiated by radical reforms and campaigns under Mao, but in the 1980s restructuring was accelerated. Labor migration allowed the younger generations to "break free" from local conventions and assert their economic superiority and position of power in relation to the senior generations. New multiple mothering formations developed, based on a clear-cut generational division of labor: the senior mothers (and their husbands) took over the "feminine" work of everyday care and vigilance, while the more junior mothers joined their husbands in focusing on the "masculine" work of earning income away from home. These new multiple mothering formations are more balanced in terms of intergenerational power structure than were their predecessors in the Maoist period. Grandmothers still enjoy the prestige of seniority (at least on certain occasions), but junior mothers now act as breadwinners. This restructuring was accompanied by the rise of a series of educational institutions and expert services that started to take over the educational responsibilities of parents and grandparents, as the former are too busy to have time for education and the latter are deemed too old and "backward" to qualify as educators.

Labor Migration and the Work of Begetting Children

Most Yellow Flower migrants see themselves as sojourners who remain strongly attached to their native township and their native lineage village. This attachment to lineage and native place is not just about a lack of resources and opportunities to move elsewhere; it is also about ethical values, cultural meanings, and a sense of collective identity. Most migrants invest a significant amount of savings back home on worldly things like building a new family house and the related work of keeping up with ever-changing notions of what the sociologist Thorstein Veblen ([1899] 1934, chap. 3) called "pecuniary decency." But their economic success is also evaluated in terms of their capacity to contribute to community-building efforts and to the vitality of "old" local formations of social organization such as lineage associations.[7]

These lineage formations have a long recorded history of ritual and political activities. Such activities were repressed during the Maoist period but have flourished since the 1980s. Today, most local lineage associations have managed to build one or several ancestral halls for communal ritual activities, financed by activities such as labor migration to the Pearl River Delta region. The recent surge in local lineage associations was thus shaped by larger national and global forces of economic restructuring, but they continue to be built around "traditional" ritual ideologies of shared patrilineal descent and ancestor worship. Historically, these ideologies have nurtured the development of a family planning culture that emphasizes the importance of having many children, especially male heirs (M. Wolf 1970, 1972, 1985; R. Watson 1985). In Yellow Flower, the overall pronatalist orientation of this "traditional" family planning culture was not significantly challenged by the reforms of the Maoist period (Harrell et al. 2011; Santos 2006b, 2011, 2016). In the late 1970s, when decollectivization was initiated, local reproductive practices remained strongly pronatalist because the economy remained primarily agricultural and thus required a continuing supply of laborers. This started to change only in the 1980s with labor migration and industrial work, along with the Birth Planning Policy (Harrell et al. 2011; Santos 2006b, 2011, 2016).

The Birth Planning Policy was not vigorously enforced in Yellow Flower until 1988, and even then, it was initially enforced as a relatively flexible "two- to three-children" policy. This policy generated significant popular discontent in Yellow Flower, and the vegetable gardens in Foshan and Guangzhou played an important role in local strategies of resistance. These vegetable gardens offered married women a safe refuge from Birth Planning Policy officials and a place to give birth to "unplanned" children. The gardens also allowed many village couples to earn enough money to pay the fines for "unplanned births" of more than the normative two or three children. By the late 1990s, however, giving birth to "unplanned children" had become extremely expensive. The boy in this chapter's opening story (a third son) had cost his mother a lot of money in Birth Planning Policy fines, not to mention the price of her sterilization.

Today, most young village couples in this part of northern Guangdong emphasize the importance of having children, especially male heirs, but most young couples tend to have no more than two children. One reason for this is that the local Birth Planning Policy has become less permissive. The other is that local reproductive ideals have changed. Most young couples say that they would like to have at least one son, but that the ideal would be one son and one daughter. Some would be happy to have only daughters, but they complain about peer pressure and parental pressure to do otherwise, a state of affairs that is somewhat different from that found by anthropologist Lihong Shi (2017a, 2017b) in rural Liaoning, where sons have become too expensive due to rising expectations in brideprice payments and the decision to stop having children after a singleton daughter is born is increasingly accepted.

Despite the shift toward fewer children per couple, the work of begetting children remains central in Yellow Flower. This is also true in major cities like Guangzhou, but there women are marrying late and having children in their thirties or later, even though everyone continues to invoke the cultural ideal of having children early (J. Zhang 2017a; J. Zhang and Sun 2014). In Yellow Flower, this ideal is also the dominant framework of action. Most local girls drop out between the end of primary school (sixth grade) and the end of junior middle school (ninth grade) and then work in factories for a few years before marriage. Most get married in their early twenties (usually to someone from the same township or from a neighboring township) and have their children within the first ten years of marriage while continuing to engage in temporary labor migration. Some manage to integrate their employment situation in the city with the duties of family life and the care of multiple children by having their own business such as running a vegetable farm, but not all migrant couples are vegetable farmers, and running a vegetable farm is labor intensive, so who takes care of the children while the parents are working?

Technologies of Multiple Mothering

Bright Moral told me in 2000 how busy he and his wife Palm Sister were taking care of sixteen grandchildren. Their situation was already quite common. More than 50 percent of the village population was working away from home, including many migrant parents who left their children "behind" under the care of grandparents. In the 2010s, many lineage communities in the township had only grandparents and children around. Palm Sister explained this phenomenon during a conversation in 2005:

> When I married into this village [around 1960], I brought with me one son and one daughter [Palm Sister's two previous husbands had passed away very early]. After marriage, I gave birth to four sons and two daughters. I am now over seventy years old and have five daughters-in-law and twenty-one [patrilateral] grandchildren—eleven grandsons and ten granddaughters. That's a lot of grandchildren, so we need to help our daughters-in-law. Without support, our sons and daughters-in-law would never be able to go out of the village to earn money, and without this money, they would never be able to have as many children or build as many new "mansions" as they did. Getting

> married and having children these days is very costly, and building a new house costs more money than ever before. . . . The only way to do it is to seek work away from the village, but we are too old to do anything. Our sons and daughters-in-law go out to make money; we can only help them take care of the children. I bathed all my grandchildren when my daughters-in-law were "sitting the month" [the period of convalescence following childbirth], and I carried all of them [grandchildren] on my back [with the support of a sling] before they started to walk by themselves [usually around two to three years old]. . . . Mothers want to stay close to their children, but this is not always possible because they need to work hard on the vegetable farms [or in factories], and the environment down there is not good for children. Once the children start to walk, or even before that, mothers prefer to leave the children in the village. We watch them and feed them and make sure they go to school.

Such "surrogate parenting" arrangements do not represent a radical departure from earlier strategies and procedures of child rearing. Palm Sister continued:

> When I had my children [back in the 1960s and 1970s], I had to take care of them largely by myself because there was no mother-in-law [Bright Moral had lost his parents at a very young age]. Everything was harder without a mother-in-law, but I had more freedom. In those days, the old still had a lot of authority in the family, and mothers-in-law were quite often in charge of household matters. . . . Children were taken care of by the mother [C: *a-me*] under the guidance of the "old mother" [C: *lou-ma*, grandmother]. Young girls usually started taking care of younger siblings at around five or six [years old]. My eldest daughter helped me take care of her younger siblings, and when I was a small child, I helped my mother and grandmother take care of my younger siblings. In those days, it was important to have a lot of people around to help take care of children because this made it easier to manage labor and coordinate the work in the fields. If a daughter-in-law needed someone to watch her young children while she was working in the fields, she could always ask the support of her mother-in-law or other close relatives in her production team. In those days, this support was not as important as it is today because mothers did not need to go out of the village to earn income, and the work in the fields was not as intensive as the work in factories or on vegetable farms.

Almost everyone in the local village society was brought up by a small army of caregivers under the control of two main characters: the mother and the grandmother. This "multiple mother" scenario forms the core of a technology or a sociotechnical ensemble of child rearing, meaning an assemblage of materials, people, ideas, and artifacts that comes together in the work of providing care, protection, and education to children. This multiple mother can take many different forms, and it can have many different functions and effects, but its overall purpose is to help young mothers cope with child-rearing duties so that their productive activities both inside and outside the household are not completely disrupted. Grandmothers, sometimes also grandfathers, are important actors in this process. In the 1960s and 1970s (when Palm Sister's children were born), just as in the 1930s and 1940s (when Palm Sister was a child), grandmothers commonly provided child-care guidance as mothers worked in the fields, but their assistance was less critical than it is today. In the era of labor migration, having both paternal grandparents alive and available to offer full-time child-care support has become a critical resource. Parents lacking this resource have their labor migration prospects significantly constrained.[8] This was the situation of Bright Gold and his wife before Full Elder Sister decided to leave her husband behind to seek work in the city with her eldest son. Some couples obtain the support of maternal grandparents, but this is still uncommon and is usually a supplementary arrangement.

Reliance on the child-rearing contributions of the senior generation also reflects a lack of alternatives. Migrant parents have limited access to social welfare and educational facilities in the city, and they cannot afford paid child care. For them, the larger family remains the most important source of social support. In urban settings too, limited day care for preschool children, expensive private babysitters, and mistrust of domestic helpers all make grandparents a comparatively trustworthy source of child care after publicly subsidized child-care support programs were dramatically cut in the 1980s and 1990s (F. Du and Dong 2013). In this new political conjuncture, there emerged a 4:2:1 child-care pattern—that is, four grandparents and two parents jointly raising one child (Goh 2011). In reality, there may not always be four grandparents caring for one grandchild—sometimes there are only two or even just one—but the term refers to a model of child care in which potentially two sets of grandparents collaborate with parents on raising a single child. This multigenerational model of collaborative child rearing became popular in the 1980s and 1990s under the One-Child Policy, and it remains popular in urban areas in the second decade of the twenty-first century under the new multiple-child policy framework.

The popularity of this model of collaborative child rearing notwithstanding, there is also a parallel trend toward what the anthropologist Hong Zhang (2017) has called "grandparenting outsourcing" through which middle-generation parents seek to reduce the child-rearing workload of grandparents. This phenomenon is particularly salient in major cities like Guangzhou among middle-class families (Zhong 2019). One reason for grandparenting outsourcing is the desire to be a good son or daughter and thus to take proper care of the senior generation by reducing their child-rearing workload—for example, by hiring nannies or simply by not letting them do any child-care work or at least certain child-care tasks (H. Zhang 2017). Another reason is that grandparents themselves are not always willing to provide child care on a full-time basis given the increasing intensity and range of activities of school-age children (H. Zhang 2017). Yet another reason is the increasing impact of intensive parenting ideologies. Experts and government officials tell parents that the senior generation is too old to do child care properly, and teachers also tell parents that the senior generation is not qualified to oversee the education of school-age children. In this new climate of intensive parenting, mothers are expected to take full responsibility for the work of overseeing the schooling of their children (Zhong 2019). Grandparents can be used for unskilled tasks such as picking up the children from school, but not for more complex tasks such as helping the children do homework. Giving too much work to grandparents is increasingly considered to be a bad thing.

Mothers in rural townships like Yellow Flower are also concerned with reducing the contributions of grandparents, but the situation there is different from in the city of Guangzhou. The Yellow Flower framework of multigenerational child rearing is based on a variation of the 4:2:1 model. Local families have many "little mosquitoes," not just one or two "little emperors," and there are only two grandparents, not four, because the family model in rural northern Guangdong remains strongly patrilineal and patrilocal, whereas the urban family model has become more bilateral under the influence of the One-Child Policy. The patricentric orientation of rural northern Guangdong families creates a situation of shortage of grandparents in which the two (paternal) grandparents are expected to attend simultaneously to the child-rearing needs of multiple middle-generation couples. This means that grandparents like Palm Sister and Bright Moral have to rotate among sets of grandchildren, negotiating who is going to help take care of whose children, when, how, and where.

Most migrant parents (especially mothers) I interviewed over the years say that they would be happy to take care of their children by themselves, but they also note that asking their parents to step in is a good solution because taking care of children is a full-time job that is best done by someone with experience and expertise. This reliance on the senior generation for child-rearing support is a form of dependency that can be selfish and exploitative at times,[9] but one should bear in mind that this dependency is strongly encouraged by the senior generation. Moreover, not all parents who choose to rely on the senior generation do so for selfish reasons. Accepting support from the senior generation allows parents to focus on another family duty, something that they consider far more important and valuable than child rearing: the work of earning income outside the village to keep the whole family running. This was true in the 1980s when villagers started to leave the township to seek work in the city, and it is still true today when rates of labor migration remain high throughout the whole of Yellow Flower township and when the economic pressures on villagers have increased due to the rising cost of living.[10]

For mothers, this strong commitment to income-earning activities outside the village is perhaps nowhere clearer than in weaning practices. In the 1960s and 1970s, mothers did not wean their children until they were around two or three years of age (with gender variations), and some older women vividly recalled the sight of children as old as five being breastfed while their mothers were working in the fields. Migrant laborer mothers almost invariably wean their infants at around three to six months, and from then onward, babies are fed solely with rice porridge and (since the late 1990s) industrial powdered milk. Back in the 1960s and 1970s, prolonged breastfeeding was considered a good option because it was affordable and did not disrupt the mother's capacity to work in the fields. This work was flexible and was performed in the vicinity of the village, so the mother could remain in close contact with the child. Today, prolonged breastfeeding is no longer considered a good option because most mothers are working very long hours in places such as factories and vegetable farms. This type of work is not very flexible and requires the physical separation of mother and child.

Most migrant mothers, as Palm Sister notes, would prefer to stay close to their children and spend more time with them, but this is not always possible because the mothers must return to work as soon as possible after childbirth.[11] It is difficult for grandparents to go to the city to offer child-care support, because they have to consider the needs of other daughters-in-law and find it difficult to live away from their villages for long periods of time (some can barely endure a bus journey to the city because of motion sickness). So the only option for migrant mothers (and fathers) is to leave young children in the care of grandparents back in the village. This option is also favored because the environment in the city (i.e., the periurban areas where factories and vegetable farms are located) is considered not very suitable for children. In 1999, for example, two children who were four and five years old were found drowned in waterways bordering the vegetable farms leased by Yellow Flower migrants, somewhere on the edges of Guangzhou. Accidents like this can happen everywhere, but in the city, people are often indifferent to what happens to their neighbors or their children. These tragedies were very powerful in making the point across the migrant community that it is better to leave one's young children safely back in the village than expose them to the dangers of the urban environment.

Leaving children with grandparents is not a form of abandonment, as assumed by expert commentators and state media news sources (see, for example, Y. Li et al. 2015). Most migrant mothers (and fathers) are convinced that they are doing what is best for their children, and they certainly do not see themselves as having renounced their maternal (and parental) duties and responsibilities. They may not be providing everyday care for their children, but they are working hard to earn the money that pays for food, clothes, education, and so on. In their view, the work of mothering, and more generally the work of parenting, can be partitioned into different roles and shared by many actors, so when they say that they are committed primarily to their income-earning duties rather than to the actual work of raising children, they are saying that they are working on their maternal and parental identity as "breadwinners" rather than as "everyday caregivers." This is not to say that they have completely dismissed the importance of acts of everyday caregiving (for example, when mothers return home from the vegetable farms, they are very keen on sleeping with their children and expressing motherly love), but they prefer to present themselves as "nurturant breadwinners" as opposed to "nurturant caregivers." Both conceptions of maternal or parental identity contribute to the "nurturing" of the child but stand in a hierarchical relation to each other. Those focusing on the work of earning money are the ones people refer to as the "boss" (C: *lou-baan, lou-sai, si-tau*).

The Decline of the Authority of the Senior Generation

When I spoke to old Bright Moral back in 2000, I had not yet met the "boss," his third daughter-in-law. When I finally got to meet her face-to-face a few weeks later, I realized that she and Bright Moral actually maintained a very good relationship and that this was the reason he had chosen his third son's place as his "official" residence after family partition a few years earlier. This was the kind of daughter-in-law who would buy a new pair of trousers for Grandpa for the Spring Festival period upon realizing that he had only three patched old pairs. I asked him a few months later, what was so scary about this daughter-in-law?

> When I was a kid [back in the 1940s and 1950s], old people were in charge of family matters. It was the duty of parents to organize the marriages of their children, and family division was delayed until all sons were married. When young women married into the village, one could see that they were afraid of their mothers-in-law. . . . By the time I got married and started to have my own children [in the 1960s and 1970s], old people were still in charge [C: *a-gung leung-gung-po wa-si*], and daughters-in-law were instructed to take proper care of their children. There were many incidents of unfilial behavior, but there was community pressure to show respect toward the senior generation. Nowadays the situation has changed. The villages are empty. Everyone is away making money. There is no community pressure anymore, and the old rules of family division no longer apply. Sons establish their own independent "stoves" immediately after marriage as they set off to the city to earn money. Old people are no longer in charge. Daughters-in-law are in charge, and they instruct the old to take care of their children.

Youngsters are not just telling old people what to do; they are instructing old people to do the job with little money:

> Daughters-in-law like to say that they work very hard in the city in order to send money to the village and pay for all expenses back home, but this is not

> what is happening. The old are complaining that they are not receiving enough money. I do not mean pocket money; I mean money to survive. Most have to farm the land to feed themselves and their grandchildren. . . . We have already reached an advanced age, but we are not being looked after by the younger generation. Having worked hard to nurture our children is not enough; we still need to farm the fields to nurture the children of our children. Old people today are facing a lot of hardships.

More than ten years later, in March 2012, I met Bright Moral at the house of one of his close village brothers, old Splendid Omen, and his wife, Third Sister, a seventy-two-year-old illiterate grandmother who, like most village grandmothers, is very proud of having bathed all her grandchildren as infants:

> We have six [paternal] grandchildren. Our three sons are all working away from the village. . . . Our second son is still a bachelor; he lives with his younger brother and his wife. . . . Our sons are all cultivating vegetables in the city to earn money; we stay in the village to take care of the children. We already took care of the four children of our eldest son [back in the 1990s and the 2000s]. . . . We are now taking care of the two children of our youngest son, a boy and a girl. The boy is eleven years old and attends primary school [grade 5] in the market town. The girl is still very young. She's three years old and needs a lot of care. We get about ¥600–¥700 per month to get by with these two children. It is not a lot of money, but many old people receive even less. The only way to get by with this money is to save money on rice, vegetables, peanuts, corn, and ginger, so we are still farming the land to have food to eat. Next year we'll stop cultivating rice. I'm half blind already [due to cataracts], so I cannot help my husband in the fields anymore. We want to help our children, but we are getting too old to do anything. . . . I know that my sons would give us more money every month if they could afford it. But what we are getting at the moment is not enough to fill the stomach. Yesterday I took the young girl to the doctor to get an injection because she was sick. Just that cost ¥50!

Although old people themselves realize that this is an exploitative relationship, they nevertheless uphold the idea that they have to help and support their children until they can give no more. Of course, their efforts to render help and support create all kinds of frictions and contradictions in practice. Old people are not simply being told to do things like take care of grandchildren on a very tight budget, Third Sister says; they are also being scolded for not doing it the right way:

> Daughters-in-law nowadays do not have to listen to what we say, and no one criticizes them when they mistreat us. They often say that we are good for nothing, and they like to scold us for all kinds of reasons. . . . They say that we are old and "backward" and that we don't even know how to take care of children. If they actually had some sense, they would think something along these lines: "They are so old already, nurtured so many children, how can they not know how to take care of children?" But this is not what they say. What they say is that we are "useless."

Third Sister gave a concrete example:

> We ate a lot of sweet potatoes over the years. . . . We could even say that without sweet potatoes, we would probably not be here. . . . We also gave a lot of sweet potatoes to our children [growing up in the 1960s and 1970s]. . . . There is nothing wrong with sweet potatoes. They nurture people. But when our daughters-in-law return to the village, they criticize us for cooking sweet potatoes. They say that sweet potatoes are not tasty and are not nourishing enough. And when we give them a bowl of rice instead of sweet potatoes, they criticize us for not adding enough salt and oil. . . . Sometimes they also say that the food lacks sugar or that it lacks soy sauce. . . . I don't really understand what they want. . . . People of our age never add sugar or soy sauce, and we are not used to adding a lot of salt and oil. All we need is a bit of salt to add taste. . . . Today a bit of salt is not enough. They also want monosodium glutamate, sugar, ginger, and whatnot. It may well be that cooking in this manner makes food tastier. . . . But our economy does not allow it. . . . You need money to cook food with all those things. . . . Who pays for it? They certainly don't!

It is not just that the middle generation is failing to show respect toward the senior generation, Third Sister says, but the junior generation (grandchildren) is also not responding to the senior generation's instructions. Local authorities commonly refer to the senior generation's lack of authority as an important factor behind recent policies and market developments in the educational sector. Starting from 2008, the Yellow Flower township government has pushed for the creation of full-day kindergartens and boarding primary schools for local children, including the children of migrant parents. These local developments are linked to larger changes in national frameworks of educational governance highlighting the lack of "quality" of the senior generation for the role of educators of children, especially school-age children (Kipnis 2009, 2011; Kuan 2015). These discourses have become increasingly widespread in China under the influence of the larger Reform-era movement known as "education for quality" (SC: *suzhi jiaoyu*), as well as under the impact of larger forces of professionalization of the educational sector.

The dominant view in China today is that the education of children (starting from nursery and kindergarten) should be fully placed in the hands of teachers and other professional experts. This ideology of professionalization was already present in the Maoist period, but it has been significantly intensified in the Reform period with the rise of mass literacy and the development of a more competitive, comprehensive, and intensive regime of education (Kipnis 2011). It should be noted, however, that the contemporary emphasis on the figure of the expert is linked to a vision of work, gender, and family that is no longer concerned with facilitating the incorporation of mothers in the formal labor force through the development of a public network of free child-care provision. The emphasis now is on getting mothers to find ways of coping with the dual burden of family and employment. In this gendered vision of intensive parenting, teaching experts cannot do the job on their own; the work of teachers needs to be followed up on a daily basis by parents, and mothers should be the ones to take up that task. This vision emphasizes that a good mother will not place this work of supervision in the hands of the senior generation because they are too old and are not really qualified to do the job. In urban middle-class circles, this educational ideology of motherhood is placing increasing pressures on working mothers to find ways of coping with the demands of a highly intensive schooling regime that combines long school hours and extracurricular classes with heavy homework duties (H. Zhang 2017; Zhong 2019).

The situation in rural townships like Yellow Flower is slightly different from what is going on in urban middle-class circles. Rural mothers are not as committed to educational ideologies of motherhood as their urban middle-class peers. The main driver of grandparenting outsourcing in Yellow Flower is educational infrastructure. Starting from the 2010s, the township has witnessed the emergence of a network of full-day kindergartens and boarding primary schools for local children. Most local mothers (including migrant laborer mothers) welcome this new development. Not every local couple can afford the costs associated with the new schooling arrangements, especially kindergartens, but it is quite clear that the trend is growing. I noticed in 2016 and 2017 that a growing number of local children (including children of migrant laborer parents) were attending full-day kindergartens in the market town, and my friends in Harmony Cave tell me that this arrangement has already become a local norm. Grandparents are still involved in picking up the children from school and other related tasks, but they no longer have the burden of supervising children during the day. This dynamic of grandparenting outsourcing is even more radical when it comes to school-age children. All primary schools at the village level were suspended or no longer offer classes beyond grade 4. After grade 4, local children have to enroll in a boarding primary school located in the market town. These children spend most of their time in school, and they go home to stay with their grandparents (or with their parents, if they are around) only on weekends and during public holiday periods.

I have asked many middle-generation mothers in Harmony Cave why they think that the boarding primary school in the Yellow Flower market town is a good educational solution for their children. Many mothers told me that they are so busy with the work of earning income that they do not have time to take care of the children. They need help, and they prefer to place their children in the hands of professional teachers (in the boarding school) than under the care of "backward" "old" grandparents. Their thinking is that grandparents are cheap but they are too old to qualify as good educators; schools and teachers are better. Some mothers told me that they would rather enroll their children in a school in the city but they know that this is not feasible because it is too expensive. Attending the boarding primary school in Yellow Flower is also expensive, but most mothers feel that it is their duty to provide the best possible education for their children. There is also the filial duty of reducing the child-care burden on the senior generation, but this point should not be overstated. Most families in Yellow Flower continue to rely on grandparents as a major source of child-care provision. Grandparental support is crucial in the first three years of age, and it continues to be important after the child starts to attend preschool and primary school because—as I was repeatedly told by local mothers—most parents are so busy with the work of making money that they do not have much time available to take care of the children on a daily basis.

This prioritizing of the work of earning income over the work of providing care and education of their children suggests that Yellow Flower mothers see motherhood differently than do urban middle-class mothers, who are increasingly committed to an ideology of motherhood that emphasizes their responsibility as educators. Yellow Flower mothers are more concerned with their own capacity to earn income and they feel that they have no choice but to delegate mothering tasks like "caregiving" and "educating" to surrogate parents like grandparents and boarding-school teachers. These findings have implications for recent debates around the work of American development economist Scott Rozelle and his Rural Education Action Program (REAP) team at Stanford University. In a series of articles widely debated in China,[12] Rozelle and his team argue that one of the best ways to bridge the educational gap between cities and rural areas is to improve conditions of child rearing by asking rural mothers working in the cities to return home to take care of their children. Critics of Rozelle have rightly noted that asking female migrant laborers to return home and abandon their role of family breadwinners would be to reproduce the idea that only mothers are supposed to take up the responsibilities and burdens of parenting. Most young mothers in Yellow Flower would add that Rozelle's proposal makes no economic sense. Why not share the work of mothering with grandparents and other surrogate parents when rural families need young mothers to work hard to earn money? If young mothers do not help their husbands earn income, who will?

Reassembling a New Patriarchal Order of Child Rearing

Changing child-rearing practices in the Yellow Flower region since the 1990s have involved a reassembling of previous patriarchal family structures and hierarchies. Labor migration played an important role in this process. I use the term "reassembling" as opposed to "breakdown" because there was no clear-cut "collapse" of patriarchal family structures, just as there was no clear-cut shift to a conjugal family system in which parenting duties became circumscribed to the conjugal couple.[13] This "triumph of conjugality"

(Y. Yan 1997) narrative of intimate modernity was first developed in western Europe and North America in the late nineteenth century and the first decades of the twentieth century (Durkheim 1895, 1898, 1900, 1921; see also Lamanna 2002). This narrative started to gain significant global popularity in the postwar period as a political model of social and economic modernization (Thornton 2005). In China, the model was turned into a blueprint for large-scale reforms under Mao and again under Deng Xiaoping and his successors. Today, the model continues to be used by the Chinese government as the developmental path that the country needs to take in order to achieve global modernity (Greenhalgh 2010). Like all models, the "triumph of conjugality" narrative of family modernization has both strengths and limitations. On the positive side, it helps make sense of phenomena such as the decline of elder power and the growing significance of affective individualism; on the negative side, it does not pay sufficient attention to the continuing centrality of gender inequality and the continuing significance of relations of interdependence between generations.

The growing power of the younger generations in places like Yellow Flower should not be conceptualized as a "triumph of conjugality" (Y. Yan 1997) but as a reconfiguration of preexisting patterns of gendered generational interdependence typical of patriarchal family formations. These interdependencies can be observed in many other parts of the world under present-day frameworks of global capitalism and a worldwide erosion of public child-care support (Attias-Donfut and Segalen 1998, 2002; Segalen 2001, 2009; Swartz 2009), but they cannot be overlooked in the contemporary Chinese context. In urban China, and in some parts of rural China, both sets of grandparents are usually involved in the work of child-care support, but in rural northern Guangdong, the task of grandparenting continues to be significantly skewed in a patrilineal direction.

This was already the case in the 1960s and 1970s, but the shift to a mode of livelihood based on labor migration from the 1980s onward has introduced important changes. Child rearing in the age of labor migration continues to be built around gendered generational interdependencies within the patrilineal joint family, but these interdependencies were significantly reconfigured. This gave rise to new multiple mothering formations in which (patrilateral) grandmothers (and grandfathers) have become largely responsible for the "feminine" work of everyday care and vigilance, and younger mothers redefined their family duties primarily in terms of the "masculine" work of earning income outside the village. This transformation has empowered the middle generation economically, but it did *not* lead to the collapse of "the intergenerational contract" (Croll 2006). If anything, it resulted in the emergence of a new patriarchal configuration in which middle-generation mothers have more bargaining power in the negotiation of patrilineal generational interdependencies. As the sociologist Deniz Kandiyoti (1988, 275) notes, "Patriarchal bargains are not timeless or immutable entities, but are susceptible to historical transformations that open up new areas of struggle and renegotiation of the relations between genders"—as well as between generations.

This opening up of new areas of struggle and renegotiation between generations has inspired young mothers to construct a whole new system of ethical values and notions of motherhood in the context of larger changes in national frameworks of family governance and education. These changes were shaped by global developments such as the emergence of an increasingly competitive educational environment in which children face increasing pressures to expand their study hours and mothers (and fathers) face increasing pressures to take a more active role in the education of their children. In China, the core idea of this educational model of intensive mothering and parenting is that the intensive work of caregiving performed by mothers and fathers as primary caregivers plays an important role in the development of psychologically balanced and educationally successful children. This idea that intensive mothering and parenting is crucial for the well-being and the success of children started to become normative in urban areas in the 1990s, and by the turn of the millennium, there was already a growing body of psychological and educational experts publishing popular books on the science of parenting and the field of child development (Naftali 2014, 2016; Kuan 2015). These expert commentaries inspired the emergence of nationwide public debates on the "inadequate" parenting practices of migrant parents who leave their children behind (see, e.g., Nie et al. 2008; Duan and Yang 2008). In these debates, the phenomenon of "left-behind children" is often depicted as a major societal problem that needs to be eradicated through the enforcement of a more "civilized" educational model of intensive mothering and parenting.

Most young mothers in Yellow Flower do not favor this urban middle-class model of intensive mothering and parenting. They are of course concerned with the education of their children, but they are more concerned with the need to earn income for the family. These mothers favor a model of motherhood that is less based on the nurturing work of daily care and guidance, or on the nurturing work of coordinating the process of education, than on the nurturing work of earning income for the family to pay daily necessities. This is not just the outcome of economic necessity; it is a moral choice. Mothers look at the nurturing work of earning income as a superior form of showing their motherly love, and they see no problem in delegating the tasks of everyday care and education to the senior generation and, increasingly, to professional educators and professional institutions such as kindergartens and boarding primary schools.

Local mothers (including those engaged in labor migration) are more and more starting to favor a strategy of child rearing that involves increasing the contact time of their children with professional educators. Not every local couple can afford the costs of enrolling their children in a local kindergarten or of getting their children to eat and sleep in the township's boarding primary school, but it is quite clear that these practices are becoming popular. Grandparents are still important components of local technologies of multiple mothering, providing crucial child-care support in the first three years of age of the child and then again when the child is old enough to go to kindergarten and primary school, but grandparents are no longer as busy doing child care as they were when I first met Bright Moral (the grandfather mentioned in the opening vignette) back in 1999–2000. One reason for this is that the senior generation nowadays has fewer (patrilateral) grandchildren, and this has reduced their child-rearing workload to about four to six grandchildren, an average of two or three per son. Another reason is that the contact time of local children with professional educators has increased. Many children aged three to six are spending a significant part of the day in the kindergarten, and many children aged six to ten are spending a significant part of their daily and weekly time during the schooling period in a boarding school in the market town. These boarding-school children go back to their home in the village only on weekends and during public holiday periods, thus reducing time spent with grandparents.

Most young mothers in Yellow Flower view this development in a positive light, largely because of the influence of urban middle-class ideologies of intensive mothering and parenting and the moral critique of the phenomenon of "left behind children." Before the 2000s, most young mothers did not question the practice of leaving their children behind under the care of the senior generation. Grandparents were considered crucial components of local multigenerational practices of parenting and child rearing. Young mothers and parents did not have time to take care of children because they were too busy working in the city and/or earning income for the family. It was up to the senior generation to step in to help take care of the "little mosquitoes" mentioned at the beginning of this chapter. After the 2000s, an important change occurred in local technologies of multiple mothering. Young mothers and parents continue to be focused on the work of earning income for the family and they delegate the work of daily care, vigilance, and education to others, but grandparents no longer play such a central role. Young mothers and parents prefer to leave their children in the hands of professional teachers (in kindergartens or in boarding primary schools) as opposed to leaving them with grandparents who are deemed too "old" and "backward" to qualify as good educators. Young mothers and parents continue to rely on technologies of multiple mothering to take care of their children, but now local teachers working for state institutions and state-policy-aligned market services are taking over as the key substitute parents, and they are committed to a more labor-intensive model of child care and education that involves structured learning activities.

CHAPTER 5

Flush Toilets

The Politics of Material Civilization

WE ALL NEED TO HANDLE MATTERS OF BODILY HYGIENE ON A daily basis, but there are different ways of organizing and governing such mundane practices. Like other metropolitan anthropologists doing field research in relatively remote locations, I was concerned with questions of bodily hygiene when I first arrived in Harmony Cave in the summer of 1999. How do villagers "go to the toilet"? What kinds of technical arrangements and procedures are in place for this purpose in rural communities in northern Guangdong? I was already quite familiar with everyday life in major cities like Guangzhou, but not with the challenges of the local countryside, and I had never lived for long periods in a rural community in China or anywhere else.

My first local guide on this issue was Bright Image, a sixty-year-old man from Harmony First. He was my first host in the village. At the time, he was living alone with six of his grandchildren because his wife, four sons, and four daughters-in-law were working in vegetable gardening enterprises in the city of Nanhai. On the day I moved to one of his two brand-new modern houses, Bright Image provided instructions. He mentioned three key places to sort out one's needs. The surrounding fields and hills are particularly convenient when one is away from the village and its residential areas. As for the village latrines, they are like public toilets that can be used whenever one is close to the village area. If a latrine is not convenient, one can use a chamber pot or plastic basin at home and then pour the waste matter into a village latrine. He added that most villagers use communal latrines because they are still living in old-style clay-brick houses that do not have private bathrooms with flush toilets. Bright Image noted proudly that only recently built modern multistory houses like his own were equipped with "advanced" (C: *sin-jeun*) toilet arrangements of the type suitable for my "high-class identity" (C: *gou-kap san-fan*) as a "Western" foreign guest, but he insisted that at night I should feel free to pee in the small plastic bucket near my bedroom to avoid the hassle of having to go to the manually flushed squat toilet on the ground floor.

I took this suggestion seriously and followed my host's advice. A few days later, however, I started to realize that what I took to be a last-minute toilet arrangement devised by my host—the bucket for nighttime peeing—was actually fairly common. Most families in the village kept one or two of these buckets in their houses for peeing purposes, not just at nighttime. Indeed, this practice was still so popular that even families like my host's who had already moved into a modern house with a private flush toilet continued to use these indoor urine buckets. I initially thought this was linked to the fact that village folks had still not adapted to the idea of having a private toilet at home, but it quickly became apparent that there was another reason.

My realization of this occurred a few weeks later when I decided to empty the urine bucket placed next to my bedroom straight into the squat toilet downstairs. When my host realized what I was doing, he became very agitated and prompted me to stop. I soon realized that I was throwing away something that he considered highly valuable. Like most village households, he was not accumulating urine in buckets simply to throw it away. Rather, he wanted to dilute the urine in water in order to produce fertilizer for his vegetable garden. This was not just about saving money; like many other villagers, he was convinced that vegetables grown with this fertilizer are tastier than those grown with chemical fertilizer. From his perspective, emptying the urine bucket into the toilet was a total waste.

A similar dynamic was in place—so I subsequently learned—in the public latrines of each village hamlet. Locally called "shit pits" (C: *si-haang*), these are usually located away from people's living quarters, often close to pigsties and cowsheds. Most latrines that were in use in the late 1990s and early 2000s were built in the 1980s (the first decade of the Reform period) as part of a collective effort by each village hamlet or village group. During the first six months of my stay in the village between 1999 and 2001, I used mostly the public latrine of the residential complex of Harmony First, because this was where the housing units of my first two host families were based. These public latrines are small buildings (10–15 square meters) made of "traditional" yellow mud bricks and tiles (figure 5.1). Inside, there is a pit, usually no more than 2 meters deep, where all waste matter accumulates. Users squat on two solid wooden boards hanging over the pit. The space inside the latrines is well ventilated because the entrance has no doors and the walls have small openings. Latrine users are expected to leave a hat or some other personal item by the entrance to signal their presence and thus avoid any embarrassing encounter.

I initially thought that the main function of these latrines was to enable villagers to sort out their bodily needs inside the village in a safe, secluded location that was sufficiently removed from people's residential quarters so as to prevent the spread of foul odors and other nuisances associated with excreta. But I quickly realized that—as with the urine buckets—an equally important function was the accumulation of human waste for use as

FIGURE 5.1. Village communal latrine, Harmony Cave, 2009

agricultural fertilizer. Once the pit is full, the waste can be turned into liquid fertilizer simply by diluting it with water to initiate the fermentation process. This diluted "shit-pit water" (C: *si-haang-seui*) can be applied directly to the rice plants in the paddies or to farm produce on dry fields, but this is a very laborious process. An alternative procedure is to treat the accumulated waste in the pit with lime, ashes, and other natural materials such as animal manure and chunks of muddy soil, and then sun-dry the resulting mixture to produce "mixed-soil fertilizer" (C: *tou-jaap-fei*). Applying this fertilizer to fields during the dry season is thought to be a cheap, effective way of maintaining and enhancing the "soil's strength" (C: *tou-lik*), but it is also laborious and time-consuming. In contrast to fertilizing procedures involving farm chemicals, very large amounts of shit-pit water and mixed-soil fertilizer need to be applied to the fields to achieve visible results, and these materials have to be transported to the fields in buckets strung on bamboo poles or in handcarts because the rice fields have no roads or paths, only narrow field ridges (Santos 2006b, 2011).

In the late 1990s, when I first arrived in the Harmony Cave region, many villages still recycled human waste for agriculture, but it was also clear that commitment to these practices was declining. Historians of science and technology have documented the long history of these practices of agricultural recycling of human waste in imperial China.[1] These practices are known to have reached particularly high levels of social and technical elaboration in provinces like Guangdong in the fertile subtropical region of South China.[2] By the late Ming dynasty (sixteenth and seventeenth centuries), an intensive trade in human excreta had emerged in many parts of this region.[3] At the time, peasant families were already relying on high levels of fertilizer input to sustain their soil-exhausting multicropping farming regime, and they had to supplement local fertilizing materials with human waste collected in cities and towns. Peasants were particularly keen on purchasing urban human waste because urbanites have a high-protein diet that was thought to improve the quality of human manure.

These rural-urban exchanges were at the heart of a sophisticated agro-urban sanitation system that was not reconfigured until after the collapse of the last imperial dynasty in 1911 under the influence of new "Western" and "Japanese" concepts of public health.[4] The move away from this agro-urban sanitation system was slow because the system was too functional and too well consolidated to be dismantled from day to night. Recent research on the history of public sanitation in the city of Guangzhou during the Republican era (1911–49) shows that the municipal government was neither able to nor interested in challenging the existing agro-urban sanitation system (J. Zhang and Santos 2018; J. Zhang 2017b). Instead, the municipal government sought to curb the power of local organizations in the human manure business, while promoting the standardization and centralization of procedures of public toilet construction and maintenance. The goal was not to dismantle the system but to centralize it and to increase the government's share of the profit in it without having to dismantle local organizations.

After 1949, the Communists continued this strategy of centralization, but they put an end to the commercial dimensions of the "old" agro-urban sanitation system. The Communists were ambivalent toward the "Western" flush-and-discharge model of human waste management, preferring instead to maintain traditional urban-rural synergies through a collectivist regime of public toilets and daily night-soil collection (FAO 1977; J. Zhu 1988; L. Zhou 2004). Only after the reforms of the 1980s and 1990s was this collectivist people-centered infrastructure of urban sanitation discarded in favor of a more high-tech, individualized approach based on private bathrooms, flush toilets, and an expanding grid of sanitary sewers. This was a key turning point in the making of China's contemporary project of "hygienic modernity" (Rogaski 2004) and more generally in the construction of a new vision of "socialist civilization" (SC: *shehui zhuyi wenming*).[5] By the late 1990s, the burgeoning middle class in China's major cities was no longer satisfied with having home bathrooms with flush toilets; they wanted to have sophisticated bathroom designs with "high quality" flush toilets (L. Zhou 2004; Lai 2016).

This nationwide "flush toilet revolution" played a part in the making of modern identities in China (Laporte 2010; F. Bray n.d.; Redfield and Robins 2016), but one should be careful not to assume a too narrow and homogeneous notion of modernity. As Japanese cultural commentator Seno Kappa (2011) shows in an insightful essay on the history of the flush toilet, just as there are many different kinds of flush toilet practices and infrastructures around the world, so are there many different conceptions and approaches to "modern civilization."[6] While the spread of industrial modernity has reached large numbers of people in many different parts of the world, it did not give rise to just one civilizational configuration—one pattern of ideological, practical, material, and institutional response—but to multiple modern civilizational configurations, or "multiple modernities" (Eisenstadt 2003), with significant variations, right down to the level of individuals, families, and communities. If the flush toilet has become an important symbolic marker of modern civilization around the world, the way each society or community constructs its own version of flush-toilet modernity reveals significant differentiations. Making sense of these differentiations requires opening the "black box" of the "technological choices" (Lemonnier 1993) shaping the construction of flush-toilet modernities in any given context.

The term "technological choice" requires clarification. Anthropologist Claude Lévi-Strauss ([1976] 1983) was one of the first to note that human societies make technological choices that are both collective and meaningful. In most instances, it is only by analogy that one can say that it seems as though a community or a society has chosen a particular sociotechnical arrangement from a whole range of possible avenues. These technological choices are rarely the product of a consensual decision but entail complex processes of moral, technical, and political negotiation at multiple levels. There are negotiations taking place at the macro level and involving actors such as national governments and international organizations, but negotiations are also taking place at the micro level and involving individuals, families, and specific communities of users (Cowan 1983; Wajcman 2016, 111–35). Most historical and social science accounts of modern technological choices focus on powerful macro-structural forces at the national and global levels. But the spread of private flush toilet arrangements in Chinese rural communities is not a mere by-product of macro-level technocratic forces such as national development policies, industrial marketing campaigns, and global aid programs; these macro-level forces are important but must also be situated in the context of complex user-mediated negotiations at the micro level (Santos 2016, 2018).

This chapter views these micro-macro mediations from the perspective of the intimate choices of Yellow Flower village communities. In the Harmony Cave region, the shift to the private bathroom and the flush toilet started to take place in the 1990s. This was the period when farm chemicals became increasingly popular and new forms of housing and village planning emerged. In this context, the villagers' decision to adopt the private bathroom and the flush toilet did not result from a consensus on the superiority of such "advanced" technologies, but from "translation" (Callon 1986) of elite social strategies and interests that promoted the private bathroom and the flush toilet as the new local standards for what counts as "modern" and "civilized" in terms of bodily hygiene and public sanitation. These elite efforts of trend-setting went hand in hand with the development of new notions of personal privacy and hygiene, but these changes did not completely dismiss earlier practices of bodily hygiene and human waste management. This coexistence of "new" and "old" practices suggests tensions between older "civilizational legacies" and newer "civilizing missions."[7]

A New Material Civilization of "Mansions" with Private Bathrooms

An important factor leading to the spread of the private bathroom and the flush toilet was the housing boom that began in the 1990s in the context of increasing labor migration to the city. Another factor was the decline of subsistence farming and the industrialization of local agricultural practices. When I arrived in Harmony Cave in 1999, most communal latrines were still operating as producers of mixed-soil fertilizer, even though there were already clear-cut signs of decline. This decline was due in large part to the rise of new forms of housing with private flush toilets, but the main factor was the increasing popularity of chemical fertilizers in local agricultural practices.[8]

Farm chemicals became available in local markets in the mid-1980s, but only in the 1990s did these so-called advanced scientific products (C: *sin-jeun fo-hok mat-ban*) enter local agricultural practices, as the local economy improved and villagers were able to afford farm chemicals and turn them into objects of "conspicuous consumption" (Veblen [1899] 1934). Villagers also were genuinely impressed by the effects of farm chemicals on food production when compared to previous techniques of fertilization such as mixed-soil fertilizer. Farm chemicals were "magical" less because they increased crop yields in absolute terms, but more because they enabled local farmers to achieve higher levels of food production with less labor. This major sociotechnical achievement allowed village families to continue farming their land at home while sending migrant workers to Guangzhou and the neighboring Pearl River Delta region to earn additional income (Santos 2011).

By the late 1990s, the first modern-style houses with private bathrooms and flush toilets were being built in Harmony Cave with savings earned mostly through temporary labor migration. I noticed that their occupants often remained regular users of communal latrines, even as they boasted about the "advanced" toilet arrangements of their new "mansions" (C: *lau*). These dwellers in modern houses saw themselves as the first local representatives of a superior "modern material civilization," and they were not shy to boast about it. These claims to superiority did not represent a consensus. Stories circulated in the village contesting the idea that the modern houses represented a superior form of residence. It was said, for example, that they were too hot during the summer because their walls and windows were excessively insulating and their location—the open fields in the middle of the valley—had too much sun exposure. These problems were often framed in terms of bad feng shui, which helped explain, for example, why so many of the modern houses were infested with ants, why their groundwater did not taste so good, or why their inhabitants were more susceptible to episodes of misfortune such as traffic accidents. These and many other criticisms were the subject of heated discussions during informal village gatherings, but the idea that the modern homes were the most "advanced" form of housing was already becoming dominant. This picture was somewhat one-sided, but like most hegemonic representations, it was partly grounded on materialities.

Materially speaking, the new houses are indeed very different from the older clay-brick houses (C: *nai-jyun nguk*), whose construction techniques were developed well before the Communist Revolution in 1949 (Santos and Donzelli 2009). Back in the late 1990s and the early 2000s, most village families were still living in these single-story structures, which they had built using the skills and labor of their personal networks of support. Mud from the local rice fields is used to shape the bricks, which are briefly fired in the village kiln. The roof tiles are also made of local mud, but they are darker than the bricks because they are fired longer to increase waterproofness and durability. Local mud-brick houses are rarely built as autonomous units; they are aggregated in compact residential compounds comprising a whole village or hamlet. Because each house unit is small (15–25 square meters), the average village family required several units including a kitchen, a bedroom, a rice granary, and more, depending on family size and holdings. This style of housing never included a separate bathroom unit.

In contrast to these small low-tech bungalow units, the modern houses rely on "higher level scientific expertise" (C: *gou-kap fo-hok ji-sik*). This form of housing originated in the more affluent southern parts of the province where most local migrant workers sojourn. In Harmony Cave, the new houses usually have two stories and a terrace on the roof that can be used to dry crops or clothes. Most have an automated system of piped water whereby groundwater is electrically pumped up into a stainless-steel water tank on the terrace. The new houses, which look like sturdy big white boxes, are constructed with industrial building materials like brick, cement, and glass windows. These materials are purchased in the city and are represented as more "advanced" and "scientific" than traditional building materials like clay bricks. Constructing one of these houses is a complex work of engineering that requires hired professional supervision. In the late 1990s, a two-story house in the village cost about ¥70,000 (US$8,400) to build, a sum that represented roughly a decade of savings of a migrant couple managing a vegetable gardening enterprise in the city. By the late 2010s, the cost had increased to more ¥300,000 (US$45,000), so it is not surprising that close to one quarter of the village population is still living in clay-brick houses.

The "home toilet" (C: *ga-geui chi-so*), also called the "home bathroom" (C: *ga-geui sai-san-gaan*), is one the most important technological innovations associated with the rise of the new-style houses. Usually located next to the kitchen in accordance with feng-shui principles, the bathroom's small space (3–8 square meters) incorporates an amalgam of old and new technology. Back in 1999–2001, the bathroom included four key components: a squat toilet fixture connected to a small underground septic tank, an outlet of piped water, a plastic bucket to store water, and a plastic ladle to flush the toilet and rinse the body. Some bathrooms already had showerheads and water heaters. At the time, I had the impression that villagers were still in the process of negotiating the best way to use these new spaces of personal hygiene. Choices had to be made, and these technological choices involved complex processes of negotiation. Through participating in daily informal discussions on the subject during fieldwork, I came to realize that there were important disagreements between villagers. These negotiations played a crucial role in shaping the present-day configuration of local material practices of bathing and bodily elimination.

The Private Bathroom and the Practice of Bodily Hygiene

In the first two decades of the Reform period (the early 1980s and 1990s), local customs stipulated that people should "wash the body" (C: *sai-san*) every evening, usually immediately before or after dinner. Adults, unlike children, were expected to wash indoors, by using a small plastic or wooden ladle to splash the body with water scooped from a plastic or wooden bucket, and to use a small cloth towel to clean the body and wipe it dry. Adults were expected to use hot water, which was usually heated with the same fire that was used to cook dinner in the kitchen's firewood stove, to avoid additional fuel costs. In the clay-brick houses, adults usually washed in a secluded corner of the kitchen, using fresh water supplied by means of a manual borehole water pump in the kitchen.[9]

These arrangements started to change in the late 1990s with the construction of the first modern forms of housing. With the new houses, villagers no longer needed to pump their water manually, and they no longer had to bathe hiding behind the kitchen cupboard; they could do it in a private room designed for that purpose. Most new house dwellers I interviewed between 1999 and 2005 welcomed the appearance of a separate bathroom because it allowed more privacy and autonomy, but they did not completely discard earlier bathing procedures. That the bathrooms of the new mansions included highly "advanced" devices like showerheads and water heaters did not make much difference, as inhabitants continued to use plastic ladles to bathe and firewood stoves to heat bathwater at dinnertime. Most villagers explained that this was more economical (less wasted water, no need to consume gas and/or electricity[10]), was easier, and produced better results. The "advanced" devices, they admitted, served primarily as indicators of wealth and social status.

These entanglements between old and new bathing procedures still have not entirely disappeared, even though the number of new houses with private bathrooms has increased quite dramatically (from six in 2001 to about three-quarters of all village households in 2018). Likewise, villagers are aware that defecation in the surrounding fields and hills is no longer considered acceptable, but many have not entirely discarded the practice, and many continue using urine buckets inside their homes for agricultural purposes. Villagers residing in clay-brick houses in the ancestral village continue using communal latrines, as one would expect, because they do not have private bathrooms in their homes. Somewhat more surprising is the fact that the practice of using communal latrines has not been entirely abandoned by villagers residing in new houses. These villagers explained their preference in 2016 by saying that flush toilets are very wasteful of household water and are expensive to maintain. Some also said that they prefer communal latrines because they find it inappropriate to poo inside the home, but this issue is controversial.

This preference for pooing outside the home is not uniformly distributed within the village population. Villagers who have moved to a house in the local market town or to an apartment in the city for a long period of time have developed a set of flush-toilet practices that is closer to urban expectations and standards of bodily hygiene. These "urbanized" villagers tend to be very critical of pit latrines or open defecation, and this is especially true of the younger generations born in the 1980s or after. My overall impression is that older villagers born in the 1970s or earlier (regardless of their regular place of residence) tend to be more accepting of earlier practices of bodily elimination. Gender is also an important factor (males tend to be more flexible), as are variables such as income and education.[11]

Even young villagers with significant city exposure through labor migration (i.e., villagers born in the 1980s or later) are not completely reluctant to use communal latrines when they return to the ancestral village. An important factor here is that their toilet experiences in the city (most live in factory dorms or in zinc huts constructed in periurban vegetable gardens) often continue to be framed around communal toilets. A case in point is the toilet situation of the vegetable gardens. The zinc huts are very small in size (a single room of about 20–30 square meters), although they sometimes accommodate a whole joint family. They usually have electricity, but until the 2010s, most did not have access to municipal water. The huts are usually located in agricultural areas that are not connected to the public sewage system. I have never encountered a zinc hut with a built-in private bathroom with a flush toilet. These huts have separate communal pit toilet structures that—like the village latrines back home—are built in a place that is sufficiently removed from people's sleeping and eating environment so as to remove all foul odors and nuisances associated with excreta. Village migrants often reproduce rural practices as they become part of urban society, but there are also significant points of rupture with the past. Unlike the village latrines back in the Harmony Cave region, the pit toilet structures of the vegetable gardens never really operated as composting reservoirs of human manure.

In 2012 and 2015, I asked many young village migrants (in their thirties or younger) based in Guangzhou and Foshan why they are not using the communal pit toilets of their vegetable gardens to produce human manure. Their answers initially echoed the economic explanations provided by villagers back in the late 1990s: that producing human manure is too labor intensive and not as effective as farm chemicals for food production. But they also remarked that the practice is "backward" (C: *lok-hau*) and "unhygienic" (C: *ng wai-saang ge*).

These hygienic discourses are particularly salient among young village migrants, but they echo a more general conceptual and infrastructural shift back in the Harmony Cave region to a model of human waste management that is no longer predominantly agricultural in orientation. The tendency nowadays is to engage in practices of pooing and peeing that take place in private and are no longer aimed at promoting the agricultural recycling of human waste. This new generation of toilet practices is fecal-phobic rather than fecal-philic, and it is said to be more "advanced" and "hygienic" because it is built around the concept of the private bathroom and the flush toilet. The trend was set by the wealthier strata of the village population, which now includes a diverse population living in new houses in the ancestral village or in the market town, or in some cases living in apartments in the city.

Emerging Flush-Toilet Infrastructures

Flush toilet technologies vary depending on context. The flush toilet in the Harmony Cave region is not a sitting toilet with a partially or fully automatic flushing mechanism, as found nowadays in most urban middle-class homes in China (L. Zhou 2004). It is a squat toilet fixture that needs to be flushed manually. This can be done by pouring water directly into the toilet hole by means of a showerhead connected to the tap or by using a plastic ladle or a plastic bucket to pour water into the toilet hole. Villagers say that flushing all excreta in this way is an act of "scientific hygiene" (C: *fo-hok wai-saang*) that is as important as cleaning the body with toilet paper instead of the wood chips used in the past. A toilet paper bin is kept next to the squat toilet fixture to avoid the toilet becoming clogged with paper and overflowing, but the paper accumulated in the bin is not always burned outside the house or in the kitchen's firewood stove. Instead, it is commonly discarded or even flushed down the toilet, thus defying the very purpose of the bin.

It is not clear exactly what about this practice constitutes "hygiene" (C: *wai-saang*). Villagers using flush toilets are not so directly confronted with excreta because they can make excreta disappear, but this does not mean that all associated nuisances disappear with water dilution and flushing. This is never really the case, even when one is using flush toilet technologies connected to centralized sewage systems. These systems are very good at transporting waste materials to faraway sewage treatment facilities for further processing, but even these systems have breakdowns.[12] Local flush toilet infrastructures, by contrast, are based on small-scale sewage systems with septic tanks and so are not capable of evacuating waste materials to faraway places. This is not a problem in itself. Small-scale sewage systems can be very efficient at handling waste materials, but this is not always the case in the Harmony Cave region. The most popular local model—as of 2018—is a "three chamber septic tank" (C: *saam-gaak-sik fa-fan-chi*) that is constructed immediately outside the house, usually next to the bathroom or the kitchen. This tank is very functional if properly maintained, but many villagers are reluctant to spend money to service and empty it.

When poorly maintained, local septic tanks lead to frequent toilet overflowing, which is exacerbated by the frequent disposal of toilet paper into the squat toilet fixture, but this is not the only aggravating factor. Too much wastewater is discharged into the septic tanks because people are using the toilet to get rid of both bathwater and sewage. As a consequence, the home is regularly invaded by all kinds of foul smells and nuisances associated with human excreta—something that did not happen when people were using communal latrines outside the home. Another consequence is the increasing prevalence of negative environmental and public health effects (Santos 2011; Lai 2016). In a septic tank without a separate soak pit or drain field, untreated wastewater seeps more rapidly and deeply into the ground. As a result, the spread of contagion to local underground water sources is a genuine risk, even though local people usually boil the water before consumption. To avoid the risk of contamination, many local rural communities have recently started to develop new piped water infrastructures connecting villages to mountain water sources and using water chlorination techniques to purify water, but the issue has still not been completely addressed and is becoming more urgent as the number of houses with septic tanks is growing in an increasingly urbanized and already densely populated rural area.

These environmental tensions point to important challenges in terms of sustainability for the local population, but it would be a mistake to think that the experience of operational and environmental uncertainties is specific to local flush toilet modernities. I wrote the bulk of this chapter while residing on the forty-seventh floor of a posh sixty-eight-floor high-rise on Hong Kong Island, where residents are regularly confronted with breakdowns of the building's toilet water supply. Residents are usually notified by the building's management of the dates of interrupted water, so that they can prepare themselves adequately, but there are also moments of unplanned breakdown. For example, storms during the typhoon season can break water pipes and lead to a situation of temporary interruption of the domestic water supply, which can generate chaos as thousands of residents suddenly find themselves having to rush out of the building to get water to flush their toilets. These practical disruptions go hand in hand with ongoing environmental tensions resulting from the fact that up until quite recently, only a small percentage of the daily sewage and industrial wastewater generated in Hong Kong received adequate treatment. A significant portion of this wastewater was dumped into the sea, close to shore, with partial or no treatment of any kind, turning the water near Hong Kong into a giant cesspool. This problem has been significantly improved from the 1980s onward but, as in most major cities in the world, it has not been completely resolved.[13]

In Hong Kong, as in the Harmony Cave region, such experiences of infrastructural tension and vulnerability are part of being a modern technological subject in the twenty-first century in the age of the Anthropocene, the age of humans, an epoch in which it is becoming increasingly clear that humans have become one of the most potent geophysical forces on the planet, and their activities are leading to increasing environmental uncertainties (Tsing 2017, 2020; Hornborg 2019).

The Flush Toilet as a Technopolitical Project

Most critical social science accounts of the spread of flush toilet infrastructures around the world focus on powerful macro-level "civilizing" forces in the fields of public health and urban sanitation (Black and Fawcett 2008; George 2008; Jewitt 2011). These accounts have shown how the global spread of modern flush toilet infrastructures from the nineteenth century onward is not adequately captured by terms like "technology-transfer" or "hardware-acquisition." Even when some kind of "technology transfer" is involved, it is a constructive process that is shaped by complex social, material, cultural, economic, and political negotiations.

The case of Harmony Cave illustrates that technological change does not follow some kind of natural drive for material progress, but involves political processes of "translation" and "domestication" that open the way for a particular kind of technological change. Although questions of "technopolitics," or the "mutual constitution" of technology and political culture (Hecht 1998, 15), are relevant here, as are questions of "co-production" of technology and society (Jasanoff 2004, 2016), what is not always acknowledged is that macro-level forces of change are themselves entangled in complex social, material, cultural, economic, and political negotiations at the local level.

The shift to flush toilet infrastructures in the village of Harmony Cave did not result from a local consensus on the superiority of these new infrastructures, but from "translation" (Callon 1986) of the social strategies and interests of a local elite. High-earning migrant workers played a key role in promoting a creative process of mimetic engagement with the new schema of bodily hygiene and public sanitation that had emerged in the more affluent parts of the province. This elite brought the first private bathrooms and flush toilets to the village and showcased the wonders of these expensive infrastructures to other villagers. This attempt to benefit from the high status associated with these new infrastructures was not straightforward, as financial resources had to be mobilized to sustain the image of superiority of these new infrastructures of bodily hygiene and public sanitation in the course of local debate and controversy. In time, the construction of more and more new houses with private bathrooms and flush toilets allowed the development of new models of human waste management and new procedures of bodily hygiene, but it has also allowed the reproduction of earlier practices and structures, considered more appropriate and efficacious.

The shift to flush toilet infrastructures in the Harmony Cave region resulted less from inherent material benefits associated with the new technologies than from cultural values and social relations associated with these technologies. Anthropologists have long challenged the idea that human technological activity is "culture free."[14] Writing about this tradition, and its intersections with constructionist approaches in science, technology, and society studies (STS),[15] Bryan Pfaffenberger (1992) notes how the work of anthropologists such as Bronislaw Malinowski (1965a, 1965b) and Marcel Mauss ([1925] 2016, 1950, 2006) opened the way for questioning the assumption that technology is primarily about the extension of human physical capacities to alter the natural world—a key assumption behind nineteenth-century evolutionist schemes of cultural evolution and technological progress. Malinowski and Mauss argued that it is misleading to evaluate technical artifacts *strictly* according to their functional efficiency as part of a system of material production, thus treating them independently of the human relations surrounding their use. The Maussian tradition is particularly helpful for grasping the linkages between micro-historical realities and large-scale historical transformations.

The Flush Toilet as Civilizational Process

It is obvious that micro-historical negotiations are connected to broader historical exchanges that one could call, following Mauss, "civilizational processes."[16] The spread of the flush toilet in rural Guangdong is such a process not in the sense that it leads to a higher stage of civilization (i.e., modernity), but because it connects many different "sociotechnical" entities—techniques, technologies, artifacts, institutions—in dynamic ways. These processes of creative assembling result in expanding networks of interdependency, which have multiple scales. When villagers in northern Guangdong introduce flush toilet technologies into their homes, they are also responding to broader national and global processes converging in the construction of a new modern material civilization built around the flush toilet and its supporting hydraulic system of human waste management.

I borrow the term "material civilization" from the French historian Fernand Braudel ([1979] 1992, 27), whose approach to the emergence of modern capitalism in western Europe differed from conventional views. Rather than diagnose a "gradual progress towards the rational world of the market, the firm and capitalist investment" (ibid., 23), Braudel drew attention to the basic aspects of life shared by all members of society, not just the capitalist and the laborer but also those outside the formal process of economic production. "This rich zone," he wrote, "like a layer covering the earth, I have called for want of a better expression *material life* or *material civilization*" (ibid.; emphasis in the original). Braudel's focus on material civilization contrasts with a tendency among historians, sociologists, and anthropologists of civilizational processes to privilege the study of religious, ethical, and cultural ideologies. As British sociologist Tim Dant (2006, 300) explains, "It is not ideas as such that are indicative of civilizational processes, it is how those ideas are manifest at the material level that is important." This Braudelian conceptualization of civilizational processes combines the ideological with the material and is at odds with approaches that divide civilizational processes in terms of a dual scheme of material civilization and spiritual civilization. This is the approach promoted by the Chinese Communist Party since the beginning of Reform and Opening in official campaigns calling for the development of a new "socialist material civilization" (SC: shehui zhuyi wuzhi wenming) and a new "socialist spiritual civilization" (SC: shehui zhuyi jingshen wenming; Dynon 2008),[17] and the central role played by this dualistic ideology in party rhetoric only highlights the need to take into consideration the normative dimensions of the concept of civilization.

The work of Braudel is useful for capturing the mundane ideal-material entanglements of civilizational processes, but it is not so useful for making sense of the strongly normative dimensions of modern transformations. Here, a new narrative about "civilization" needs to be introduced, one that is usually associated with the work of Norbert Elias ([1939] 1994) on postmedieval European court society. Like Mauss and Braudel, Elias is interested in the intricate connections between habitus as the socially organized basis of physical movement—how people walk, sit, pee, poo, et cetera—and the use of instruments or technologies. But he approaches modern material civilization as inherently transformational, a "civilizing process" that brings about important changes in everyday behavioral standards as well as material practices, as human societies become larger. These changes are usually initiated by elite social groups who become trendsetters and succeed in establishing new terms for the incorporation of ordinary individuals and communities into larger chains of inclusion and civilization. The work of Elias has been criticized for contributing to the reproduction of a Eurocentric view of the making of modernity (J. Goody 2006), but there are reasons to believe that his theorization of the civilizing process can be applied productively in a variety of settings including China (Brandtstädter 2003; Mennell 2007).

Elias's approach to modern material civilization allows us to connect the "civilizing" aspirations of local-level trendsetters in rural northern Guangdong to a broader national and international civilizing mission promoting the flush toilet as the global standard of bodily hygiene and public sanitation. Private flush-toilet schemas of bodily hygiene and public sanitation have become globally hegemonic under the influence of technocratic ideologies of development and modernization (Black and Fawcett 2008; George 2008; Jewitt 2011). These schemas have become so powerful globally that they are rarely questioned and block the development of alternative visions of bodily hygiene and public sanitation. Most development projects in the field of water, sanitation, and hygiene (WASH) promoted by governmental agencies and civil-society organizations, as well as by international nongovernmental organizations like the United Nations and the World Bank, are committed to the dissemination of flush-toilet schemas of bodily hygiene and public sanitation. China has received various forms of aid to promote this civilizing mission. In 1996, to give just one example, UNICEF supported the implementation of a development program in eight provinces to improve the sanitary conditions of rural villages, and a key part of this program involved introducing flush toilets and small-scale sewage systems to the Chinese countryside (L. Zhou 2004, 83).

It would be a mistake to ignore the impact of organizations such as UNICEF on China's national policies of public sanitation, but the effects of such international organizations are themselves mediated by technopolitical negotiations at the national level. From very early on, possibly since the first known Chinese descriptions of Western flush toilets were written in the 1860s, Chinese elites developed their own vision of a new hygienic modernity built around Western-style flush toilet technologies (L. Zhou 2004, 76). These visions of modernity were based on Western Enlightenment ideas of evolutionary progress as well as an older Confucian vision that Prasenjit Duara (2001, 122) describes as an active engagement with "bringing true and proper civilizational virtues to all." This project was significantly expanded and strengthened throughout the early twentieth century. Early twentieth-century intellectuals and officials advocated "civilization" (SC: *wen-ming*) as a national strategy for radical social transformation, and flush toilets were an important aspiration of this "civilizing mission" (Harrell 1995; Friedman 2004). As early as 1933, in a special issue of *Dongfang Magazine*, the historian Yucheng Zhou describes the flush toilet as one of the key goals of China's project of modernization, expressing the hope that "everyone will one day be able to have their own flush toilet bowl to poo" (cited in J. Zhu 1988, 18), but this was a very costly ambition, and municipal governments continued to favor the agro-urban system of human waste management because this system worked and was a good source of revenue and power (J. Zhang and Santos 2018).

After 1949, many Chinese continued to dream about the day in which everyone would have their own flush toilet bowl to poo, but the government favored once again the temporary adaptation of existing agrarian infrastructures of human waste management and public sanitation (L. Zhou 2004). Under Mao, the urban population was expected to poo for the most part in public toilets under a collectivist regime of daily collection, and night-soil workers such as Shi Chuanxiang (1915–1975) were celebrated in official propaganda as national heroes and model workers. But even in the Mao era, as Chinese economist Jiaming Zhu (1988, 2) vividly recalls, it was difficult for urbanites to understand why night-soil workers were still necessary and why China was not using the power of science and technology to develop flush-toilet waste disposal systems. By the 1980s, the idea that national toilet standards were "backward" was widespread in urban contexts, and the government started to increase investment in public sanitation as part of a larger effort to promote the development of a new "socialist civilization" that—in official party rhetoric—included both a material and a spiritual dimension: a "socialist material civilization" and a "socialist spiritual civilization" (J. Zhu 1988, 3; Dynon 2008). Investment in public sanitation was part of official material civilization development programs, and this investment was intensified in the 1990s and 2000s when a housing construction boom started to take shape. During this period of infrastructural expansion, a large number of urban homes were connected to sewers, and the concept of the private bathroom with a flush toilet—as envisioned by early-twentieth-century Chinese elites—started to become an essential component of everyday life, not just in urban areas. The government also started promoting mass campaigns to improve national toilet standards, using a five-grade system of classification of public toilets that would establish the normativity of the flush-toilet model in the popular imagination.

An emerging elite of high-earning migrant workers in the Harmony Cave region started to construct modern new houses in their villages, arguing that their brand-new flush toilets were superior to earlier local toilet practices. This elite took advantage of state-managed programs to improve village housing and public sanitation infrastructures. One of these programs—the "Civilized Village" program—provides subsidies to improve housing conditions and build housing with home toilets (Perry 2011). One of the most affluent village groups in Harmony Cave, Harmony First, applied successfully to this program in 2010 and went on to build a new village hamlet in the old part of the village with more than thirty new houses with flush toilets. More recently, in 2018 two village groups, Harmony Fourth and

Harmony Fifth, contracted with a metropolitan construction company to build two multistory apartment buildings next to their recently renovated ancestral hall in the old part of the village. The new buildings will accommodate more than forty households, and the apartments will include the latest flush-toilet technologies. Macro-level forces are thus entangled in local negotiations, constituting flush-toilet modernities on the ground.

Flush Toilets and the Politics of Material Civilization

Similar flush-toilet civilizing transformations are taking place in other parts of rural China, especially in the richer eastern and southern coastal areas (Y. Liu et al. 2014). Yet there remain tensions. The spread of flush-toilet infrastructures in rural China is not just about the making of a new material civilization built around a fecal-phobic hygienic model of waste disposal. It is also about the transformation or, better still, the reinvention of an older material civilization built around a fecal-philic agricultural model of human waste management that emphasizes the value of "turning waste into treasure" (C: *bin-fai wai-bou*).[18]

The agricultural recycling of human waste has declined since the 1990s (when an estimated 95–100 percent of rural households were engaging in this practice), but overall levels of human manure usage in 2007 were still high, amounting to 85 percent of all rural households interviewed in different provinces in one study (Y. Liu et al. 2014, 437). Since then, the shift toward an urban-like "flush-and-discharge" model of waste disposal was significantly intensified due to the combined effects of economic growth, urbanization, agricultural industrialization, and various development policies aimed at improving rural toilet facilities, but there are significant regional variations. In the richer eastern and southern coastal areas, the shift to the flush toilet seems to be proceeding at a very fast pace, but in more peripheral regions, the shift to the flush toilet is slower. Variations within provinces and regions are shaped by local variables such as household income and education levels, population density, migration, and quality of transportation networks. Although there is an overall trend toward increasing engagement with flush-toilet infrastructures, this shift is accompanied by reinvention of earlier traditions of agricultural recycling of human waste.

In addition to the choice between discharge and recycling, there is also the possibility of using human excreta to produce biogas. This practice is now becoming more common in the Harmony Cave region and is a good way to show how older civilizational legacies of "turning waste into treasure" are being reinvented in present-day China. The first Chinese biogas digesters were assembled as early as the 1930s, but it was only in the 1970s—following a series of experiments in the 1950s and 1960s in Sichuan—that these digesters started to attract wider attention due to the development of cost-efficient methods to produce methane gas (Van Buren [1979] 1997; Santos 2011). In 1981 the government established the Institute of Biogas, or BIOMA, in Sichuan, and since then, the popularity of these digesters has extended to other provinces, even though their overall dissemination in 2007 remained limited: only about 3.7 percent of all rural households surveyed (Y. Liu et al. 2014, 437). There has been significant growth in the last ten years due to further technical improvements and heavy government investment. Today, China is the world's largest producer and consumer of household biogas plants, with more than 30 million rural households using biogas digesters to produce clean cooking fuel and organic fertilizer through the fermentation of human, animal, and plant wastes (H. Chen et al. 2017; Xia 2013; George 2008, 123–44). This biogas revolution is fully compatible with contemporary flush-toilet aspirations in rural areas, but it also highlights the continuing significance of earlier fecal-philic civilizational legacies. These ambiguities lie at the heart of the making of China's contemporary technocratic modernities, and the way they unfold in the coming years will be crucial in helping rural populations to cope with growing environmental uncertainties.

Without really thinking about it, people around the world have come to assume that the flush toilet and its hydraulic system of waste disposal is one of the basic requirements of modern life. Yet it is becoming increasingly clear that dumping excreta into any convenient body of water may not be the best way to handle both local and global sanitation problems in times of increasing environmental uncertainties and rising water stress levels. One may think that the solution to the challenge of global sanitation and public health is just a matter of improving sewage infrastructure and sewage treatment technology, but this solution is very costly and largely out of reach for people living in peripheral areas. Most importantly, despite the promises of increasing both efficiency and sustainability of centralized sewage infrastructures, the history of these infrastructures is one of moving the problem downstream and rendering it invisible until someone notices it and blows the whistle. Given that there is more wastewater generated and dispersed today than at any other time in the history of the planet, it seems strange that so many people continue to insist on the efficacy of a system that will only generate more wastewater. There is of course no single solution to local and global sanitation problems, but more seriously studying the agricultural traditions of human waste management in village China, instead of dismissing these traditions as "backward" and "unhygienic," may be useful in thinking about alternative models of human waste management for a more sustainable future in an age of increasing anthropogenic environmental uncertainties.

CHAPTER 6

Popular Religion

Technologies of Ethical Imagination

POPULAR RELIGION PLAYS AN IMPORTANT ROLE IN SHAPING THE ethical life of village communities in South China.[1] All villages in Yellow Flower township are part of local deity temple associations whose ritual activities have increased since the 1990s. An important component of these activities is the observation of periodic festivals of communal cleansing and thanksgiving that are funded by monetary donations from members. A popular form of fund-raising is the auctioning of symbolic mirrors inscribed with words representing key values and moral ideals. Here I approach these ceremonial auctions as "sociotechnical ensembles" (Bijker 2010) or *technologies of ethical imagination* (my term) that involve the mobilization of multiple actors, skills, resources, and artifacts to promote the construction of an authoritative list of values representing the local system of ethical imagination. In chapter 5, I look at bodily hygiene and public sanitation as a field of technical intervention that can be subject to larger civilizing forces of hygienic modernization promoting the construction of a new "socialist material civilization" (SC: *shehui zhuyi wuzhi wenming*). In this chapter, I approach ethical imagination as a field of technical intervention that can be subject to larger civilizing forces of ethical modernization and standardization promoting the construction of a new "socialist spiritual civilization" (SC: *shehui zhuyi jingshen wenming*) that mixes socialist ideals with traditional values of familism, social harmony, and national stability and unity.

There is much to be learned about the complexities of rural China's—and, more generally, China's—contemporary moral-ethical landscape by looking at popular religion, in which morality and ethics are operative. "Morality" is a term sometimes used to refer to socially authorized codes, rules, and norms, and "ethics" to active processes of self-reflection and self-cultivation (Laidlaw 2014, 11–19; Robbins 2007, 2012). Here these two terms are used interchangeably, but I continue to make an analytical distinction between active processes of (individual and collective) reflective self-formation and socially endorsed hegemonic codes, disciplines, and norms. This distinction is necessary because it is not always clear what counts as moral or ethical in a given context. As shown by anthropologist Charles Stafford (2010), people around the world often engage in practices that are both ethical/moral (i.e., part of a larger project of reflective self-formation) and immoral/unethical (i.e., violate a dominant system of codes, disciplines, and norms), and these contradictions are an important source of tensions in society. Such tensions can lead to frictions or even conflicts, as illustrated here in the context of local festivals of popular religion: what happens when a villager publicly articulates an ethical position that goes against the dominant system of codes, disciplines, and norms supported by his family members, his village peers, and the members of his deity temple association? Such incidents are part and parcel of the process through which villagers and their households come together as a community to construct their own meaningful frameworks of ethical imagination in the face of larger technocratic efforts of authoritarian governance aimed at promoting national moral unity and containing moral tensions and contradictions in the larger society.[2]

Tensions and contradictions are not just the product of domestic developments but reflect a larger trend around the world under processes of increasing cultural polarization, rising social inequalities, and increasing environmental conflicts (Madsen 2020). In parts of Europe and North America, these tensions and contradictions have already turned into open social conflicts and populist movements, but in China, the authoritarian state makes use of various "stability maintenance" (SC: *weiwen*) mechanisms to keep these forces in check. Popular religion was once on the list of social movements that need government restraint. For much of the Maoist period (1949–76), nationwide policies and campaigns aimed at restricting practices of popular religion led to the destruction of hundreds of thousand of deity temples around the country. The government has continued to dismiss popular religion as a "backward feudalist superstition" (SC: *luohou fengjian mixin*) after the beginning of Reform and Opening, but the overall attitude of repression and containment has receded, which has allowed the informal growth of popular religion as a major expression of ethical life in village China. The increasing centrality of popular religion festivals in constructing frameworks of ethical imagination has given village communities a more meaningful blueprint for thought and action than have nationwide efforts to promote the official notion of "socialist spiritual civilization."

"Ethical imagination" refers to forms of moral reasoning that entail the use of complex metaphoric concepts and structures depending on the human capacity for imagination.[3] This capacity is shaped not only by species-specific cognitive affordances but also by larger social, cultural, and material processes that vary from context to context. Relevant to the current "ethical turn in anthropology,"[4] and a novel contribution to this turn, is the idea that ethical imagination, like most human activities (Latour 1994, 2005), is mediated by various kinds of "socio-technical ensembles" (Bijker 2010) that operate like technologies capable of bringing together multiple human and nonhuman elements in a seamless whole.

This insight draws on a long-standing tradition of anthropological studies of skills and techniques that challenged conventional understandings of technology as material production and material progress (Pfaffenberger 1992; Lemonnier 1992).[5] This tradition, as anthropologist Francesca Bray (2013b) explains, "has developed a practical and flexible analytical method for linking the material, social and symbolic dimensions of technical practices and skills, regardless of whether they are high-tech or low-tech" and regardless of whether they relate to agricultural production or ancestor worship. Technology in this tradition refers not to modern machinery and equipment but to larger sociotechnical articulations, and the scope of these seamless articulations goes well beyond the pursuit of material rewards. Technology in this sense is not confined to material production and progress, but is defined more generally as "the pursuit of intrinsically difficult-to-obtain results by roundabout or clever means" (Gell 1988, 8). This definition makes no distinction—from the standpoint of degree of technicality—between the pursuit of material rewards through technical activity and the equally technical pursuit of symbolic rewards through activities like rituals.

Popular religion auctions of small decorative mirrors with a high symbolic value are a type of ritual technology. These ceremonial auctions help construct a locally shared framework of ethical imagination that draws on a language and repertoire that are very different from those used in official frameworks of ethical imagination. Since the beginning of Deng Xiaoping's Reform and Opening, the Chinese Communist Party (CCP) has been committed to not only promoting a vision of economic and material modernization but also to building a new "socialist spiritual civilization" with a well-developed educational system and thriving realms of science, literature, and art, along with strong social ethics, traditions, and customs (Dynon 2008).[6] This notion of socialist spiritual civilization has gone through many different incarnations in the last four decades, with each paramount leader adding a dizzying array of ideological innovations, including Deng Xiaoping's Theory, Jiang Zemin's Three Represents, Hu Jintao's Socialist Harmonious Society, and most recently Xi Jinping's China Dream and his "core socialist values" (SC: *shehui zhuyi hexin jiazhiguan*). These visions of socialist spiritual civilization do not include substantial references to Marxism, revolution, class struggle, or communism, but they are defined as socialist and refer mostly to pragmatic governance issues such as modernization, development, national strength, prosperity, stability, order, social harmony, and well-being (Pieke 2016, 23–24). Up until recently, this socialist civilizing mission supported the antitraditionalist ethos of the Maoist revolutionary period, but this antitraditionalism has been receding, and under Xi Jinping, the CCP started to depict itself as the rightful beneficiary of and successor to dynastic rule and China's cultural and civilizational traditions (Kubat 2018).

This traditionalist twist may seem to bring the official project of constructing a new socialist spiritual civilization closer to local ethical frameworks of popular religion, but the gap remains. Both phenomena—local popular religion rituals and national campaigns of socialist spiritual civilization—are technologies of ethical imagination that promote moral standardization, but they operate in different ways and at different scales, and they draw on different frameworks of authority. The CCP's campaigns of socialist spiritual civilization represent a top-down technocratic effort to create a shared sense of social harmony and promote the standardization of national frameworks of ethical imagination. The party's tight control of the national media industry and the educational system suggests that official campaigns like Xi Jinping's "core socialist values" are having an important impact on local articulations of ethical modernity in different parts of China, including rural areas, but one should be careful not to overstate this impact. Popular religion offers rural communities a meaningful set of infrastructures and frameworks of ethical imagination that lies outside the "iron cage" of official visions of socialist spiritual civilization, but this does not mean that local traditions are spaces of moral harmony and cohesion. Popular religion helps bring villagers together and generate a significant amount of social cohesion and social solidarity, but this process has to be negotiated and sometimes leads to moral frictions and conflicts.

Such moral frictions and conflicts arose during a local auction of inscribed words in 1999, an event with a complex afterlife. This is the story of a villager who chose to challenge the validity of local popular religion rituals on the basis of ethical arguments that invoked Maoist revolutionary ideals and that clashed with the views of his family members, the elite of his village, and the general moral orientation of China's political economy since Deng Xiaoping. Now part of village legend, the incident involved the family of Bright Gold, whose story is introduced in chapter 2 in a discussion on changing assemblages of love, marriage, and family planning.

The Temple of the Old Woman Lam and Its Jiao Festivals

When I first met Bright Gold (born in 1962) in July 1999 at the beginning of my first and longest stay in Harmony Cave, there were already a few new modern houses constructed in the "outer base" of the village (all of them owned by Harmony First families), but the family of Bright Gold, also from Harmony First, was still living in the clay-brick residential hamlet constructed by this village group in 1984, the year when electricity and landline phones were installed in the village.

Most villages in Yellow Flower township are part of local deity temple associations with a long history. Most local deity temples were built during the Qing dynasty (1644–1911) and were destroyed during the revolutionary campaigns of the Maoist period (1949–76), only to be renovated and reopened as sites of worship from the late 1980s onward. Today, most local deity temple associations are made up of alliances between five to ten neighboring villages belonging to the same rural administrative area or to two or three neighboring rural administrative areas. Yellow Flower boasts thirteen deity temple associations, each of which represents an independent cult that has no institutionalized relationship with other temples or social organizations (Dean 2003; Goossaert 2004). These temple associations have a high degree of organizational autonomy because they are largely self-managed and fall outside of China's five officially recognized religions (Buddhism, Daoism, Protestantism, Catholicism, and Islam). The temples are shaped by local traditions of popular religion and are increasingly recognized as "objects of cultural value" under the influence of new regimes of cultural governance and rural tourism (S. Chan 2011; S. Chan and Lang 2015).

The village of Harmony Cave is affiliated with the Temple of the Old Woman Lam, an old deity temple that was reconstructed in 1988 after having been destroyed during the Great Leap Forward in the late 1950s and 1960s. The temple community includes households from twelve different villages located across two neighboring rural administrative areas, and in 2018 it had an estimated total population of more than 3,500 individuals. The temple has its own land and is physically situated within walking distance from Harmony Cave. I first visited the temple with Bright Gold in July 1999, and during my stay in his house until January 2000 we often went together to the temple during the day to chat with other villagers. At the time, his household included him, his wife (Full Elder Sister), and their three sons and one daughter, but his wife and eldest son were working away from the village. When I moved into their house in July 1999, they were in a difficult economic position, but there were other personal issues that affected his involvement in the ritual activities of the local deity temple association.

Bright Gold had been seriously ill during the winter of 1998–99, and I was told that his recovery had taken place just a few days before a major public assembly was held on March 16, 1999, at the Temple of the Old Woman Lam. This public assembly was part of the preparations for a major ritual festival announced earlier that same year: this would be the third Jiao festival since 1988 and, as usual, there would be a large-scale ritual celebration aimed at protecting the safety and prosperity of the temple's population. As elsewhere in rural South China,[7] the performance of Jiao festivals started reemerging during the 1980s together with other local practices and performative acts of popular religion. Jiao festivals are large-scale periodic sacrificial offerings in honor of the gods of local deity temples. Through a series of rituals performed by a troupe of ritual experts over a period of days, the community seeks to renew its alliance with the gods, thanking them for the graces obtained in the past and asking for further support. The exact goal, duration, and periodicity of the Jiao festival are clearly stated in a handwritten memorial posted on the outer wall of the temple that includes information about all temple community households. These data are transferred to the records of the celestial bureaucracy of the local deity temple during the ritual proceedings through recitation and burning.

The term "celestial bureaucracy" reflects the strong metaphor based on imperial bureaucratic imagery that influenced historical development of popular religion rituals (A. Wolf 1974; Feuchtwang 2001), a metaphor still used today by villagers to explain their relation to the world of the gods. Just as the world of the living was once ruled by a powerful imperial bureaucracy—and now by a powerful CCP bureaucracy—so the spirit world is ruled by a mighty celestial bureaucracy of gods whose temple dwellings are modeled on imperial palaces and buildings. Xi Jinping's recent move to symbolically depict the CCP as the rightful successor to China's imperial tradition reinforces this metaphorical association between the gods and the party, thus reproducing and naturalizing the power of the party in local imaginaries of popular religion. But the parallels between the CCP and celestial bureaucracies should not be overstated. Both have a central and a local dimension, but the part of the celestial bureaucracy that concerns villagers is local. Most deity cults at the community level are concerned only with local gods or local manifestations of well-known deities, and these gods are considered to be very powerful and to reflect the power of local traditions and communities. Fear of local gods and respect for their powers inspire attempts to influence their behavior through worship by means of offerings of incense, food, and spirit money. These offerings are a way of asking the gods for benevolence and for protection from wandering ghosts (a major cause of misfortune).

Jiao festivals are one of the ways through which communities make petitions to the celestial bureaucracy. The rituals themselves derive in large part from the Daoist liturgical tradition, but their development was also shaped by Buddhist and shamanist elements, displaying significant regional variations (Lagerwey 2010, 95–152; Tam 2006; Tan and Zeng 2010).[8] Since its reconstruction in 1988, the Temple of the Old Woman Lam has organized a Jiao Festival for the Population (C: *yan-hau ching-jiu*) every five years.[9] The first was staged in 1989, and the second in 1994; the third was the one everyone was talking about when I first arrived in the village in July 1999.[10] This Jiao was scheduled for the autumn of 1999, and the above-mentioned public assembly on March 16, 1999, had been a fund-raising initiative by the temple's management committee, always composed of laypeople. This committee had been "elected" in January 1999 with the blessing of the gods, and it included—as usual—a small group of local male notables and their followers.[11] It is not uncommon for the most prominent members of these committees to be over sixty, but age is not the only factor in determining access to office. Wealth, prestige, reputation, skills, and connections are as important, if not more so.

Pledging Money in Ceremonial Auctions of Inscriptions

More than a hundred men attended the March 16 fund-raising assembly at the Temple of the Old Woman Lam. Bright Gold was one of them, and he surprised many when he pledged money for the upcoming festival despite his family's well-known economic difficulties. At this time in the late 1990s, fund-raising assemblies to mobilize donations for local temple activities were already common in the township (cf. Dean 2003; Tam 2006; Aijmer and Ho 2000, 187–236). Such initiatives were restricted during the Maoist period, but they had been common in the pre-Communist era. Traditionally, most local temple activities relied not only on corporate assets (if any) but also on the ability of each temple's committee to collect both obligatory contributions "pooled" (C: *gaap ge*) among temple community households and voluntary contributions "donated" (C: *gyun ge*) by local or nonlocal individuals and households. If the first type of contribution was like a compulsory tax shared by all insiders, the second resembled charitable donations (cf. Goossaert 2004, 135–51).

This same dynamic of obligatory and voluntary contributions applies to present-day Jiao festivities, but there are significant departures from the traditional fund-raising pattern. Obligatory payments and voluntary donations are now almost exclusively in the form of cash and seldom in labor or agricultural resources. Moreover, temple activities have become strongly dependent on donations because most local temples never regained the corporate assets lost during the Maoist period, and the income derived from *obligatory* payments covers only a meager portion of the mounting costs of festivals. By and large, the major sources of funding are voluntary donations. In some parts of South China, donations from nonlocals, including overseas Chinese, have become important (Ku 2003; M. Chen 2013), but this is not the case in Yellow Flower.

A major incentive behind this thriving culture of donations is the desire for divine redemption from previous moral wrongdoings (including those from past lives) by means of charitable deeds (C: *sin-hang*) like donating money to temples. This belief in the cosmic effects of monetary donations—strongly associated with the Buddhist tradition—is popular but not universally held. A more important factor is the desire to have one's economic success and generosity publicly recognized through artifacts of symbolic distinction issued by the temple's management committee. Production of artifacts such as placards or stone inscriptions with detailed lists of "fragrant names" (C: *fong-ming*)—the names of all donors—together with their native places and the exact amounts of their donations, is linked to very old traditions of religious fund-raising, ritual accountancy, and memory inscription (Goossaert 2004). However, it seems clear that the contemporary concern with the symbolic recognition of acts of monetary donation has reached unprecedented dimensions and levels of commercialization.

Donations are handled by the Jiao festival's presiding committee. In Yellow Flower, a popular strategy to attract donations is to organize ceremonial auctions in which temple community members compete for the acquisition of a limited number of small decorative "mirror screens" (C: *geng-ping*). These contain one or a few written characters making up a word or phrase whose meaning is associated with a specific element of the local code of goodness and right action. Hence, locals refer to these ritual auctions with the expression "bidding for written words (inscriptions)" (C: *biu-ji*), because what is really at stake is the possibility of being granted the title of "major contributor" (C: *jyu-yun*) or patron of an inscription of goodness and right action.[12] Within the festival's organizational hierarchy, the title of patron of an inscription of goodness and right action stands between the presiding committee and the crowd of devout believers (C: *seun-si*).

Bright Gold's pledge was made at one of these auctions of mirror screens with inscriptions. These used to consist of actual mirrors with characters painted in red ink. Today, as shown in Figure 6.1, they are no longer actual mirrors but framed images with computer-designed inscriptions, though people continue to call them mirror screens because of the symbolic appeal of mirrors in the local imagination. Mirrors are said to have magical properties, such as attracting good fortune and warding off evil spirits, and it is hoped that the framed inscriptions auctioned by local temples have similar

FIGURE 6.1. Computer-designed mirror screens with inscriptions, 2009

magical properties. The power of mirror screens lies in their inscribed characters, which are considered sacred and magical.

All major Chinese ritual traditions emphasize the power of the written word,[13] and today this is still visible in religious practices such as that of talismanic writing (C: *fu-luk*) in which written characters are invested with supernatural powers such as deterring evil spirits from entering the household, guarding the body-person, or fulfilling personal desires (Yen 2005). The inscriptions painted or printed on mirror screens in the context of Jiao festivals are said to have similar supernatural powers, so the presence of such a mirror screen on the wall in one's household is like keeping a piece of talismanic writing close to one's body, ensuring divine protection.

When describing the auctions, villagers compare the figure of the owner, issuer, and auctioneer of the inscriptions (i.e., the temple's management committee) to a CCP-like organization with a "big president" (C: *daai jung-lei*), a number of "premiers" (C: *jung-lei*), and many "deputies" (C: *yun-sau*). Such committees are elected to represent the temple's tutelary deities. The mandate of the members of this committee is not permanent and must be sanctioned by the deities themselves. These deities also must approve the final list of winning bidders. Money is the determining factor in selecting a winning bidder, but this explanation is often complemented by a less secular narrative that depicts each winning bid as a sign of divine reward for proper moral conduct—the kind of conduct worthy of moral redemption and symbolic distinction.

In practice, this work of symbolic distinction is achieved and materialized in different ways.[14] The name of the winning bidder is painted or printed on the surface of each mirror screen after the auction (see figure 6.1). When the mirror screens are on public display at the temple during the ritual festivities before being given to their patrons, visitors learn who is the patron of which inscription. This information, together with the final price of each inscription, can also be found on a large sheet of red paper posted on the outer wall of the temple. Toward the end of the Jiao ritual festivities, a ceremony to "deliver the words" (C: *sung-ji*) takes place, during which each mirror screen is delivered to the door of its respective patron by a lion dance troupe performing a ritual show combining music, firecrackers, and martial arts.

Constructing a Shared Framework of Ethical Imagination

The management committee selects the inscriptions for auction, usually with the help of a trustworthy community member with ritual knowledge. The final list is said to reflect the wishes of the tutelary deities and has to be approved in consultation with representatives of the local elite. State authorities do not have a direct say on the inscriptions selected or on the composition of the temple's committee, but they constitute an important background actor, and they may interfere at any point. Most of the inscriptions evoke traditional concepts or expressions with strong ritual, literary, and philosophical connotations, neatly recycled in light of contemporary realities. I have seen more than twenty lists of inscriptions auctioned in different local temples between 1999 and 2018, and these lists are similar in content, with the total number of inscriptions auctioned usually not higher than forty. Most consist of single-character words (C: *daan-ji*) or double-character words (C: *seung-ji*). In some auctions, there are also traditional idioms made up of three or more characters. All are meant to be pronounced in the local Cantonese language and not in standard Chinese.[15]

The March 16, 1999, auction at the Temple of the Old Woman Lam included thirty-seven inscriptions: twelve with single characters (Table 6.1a) and twenty-five with double characters (Table 6.1b). The selection of these words was the product of the reflective work of ethical imagination of one or a few individuals, but the words selected were publicly presented as divinely sanctioned products of collective ethical imagination, approved by local state authorities.

These inscriptions not only define the components of what counts as a good life (e.g., prosperity, descendants, luck) but also identify principles of right and wrong (e.g., justice, fairness, impartiality) and things that are worth pursuing in themselves (e.g., sincerity, happiness). In other words, to use a distinction drawn by philosopher Alasdair MacIntyre (1981), the

TABLE 6.1A. Auctioned words and respective prices, Jiao Festival, 1999

SINGLE-CHARACTER WORDS (C: DAAN-JI 單字)			
	WRITTEN WORD (C)	KEY MEANINGS	WINNING BID (¥)
1	丁 ding	Population; male descendants	1,200
2	財 choi	Wealth, riches	1,000
3	貴 gwai	Expensive, noble	880
4	旺 wong	Prosperous, flourishing	620
5	福 fuk	Good fortune, prosperity, blessing	580
6	祿 luk	Luck; official salary	460
7	壽 sau	Longevity	350
8	全 chyun	Complete, perfect	500
9	金 gam	Gold	450
10	玉 yuk	Jade	280
11	滿 mun	Full, complete, satisfied	480
12	堂 tong	Main room of building or house; also used to mean "of the same clan"	420
Total ¥			7,220

Note: ¥8 = US$1

TABLE 6.1B. Auctioned words and respective prices, Jiao Festival, 1999

DOUBLE-CHARACTER WORDS (C: SEUNG-JI 雙字)			
	WRITTEN WORD (C)	KEY MEANINGS	WINNING BID (¥)
1	元亨 yun-hang	Prosperous and smooth; a literary reference to the first trigram of the Book of Changes: the qian (乾) or "creative force"	380
2	利貞 lei-jing	Loyal and beneficial; a literary reference to the first trigram of the Book of Changes: the qian (乾) or "creative force"	420
3	勝意 sing-yi	"successful ideas"	1,250
4	吉祥 gat-cheung	Lucky, auspicious, propitious	580
5	誠心 sing-sam	Sincerity, good faith	780
6	公正 gung-jing	Just, fair, impartial	180
7	福德 fuk-dak	"prosperity and virtue, good fortune and kindness"	620
8	安樂 on-lok	Peace and happiness	260
9	萬事 maan-si	Everything (everything according to one's wishes)	650
10	恭喜 gung-hei	Congratulations, as in the traditional New Year greeting gung-hei faat-choi, or "congratulations and best wishes for a prosperous New Year"	350
11	發達 faat-daat	Flourishing, prosperous, developed	880
12	百福 baak-fuk	"hundred good fortunes"	380
13	禎祥 jing-cheung	Lucky and auspicious	520
14	招財 jiu-choi	"inviting wealth." as in the idiom jiu-choi jeun-bou (招財進寶) or "ushering in riches and treasures"	580
15	延壽 yin-sau	To prolong life	560
16	添丁 tim-ding	To have another (male) descendant	880

TABLE 6.1B. (continued)

DOUBLE-CHARACTER WORDS (C: SEUNG-JI 雙字)			
	WRITTEN WORD (C)	KEY MEANINGS	WINNING BID (¥)
17	富貴 fu-gwai	Riches and honor, wealth and rank	1,300
18	福星 fuk-sing	Lucky star; mascot	700
19	興隆 hing-lung	Prosperous, thriving, flourishing	680
20	永安 wing-on	Always content, calm, peaceful, and safe	960
21	生財 saang-choi	To amass wealth, to make money, as in the idiom wo-hei saang-choi (和氣生財) or "good manners bring riches"	1,100
22	順遂 seun-seui	Everything is going smoothly; just as one wishes	480
23	和氣 wo-hei	Gentle, kind, courteous, polite; harmonious, friendly, amiable; as in the idiom wo-hei saang-choi (和氣生財) or "good manners bring riches"	880
24	如意 yu-yi	According to one's wishes (everything according to one's wishes)	680
25	揭榜 kit-bong	To be recognized as the best; traditionally, to come first in the highest imperial examinations	2,500
Total ¥			18,550

Note: ¥8 = US$1

"virtuous" here refers not just to "goods internal to a given practice"—such as sincerity, fairness, or justice, whose achievement is said to benefit the whole community—but also to "goods external to practices": things like fame, wealth, or state nobility, of which it is said that the more someone has of them, the less there is for others. This all-encompassing conceptualization of the "virtuous" is the product of intimate choices made by a few elite villagers, but the choices of these villagers reflect widely shared ideals in the local rural society. Most local families are concerned with the pursuit of both "internal goods" and "external goods." This pragmatic view of the realm of the "virtuous" clashes with MacIntyre's emphasis on the superiority of "internal goods" and is closer to the conceptualization developed by practice theorists such as anthropologist Pierre Bourdieu (1998, 75–145) for whom the pursuit of "goods internal to a given practice" is never fully disconnected from the pursuit of "external goods" like money—and vice versa.

One might think that the bids offered for these various "goods" would not be significant in size, but this is not the case. The budget sheets of auctions confirm that people take these ritual contests quite seriously. The 1999 auction, for example, made a total of ¥25,770 (US$3,200)—an impressive amount by local standards that represented almost 50 percent of the festival's revenue. The payment for each word was also significant. Table 6.1b shows that the most expensive written inscription auctioned in 1999 was *kit-bong* (C), meaning "to score highest in the imperial examination" and thus to be recognized as the very best—the only inscription that can be acquired only by a household with a specific profile: one with good reputation, economic affluence, plentiful offspring, and educational success (of the kind leading to government posts). The final bid for this inscription was ¥2,500 (US$310), a very significant amount of money by local standards, representing four to five months' salary for a migrant factory worker in 1999. At the other end of the spectrum, the least expensive inscription was *gung-jing* (C), meaning "justice and fairness," which was acquired for ¥180 (US$22), which—back then—was close to half the monthly salary of a migrant factory worker.

Tables 6.2a, b, and c and 6.3a, b, and c, listing the inscriptions auctioned at the Temple of the Old Woman Lam in 2009 and 2018, respectively, show a dramatic process of monetary inflation. In 2009 the most expensive inscription was still *kit-bong* (see Table 6.2b), but its price went up from ¥2,500 (US$310) in 1999 to ¥6,000 (US$880). At the other end of the spectrum, the cheapest word in 2009 was *chyun* (C), meaning "complete" or "perfect," at ¥320 (US$45), shown in Table 6.2a. This number was still a significant amount of money by local standards in 2009 (close to half of the monthly salary of a migrant factory worker), but it was not entirely outside the financial horizons of many village families. Indeed, one could say that in 2009 it was still possible for a village family with low income to become the patron of a lower-priced inscription, and there was a wide range of inscriptions to bid for, including those with three-character idioms (Table 6.2c).

As one compares the 2009 auction to the 2018 auction, it becomes clear that there is a dramatic increase in the prices of inscriptions, an increase

TABLE 6.2A. Auctioned words and respective prices, Jiao Festival, 2009

SINGLE-CHARACTER WORDS (C: DAAN-JI 單字)			
	WRITTEN WORD (C)	KEY MEANINGS	WINNING BID (¥)
1	丁 ding	Population; male descendants	2,500
2	財 choi	Wealth, riches	1,300
3	貴 gwai	Expensive, noble	1,200
4	旺 wong	Prosperous, flourishing	2,380
5	福 fuk	Good fortune, prosperity, blessing	900
6	祿 luk	Luck; official salary	500
7	壽 sau	Longevity	500
8	全 chyun	Complete, perfect	380
9	金 gam	Gold	500
10	玉 yuk	Jade	420
11	滿 mun	Full, complete, satisfied	1,030
12	堂 tong	Main room of building or house; also used to mean "of the same clan"	680
Total ¥			12,290

Note: ¥6.8 = US$1

TABLE 6.2B. Auctioned words and respective prices, Jiao Festival, 2009

DOUBLE-CHARACTER WORDS (C: SEUNG-JI 雙字)			
	WRITTEN WORD (C)	KEY MEANINGS	WINNING BID (¥)
1	萬事 maan-si	Everything (everything according to one's wishes)	1,080
2	勝意 sing-yi	"successful ideas and thoughts"	2,280
3	富貴 fu-gwai	Riches and honor, wealth and rank	1,880

(*continued*)

TABLE 6.2B. (continued)

DOUBLE-CHARACTER WORDS (C: SEUNG-JI 雙字)			
	WRITTEN WORD (C)	KEY MEANINGS	WINNING BID (¥)
4	興隆 hing-lung	Prosperous, thriving, flourishing	1,120
5	恭喜 gung-hei	Congratulations, as in the New Year greeting gung-hei faat-choi (恭喜發財) or "congratulations and best wishes for a prosperous New Year"	1,100
6	發財 faat-choi	To get rich, as in the traditional New Year greeting gung-hei faat-choi (恭喜發財) or "congratulations and best wishes for a prosperous New Year"	2,090
7	敬壽 ging-sau	To respect longevity	420
8	神明 san-ming	Gods, deities, divinities	420
9	福德 fuk-dak	"prosperity and virtue, good fortune and kindness"	880
10	平安 ping-on	Well; safe and sound, without mishap	3,050
11	德心 dak-sam	"virtuous heart," as in the idiom dak-sam ying-sau (德心應手) or "what the heart wishes, the hand accomplishes" meaning "skilled at the job," "entirely in one's element," "going smoothly and easily"	500
12	應手 ying-sau	"responsive hand," meaning "skilled," as in the idiom dak-sam ying-sau (德心應手) or "what the heart wishes, the hand accomplishes," meaning "skilled at the job," "entirely in one's element," "going smoothly and easily"	780
13	如意 yu-yi	According to one's wishes (everything according to one's wishes)	500
14	吉祥 gat-cheung	Lucky, auspicious, propitious	1,500

TABLE 6.2B. (continued)

DOUBLE-CHARACTER WORDS (C: SEUNG-JI 雙字)			
	WRITTEN WORD (C)	KEY MEANINGS	WINNING BID (¥)
15	東成 dung-sing	"to succeed in the east," as in the idiom dung-sing sai-jau (東成西就) or "to have success in the east and in the west (or all around)"	810
16	西就 sai-jau	"to succeed in the west," as in the idiom dung-sing sai-jau (東成西就) or "to have success in the east and in the west (or all around)"	650
17	和氣 wo-hei	Gentle, kind, courteous, polite; harmonious, friendly, amiable; as in the idiom wo-hei saang-choi (和氣生財) or "good manners bring riches"	1,500
18	生財 saang-choi	To amass wealth, to make money, as in the idiom wo-hei saang-choi (和氣生財) or "good manners bring riches"	1,880
19	善慶 sin-hing	"celebration of charity, kindness, virtue"	800
20	誠心 sing-sam	Sincerity, good faith	880
21	發達 faat-daat	Flourishing, prosperous, developed	1,680
22	揭榜 kit-bong	To be recognized as the very best; traditionally, to come first in the highest imperial examinations	6,000
Total ¥			31,800

Note: ¥6.8 = US$1

fueled by growing income disparities in the local society. If in 2009 it was still possible for a village family with low income to become the patron of a lower-priced inscription, by 2018 this had become impossible (compare, for example, the prices of Table 6.2b for 2009 with those of Table 6.3a for 2018). In 2018 the most expensive inscription was *fu-gwai mun-yun* (C, meaning "riches and honor everywhere in the garden"), at ¥32,000 (US$4,850), close to the average annual income of a village household (Table 6.3b). The

TABLE 6.2C. Auctioned words and respective prices, Jiao Festival, 2009

POPULAR THREE-CHARACTER IDIOMS			
	WRITTEN WORD (C)	KEY MEANINGS	WINNING BID (¥)
1	丁財貴 ding-choi-gwai	Male descendants, wealth, nobility	3,000
2	福祿壽 fuk-luk-sau	Fortune, luck, longevity	1,800
Total ¥			4,800

Note: ¥6.8 = US$1

household that paid for this inscription had an annual income more than ¥300,000 (US$45,450), but this kind of spending is not possible for most households in the whole of Yellow Flower township. At the other end of the spectrum, the cheapest inscription sold at the 2018 auction (see Table 6.3b), *chung-ying fu-gwai* (C, meaning "pine welcoming riches and honor"), cost ¥3,800 (US$575), an amount that most village families in the township of Yellow Flower struggle to save annually.

These numbers show that the major players of the auctions are the successful families of the local economy at different periods of the local agrarian transition. In 1999 those families had already managed to save enough to build at least one modern two-story house in the village. Most of these families had members engaging in labor migration. A decade later, successful families could afford the purchase of several new houses in the village and/or the market town. Most of these families had members engaging in labor migration, but a few made their living in the township. Up until this period, it was still possible for a village family with low income to acquire a lower-priced inscription at an auction. This stopped being the case in the 2010s. Being successful nowadays is no longer about being the owner of one or several new houses or apartments in the village and/or the market town (or even in the city); it is primarily about having a high annual income. Most inscriptions sold at the 2018 auction cost more than ¥8,000 (US$1,200). This is an extraordinary amount of money by local standards, equal to a year's savings for a household with an above-average annual income of ¥50,000 (US$7,500). Most households are not willing to spend a year's savings on an inscription, and this is why most successful bidders in the 2018 auction have an average annual household income higher than ¥100,000 (US$15,100).

TABLE 6.3A. Auctioned words and respective prices, Jiao Festival, 2018

DOUBLE-CHARACTER WORDS (C: SEUNG-JI 雙字)			
	WRITTEN WORD (C)	KEY MEANINGS	WINNING BID (¥)
1	如意 yu-yi	According to one's wishes	25,000
2	吉祥 gat-cheung	Lucky, auspicious, propitious	20,000
3	招财 jiu-choi	To attract wealth	18,000
4	进宝 jeun-bou	To receive a treasure	9,000
5	丁财 ding-choi	Male descendants; wealth	23,800
6	富贵 fu-gwai	Riches and honor, wealth and rank	21,000
7	兴家 hing-ga	Happy family	13,800
8	祈禄 kei-luk	To pray for luck	13,500
Total ¥			144,100

Note: ¥6.6 = US$1

TABLE 6.3B. Auctioned words and respective prices, Jiao Festival, 2018

POPULAR FOUR-CHARACTER IDIOMS			
	WRITTEN WORD (C)	KEY MEANINGS	WINNING BID (¥)
1	祈寿康宇 kei-sau hong-yu	Pray for longevity and health	13,800
2	功成名就 gung-sing ming-jau	To win success and recognition	10,600
3	步步高升 bou-bou gou-sing	To rise steadily step by step	10,800
4	风生水起 fung-sang seui-hei	To get great fortune	16,000
5	松鹤延年 chung-hok yin-nin	Attaining the longevity of the pine and the crane	7,500
6	大展鸿图 daai-jin hung-tou	To carry out and achieve a great plan or aspiration	8,800
7	年年有余 nin-nin yau-yu	Have a surplus year after year	8,800

(*continued*)

TABLE 6.3B. (continued)

POPULAR FOUR-CHARACTER IDIOMS			
	WRITTEN WORD (C)	KEY MEANINGS	WINNING BID (¥)
8	松迎富贵 chung-ying fu-gwai	Pine welcoming riches and honor	3,800
9	锦上添花 gam-seung tim-fa	On brocade add flowers; to decorate something already perfect	5,000
10	马上好运 ma-seung hou-wan	Good fortune all at once	6,200
11	心想事成 sam-seung si-sing	To have one's wishes come true	10,000
12	财源广进 choi-yun gwong-jeun	Profits advancing and expanding	12,800
13	富贵平安 fu-gwai ping-on	Riches, honor, and safety	12,800
14	花开富贵 fa-hoi fu-gwai	Riches and honor blossom	7,000
15	竹报平安 juk-bou ping-on	Letter from the family carrying the good news	8,800
16	七仙赐福 chat-sin chi-fuk	Seven immortals give blessing	6,800
17	八仙送宝 baat-sin sung-bou	Eight immortals give blessing	7,000
18	吉星高照 gat-sing gou-jiu	Be blessed by a lucky star	6,000
19	丁财两旺 ding-choi mun-wong	Lots of sons and prosperity	10,800
20	鸿运当头 hung-wan dong-tau	Good luck right overhead	8,000
21	金桥富路 gam-kiu fu-lou	Golden bridge and road of prosperity	6,000
22	好乃成双 hou-naai sing-seung	Good is in pairs	8,300
23	一帆风顺 yat-faan fung-seun	Smooth sailing; good journey	8,000
24	富贵满园 fu-gwai mun-yun	Riches and honor everywhere in the garden	32,000
25	锦绣山河 gam-sau saan-ho	Land of splendors	22,000
26	和合昌盛 wo-hap cheung-sing	Harmonious and prosperous	22,000

TABLE 6.3B. (continued)

POPULAR FOUR-CHARACTER IDIOMS			
	WRITTEN WORD (C)	KEY MEANINGS	WINNING BID (¥)
27	文武双全 man-mou seung-chyun	Master of pen and sword, well versed in the letters and the military	20,000
28	仙娘送子 sin-leung sung-ji	Celestial woman who delivers a son	20,000
29	流水生财 lau-seui saang-choi	Flowing water making money	16,000
30	鸟语花香 niu-yu fa-heung	Birds sing and flowers give fragrance	6,800
31	鸳鸯祈福 yun-yeung kei-fuk	Mandarin duck pray for good fortune	8,500
32	花好月圆 fa-hou yut-yun	Blooming flowers and full moon, conjugal bliss	6,000
33	红日鸿运 hung-yat hung-wan	Rising sun bringing good luck	9,000
34	栋梁花瓶 dung-leung fa-ping	Flower vase on the ridgepole, combining strength with beauty	14,900
Total ¥			380,800

Note: ¥6.6 = US$1

Being able to afford an inscription is an important factor in the intimate choices of villagers, but it is not the only factor. For the outside observer, the reason to spend so much money on poor-quality mirror screens is not entirely obvious. One important point to bear in mind—to echo an argument made by anthropologist Clifford Geertz (1973) in an essay on Balinese cockfighting—is that from the perspective of villagers, the money spent on these mirrors is not being wasted but is being converted into two things that are far more important than money in the context of local cosmologies of value: divine protection and redemption, and local public recognition and symbolic capital following from the status of being a patron of an auctioned inscription. But what is most fascinating about these short-term transactional processes of capital conversion is that they explicitly

TABLE 6.3C. Auctioned words and respective prices, Jiao Festival, 2018

PILLARS (C: *CHYU* 柱)			
	WRITTEN WORD (C)	KEY MEANINGS	WINNING BID (¥)
1	丁财柱 ding-choi chyu	Pillar of "male descendants and wealth"	23,800
2	富贵柱 fu-gwai chyu	Pillar of "fortune and nobility"	21,000
3	如意柱 yu-yi chyu	Pillar of "according to one's wishes"	25,000
4	吉祥柱 gat-cheung chyu	Pillar of "prosperity"	20,000
5	招财柱 jiu-choi chyu	Pillar of "attract wealth"	18,000
6	进宝柱 jeun-bou chyu	Pillar of "receive treasure"	9,000
7	兴家柱 hing-ga chyu	Pillar of "happy family"	13,800
8	祈禄柱 kei-luk chyu	Pillar of "pray for luck"	13,500
9	财源柱 choi-yun chyu	Pillar of "source of wealth"	12,800
10	富贵柱 fu-gwai chyu	Pillar of "fortune and nobility"	12,800
Total ¥			169,700

Note: ¥6.6 = US$1

sponsor the ritual reproduction of something that has little to do with worldly exchanges—namely, the construction of a locally shared moral compass and framework of ethical imagination.

Through a series of complex operational sequences, the auctions produce a highly authoritative, divinely sanctioned picture of collective ethical imagination that circulates in the local community with the approval of state authorities, conveying a sense of moral unity and social cohesion. This sense of moral unity and social cohesion is partly illusory. Villagers disagree on which inscriptions should be included and/or are most valuable and on how inscriptions relate to real-life situations. They also disagree on bidding preferences, as different individuals or households are not necessarily interested in the same inscriptions for the same reasons. These qualifications do not imply that the idea of a unified framework of collective ethical imagination is an illusion or has no sociological force (Zigon 2009); they only call for a theoretical acknowledgment of moral disagreements.

A Story of Moral Frictions and Contentious Negotiations

The 1999 auction at the Temple of the Old Woman Lam illustrates such moral frictions. On the day of the auction, Bright Gold felt like celebrating his recent recovery from illness, and he did so without thinking too much about the consequences. He was interested in two specific inscriptions: *on-lok* (C), meaning "peace and happiness," and *gung-jing* (C), meaning "justice and fairness," and to everyone's astonishment (including his own), his bids proved victorious despite the fact that he made only a single offer for each word. Bright Gold agreed to pay the following day, but after a few days, it became clear that he would not be able to make any payment at all. While all other winning bidders settled their payments immediately, he still had not done so several months after the auction, despite having been repeatedly admonished both by close relatives and by the festival's presiding committee. He also failed to show up at two important temple assemblies just a few weeks before the beginning of the Jiao ritual festivities in November.

As the Jiao ritual festivities drew near, more and more people started gossiping about his lack of "sincerity" (C: *sing-sam*), one of the inscribed words on sale at the 1999 auction. Many started referring to him derogatorily as someone who "says things without doing the arithmetic," that is, without keeping his word (C: *gong-ye ng syun-sou*), someone who "has no money to say things (that matter)" (C: *mou chin gong-ye*). Many in his village (including close relatives) also began referring to him as a "dead son" (C: *sei-jai*), that is, a very bad boy, one of those who brings "loss of face" (C: *diu-ga*) and does not care about the maintenance of harmonious relations with his relatives and neighbors. Even his wife and children were turning their backs on him.

It was clear that Bright Gold had made a mistake. Besides making a pledge he could not honor, he also did not provide any public excuse and acted as though he had done nothing wrong. He found himself in a complex double bind: how could he reconcile the desire to express his individual view with the desire to reaffirm his ties to larger moral collectives? I am convinced that Bright Gold's bids and pledge to donate money were sincere, probably the product of wishful thinking and a few unrealistic assumptions. To begin with, Bright Gold underestimated the extent to which his family was in economic difficulty. At the time of the auction, they could not even afford to eat pork with any regularity, let alone engage in public acts of charitable giving. Perhaps more importantly, Bright Gold overestimated the extent to which he was in control of his family's finances. His wife, Full Elder Sister, had already taken over the role of breadwinner a few years earlier, in 1997, when she decided—against Bright Gold's wishes—to venture into the suburbs of the provincial capital to make money (described in chapter 2).

The couple's close relatives in the village also thought that Bright Gold's failure to "assume responsibility" (C: *fu-jaak-yam*) as the household's breadwinner was unacceptable. In their view, Full Elder Sister's decision to leave the village was the only way forward. Of course, this move also represented a major turnabout in the couple's power dynamics. As Full Elder Sister became the family's breadwinner, Bright Gold's authority diminished. Two years later, when the auction incident occurred, Full Elder Sister was still in charge of household expenses, and her take on the incident was that giving money to the festival's committee would be a waste of savings on things the family clearly could not afford. She also believed that Bright Gold would eventually find a way to negotiate the payment of his bids with money coming from the monthly rental payments I was making to them as a tenant.

Bright Gold had a different opinion. He insisted on not paying the money and he continued to deny any wrongdoing. Most importantly, he provided specific moral arguments to explain his positions. One could dismiss these moral arguments as evidence of bad faith, but I am more inclined to read them as evidence of an individual and collective project of self-cultivation that cannot be separated from the larger moral transformations triggered by the Communist Revolution of 1949. This reading adds significant historical and moral complexity to the episode.

Bright Gold was one of the few villagers of his generation (growing up during the Great Cultural Revolution, 1966–76) who managed to graduate from middle school.[16] Several villagers told me he was strongly committed to Maoist thought during his schooling, a commitment that does not appear to have faded away. Recalling a famous 1945 speech by Chairman Mao, Bright Gold would often alert me (during fieldwork between 1999 and 2001) to the continuing need to fight for the removal of the "big mountains" obstructing China's socialist transformation (see Mao [1945] 1965). In his speech, Mao refers to feudalism and imperialism as two "big mountains" that have to be removed through the unity, hard work, and perseverance of the Chinese people. Bright Gold was also concerned with eliminating the "big mountain" of feudalism, but he replaced the "big mountain" of imperialism with that of capitalism, another major target of Mao's socialist ideology. Bright Gold was convinced that the process of Reform and Opening initiated in the late 1970s had led to the resurgence of popular religion practices (based on "feudalist superstitious beliefs") together with an increasingly commoditized economy (inspired by "capitalist worship of money and commodities"), and these two processes signaled a full-fledged reappearance of Mao's "big mountains" and represented an unacceptable retreat from the chairman's virtuous teachings.

Bright Gold's challenging of the authority of the temple's management committee can be read in light of these "revolutionary" ideals. He looked at the Jiao auctions as evidence of the "feudalist" and "capitalist" activities of the temple committee, and he wanted to expose the fictitious nature of gods and money in order to overcome Mao's big mountains. His plan was to arrange a public assembly at the temple in which he would pay his two winning bids with "spirit money" (banknote-shaped strips of white paper used to worship gods and ancestors). He wanted to make the point that the standard renminbi banknotes used to pay auction bids are as fictitious as the fake paper money burned in honor of nonexistent supernatural creatures and to argue—against the picture of ethical imagination celebrated in Jiao auctions—that money is *not* a reliable measure of virtue. In his view, the monetization of the local society and of the local moral landscape had led to increasing levels of corruption and moral decay not just among the local authorities but also among the local elites (the leading organizers of Jiao festivals).

Bright Gold was determined to go ahead with his plan, but his children (under the domineering influence of their mother) begged him to abandon it, arguing—quite realistically—that he would only make a fool of himself and his family. That same morning, the children came crying to me and asked me to lend money to their father. After a series of complex negotiations coordinated by his close village relatives and the temple committee, Bright Gold ended up paying his two winning bids with financial support from me and another villager—each of us paying for one mirror.

This solution was the product of an intimate choice. All intimate choices involve complex moral negotiations between multiple actors, but not all intimate choices are so contentious. In some cases, the dialectics of personal liberties and social responsibilities result in a balanced, harmonious solution that pleases almost everyone involved in the decision-making process. In other cases, the dialectics of personal liberties and social responsibilities require one or several villagers to sacrifice their own personal views for the sake of the interests of the larger moral collectives to which they are tied. This is ultimately what happened to Bright Gold, but before it got to this point, he tried to have it his way. He tried to make a choice that not only went against the views of his family members and the views of his close village relatives but that questioned the authority of his deity temple association. This decision led to an open conflict that had significant costs for Bright Gold, but he continues to hold on to his views.

An Action-Oriented View of the Construction of Intimate Moral Communities

When I visited Harmony Cave in November 2009 and again in November 2016 to attend Jiao festivals at the Temple of the Old Woman Lam, Bright Gold's two mirrors were still hanging on the wall of his kitchen, but a few things had changed since the 1999 auction. Most importantly, in 2003 Bright Gold had joined his wife in the city to help her run their vegetable gardening business. His views on Mao's "big mountains" have not changed, but his worries and energies are now focused on his wife's increasingly poor health and his eldest son's lack of marriage prospects. Bright Gold's reputation never fully recovered after the 1999 auction incident, not least because his economic situation has not improved, and money—as he himself continues to argue—has become a major indicator of virtue, respectability, and power.

If back in 1999 Bright Gold had not found any powerful allies to support his cause, it was certainly not because his ethical positions were unusual. My field notes from that period are filled with references to informal conversations during which many villagers showed empathy for and understanding of some of Bright Gold's positions, especially his critique of the unequal and corrupt dimensions of capitalism. His critique resonated with the widely accepted view among members of Bright Gold's generation, and among older generations, that one of the greatest achievements of the Maoist era was creating a society with low levels of social inequality and corruption. This critique remains salient in contemporary village society, and my impression is that the number of villagers who criticize rising societal levels of social inequality and corruption has significantly increased after the turn of the millennium. Although social inequality and corruption have become major CCP concerns under Hu Jintao (2002–12) and now Xi Jinping (2012 to the present), there is a generalized feeling in the village that inequality and corruption have not ceased to increase in the last two decades, with rising accumulation of wealth among the super rich, rising urban and rural income disparities, and increasing socioeconomic differences between villagers. This inequality is evident in the inflation in the prices of auctioned inscriptions in the Jiao festivals between 1999 and 2018. If in 1999 it was still possible for a village family with limited income to become the patron of a written word of virtue, this was no longer possible in 2018, as the cheapest word cost an amount of money that most village families in Yellow Flower struggle to save annually.

It is hard to say whether this experience of growing social inequality will lead to more incidents and open conflicts in local deity temple associations, but it is important to make a distinction between expressing one's discontent about someone or something and expressing one's discontent in a way that is confrontational and that challenges the foundations of the authority of local deity temple elites. As far as I know, no other villager has followed Bright Gold's example in openly confronting the structures of inequality that shape the organization of local Jiao festivals, and this is certainly not because villagers are unaware of these structures. The main issue is that any open challenge will be perceived as an attack on one's own moral community, and it may lead to forms of retaliation and public criticism that will cast one's actions as those of a bad community member, someone who does not keep promises and does not contribute to the well-being of community. This last point can be illustrated with a phrase that is regularly auctioned in local deity temples: *wo-hei* (C), meaning "amiable, peaceful, and polite" (see, for example, Tables 6.1b and 6.2b). This phrase points to an aspect of the local framework of ethical imagination that highlights the importance of knowing how to live in a collective, seeking agreement, and, for the sake of harmony and unity, claiming agreement even when it does not exist. In such a context, openly challenging the ideal of the desirability of an imagined orthodoxy renders one vulnerable to being called a bad community member, someone who does not care about the maintenance of harmonious relations with relatives and neighbors.

This point about what makes a person a bad community member helps in understanding better the exact nature of the wrongdoing of Bright Gold.

Invoking Maoist revolutionary ideals to talk about growing social inequalities in society was bound to generate controversy, but what really damaged Bright Gold's reputation in the eyes of most villagers was the fact that he failed to honor his pledge to the deity temple committee and thus made a fool out of the whole deity temple community. That made him a bad community member, and the fact that he (and his family) lacked the status and the resources to have a say in community affairs only made things worse, because it made him look foolish as well. Stories of bad community members like Bright Gold remind us that moral communities are not static and that moral frictions and negotiations play an important role in the larger collective effort to build an intimate moral community in the face of larger forces of change.

Popular Religion and the Politics of Socialist Spiritual Civilization

In action-oriented conceptualizations of moral communities, moral unity and togetherness coexist with moral divisions and negotiations, as echoed in recent developments in the anthropology of ethics. Anthropologist Michael Lambek (2010, 12–13) notes that earlier approaches favored structural visions of ethics either as a system of rules and obligations or as a system of values and categories. These structural visions approached ethics primarily as a property or function of abstract reason and led to an impoverished conception of ethical life as a matter of following either a system of rules or a system of values. But ethical life is more unpredictable and uncertain than this, and Lambek (ibid., 16) suggests that one can do more to acknowledge this unpredictability and uncertainty by seeking inspiration in the work of ancient philosophers such as Aristotle for whom ethics is "fundamentally a property or function of action rather than (only) of abstract reason."

China has its own ancient tradition of virtue ethics, and the major figure in this tradition—Confucius—developed an approach that is both similar to and different from that of Aristotle. Like Aristotle, Confucius approaches ethics as a property or function of action, but unlike Aristotle, as shown by philosopher of science Yuk Hui (2016), Confucius devotes special attention to the linkages between ethics, ritual action, and artifacts/technical procedures. This innovative grounding of the realm of artifacts and technical procedures in a philosophical project of virtue and ritual action, as opposed to a philosophical project of nature and material production, points to a new way of thinking about ethics. Like Aristotle, Confucius approaches ethics as a property or function of action, but he is more concerned with defining ethics in relation to ritual action and ritual artifacts/technical procedures and their relation to lived experience.[17] Approaching ethics through the lens of ritual action and ritual artifacts/technical procedures, and their relation to lived experience, is a good way to describe the sociotechnical approach to the rituals of ethical imagination discussed in this chapter.

Writing about traditional Chinese society, anthropologist C. K. Yang (1961, 282–83) famously argued that popular religion for common people was less a source of moral ideals than of highly ingenious techniques (what he called "magic") for obtaining happiness and warding off evil—that is, for getting closer to the ideal of a good, virtuous life. Deity temple rituals in northern Guangdong illustrate a slightly different type of sociotechnical ensemble, though no less magical: a machine-like ritual infrastructure that is capable of bringing together human and nonhuman elements in a seamless whole. The main goal of this ritual infrastructure is to produce a collectively approved vision of the notion of the "good, virtuous life" itself, creating an image of collective ethical imagination that appears to be natural and the only one possible. This ritual technology of collective ethical imagination is built on a deeper reality of moral frictions and negotiations, but it creates an image of moral unity and social cohesion that makes ethical life look more static and stagnant than it actually is in practice.

Developing an action-oriented pluralistic conception of ethical life is crucial for understanding the micro-level politics of ethical imagination that shapes the development of small-scale projects of moral self-cultivation supported by local deity temple associations such as the Temple of the Old Woman Lam. But it is also crucial for understanding the macro-level politics of ethical imagination that shapes the development of much larger technocratic projects of national ethical standardization steered by the Chinese Communist Party and supported by many other actors and organizations in civil society.

A good example of these larger technocratic initiatives is the project—initially launched under Deng Xiaoping—to improve the "quality" (SC: *suzhi*) of the Chinese population and to promote the construction of a more developed and cohesive "socialist spiritual civilization" (Kipnis 2006; Dynon 2014). This project is not entirely coherent and comprises multiple elements and components that changed over time under different leaderships. The scope of the project was significantly expanded under the leadership of Hu Jintao after 2002, and since 2012 Xi Jinping has launched a number of far-reaching mass campaigns of moral education promoting "core socialist values" and the "China dream" (Gow 2017; Callahan 2013; Pieke 2016). The "core socialist values" campaign is an interesting example because it operates in ways that resemble the ritual auctions of written words in northern Guangdong, but it forms a much more complex technological apparatus that requires the input of large bodies of professional experts and that targets the whole of the Chinese population by means of massive nationwide infrastructures of media broadcasting and moral education.

Contrasted, these two types of technologies of ethical imagination illustrate why low-tech popular religion rituals and not high-tech visions of "socialist spiritual civilization" have become the language of intimate moral community in present-day village China. Xi's project to promote the spread of "core socialist values" involves the selection of words, like those of the auctions in northern Guangdong, but the words of Xi's campaign are very different from those selected by local deity temple committees. The "core socialist values" campaign promoted by Xi Jinping is based on four national goals (prosperity, democracy, civility, and harmony), four social goals (freedom, equality, justice, and the rule of law), and four individual values (patriotism, dedication, integrity, and friendship). Northern Guangdong villagers share some of these goals and values (e.g., prosperity, harmony, and justice), though others (e.g., freedom, democracy, and the rule of law) are too abstract to be popular in northern Guangdong. But the key difference between the general value orientation of Xi's campaign and the general value orientation of local popular religion rituals lies elsewhere. Xi's campaign is primarily concerned with subordinating the small self of individuals, families, and communities to the larger self of a CCP-led narrative of the Chinese nation and civilization. By contrast, the ceremonial auctions organized by deity temple associations in northern Guangdong are primarily concerned with celebrating the achievements and aspirations of local individuals, families, and communities and their ancestral traditions.

This contrast illustrates why it is the language of popular religion rituals and not the language of "socialist spiritual civilization" that has become the language of moral intimacy in village China, and it also says something about the current nationwide quest for a new moral compass capable of filling the void left by four decades of postsocialist reforms favoring the achievement of material wealth. Xi's "core socialist values" campaign is a powerful attempt to develop such a new moral compass capable of reaching the whole of the Chinese nation, but it is questionable whether this technocratic effort to define the terms of what counts as "the new Chinese socialist spiritual civilization" will be accepted without modification. The language of "core socialist values" is already having an important impact on local articulations of ethical modernity in many parts of China, but in village China it cannot compete with popular religion repertoires of ethical modernity and spiritual civilization. The fact that Xi Jinping's leadership is increasingly depicting the CCP as the rightful successor to China's dynastic rule and as the protector of China's cultural traditions might arise from the realization that the only way to govern popular religion in rural China and bring it under the framings of CCP's discourses of socialist spiritual civilization is to make sure that the party claims its position of authority next to local celestial bureaucracies. This marks a new beginning in the relation between popular religion and China's ongoing colonizing macro-level politics of socialist spiritual civilization.

GLOSSARY OF CHINESE TERMS

ABBREVIATIONS

C	Cantonese, Yue Chinese
SC	standard Chinese (Putonghua, Mandarin)

Note: literal translations are indicated with quotation marks.

a-gung leung-gung-po wa-si (C) 阿公两公婆话事 (paternal) grandfather and his wife call the shots

a-me (C) 阿嬷 mother; prestige Cantonese variety pronunciation, *a-ma*

Ba Ma Ying (SC) 爸妈营 Father Mother Camp (WeChat public account)

bin-fai wai-bou (C) 变废为宝 turning waste into treasure

biu-ji (C) 標字 "bidding for written words (inscriptions)"

chengzhen zhigong jiben yiliao baoxian (SC) 城镇职工基本医疗保险 Urban Employee Basic Medical Insurance Scheme

chiu-saang-fai (C) 超生费 unplanned-birth fine

chung-ying fu-gwai (C) 松迎富贵 "pine welcoming riches and honor," longevity with riches and honor

chyun (C) 全 "complete" or "perfect"

chyun-man siu-jou (C) 村民小组 village groups (Reform-era administrative unit, cunmin xiaozu in SC); usually refers to a small group or a residential hamlet within a natural village

chyun-wai-wui (C) 村委会 village committees (Reform-era administrative unit, cun-wei-hui in SC); usually refers to a small cluster of neighboring villages

Da J Xiao D (SC) 大J小D Big Sister Small Brother (WeChat public account)

daai-deui (C) 大队 village committees, brigades (Maoist administrative unit, da-dui in SC)

daai-deui jip-saang-po (C) 大队接生婆 brigade midwife, government-certified lay midwife
daai-huk (C) 大哭 ritual wailing
daai jung-lei (C) 大總理 "big president," leading figure of the management committee of a Jiao festival
daai-po (C) 大婆 "big wife," official wife
daan-ji (C) 單字 single-character inscription or written word
Daoguang (SC) 道光 Qing dynasty reign period (1820–50)
dawo (SC) 大我 "big self"
Di Yi Fu Chan (SC) 第一妇产 Number One Gynecology (WeChat public account)
Dian Dian Jia De Tu Xiao Dou (SC) 点点家的土小豆 Little Home Bean (WeChat public account)
Ding Xiang Ma Ma (SC) 丁香妈妈 Clove Mother (WeChat public account)
diu-ga (C) 丢架 loss of face

faat-yuk (C) 发育 bodily growth, associated with the capability of reproduction
fangyan (SC) 方言 regional dialects, regional languages
fo-hok wai-saang (C) 科学卫生) scientific hygiene
fong-ming (C) 芳名 "fragrant names," distinguished list of donors
fu-gwai mun-yun (C) 富贵满园 "riches and honor everywhere in the garden"
fu-jaak-yam (C) 负责任 to take or assume responsibility
fuke (SC) 妇科 "medicine for women," gynecology
fu-luk (C) 符籙 practice of talismanic writing
fung seui (C) 风水 feng shui, geomancy
gaan-gaak-fai (C) 間隔費 birth-spacing fine
gaang-tin (C) 耕田 to plough the fields
gaap ge (C) 夾嘅 "pinched," pooled
ga-geui chi-so (C) 家具厕所 home toilet
ga-geui sai-san-gaan (C) 家具洗身间) home bathroom
ga-heung (C) 家乡 native place
gan-gei (C) 根基 foundation
gaoling chanfu (SC) 高龄产妇 "advanced age pregnant woman"
gau se-wui (C) 旧社会 old society
geng-ping (C) 鏡屏 mirror screens
gongfei yiliao (SC) 公费医疗 social health insurance scheme
gong-ye ng syun-sou (C) 講嘢唔算數 "to say things without doing the arithmetic," to say things without really meaning it, to say things without keeping one's word
gou-kap fo-hok ji-sik (C) 高级科学知识 higher-level scientific expertise
gou-kap san-fan (C) 高级身份 high-class identity
gung-dak (C) 功德 merit
gung-jing (C) 公正 "justice and fairness"
gung-taai (C) 公太 great-grandfather
Guo Ma Xiu Lian Ji (SC) 果妈修炼记 "Fruit Mum Practice" (WeChat public account)
gwai-po (C) 鬼婆 "ghost wife," widow
gyun ge (C) 捐嘅 (something) donated

ha-dai (C) 下底 "lower area" (also called *ngoi-bin*, meaning "outer area")
hei (C) 气 vital energy of life force, operates like an invisible gas
hei haizi (SC) 黑孩子 "black children," children without any official documentation, unplanned children

hing-dai suk-baak (C) 兄弟叔伯 "brothers and uncles," expression used to refer to male village relatives who descend from a common patrilineal ancestor

hukou (SC) 户口 household; also household (*hukou*) booklet or household (*hukou*) registration system

ji bu wan nai de niu, zhang bu da de gaoyang (SC) 挤不完奶的牛，长不大的羔羊 "cows with inexhaustible milk and lambs that never grow up," a metaphor for how adult children treat their parents and how adult children view themselves

Jiao (SC) 醮 major ritual festival with large-scale sacrificial offerings to gods of a local temple association; rituals themselves derived from Daoist liturgical tradition, but include Buddhist and shamanist elements

jieshengpo (SC) 接生婆 lay midwife, village midwife

jihua shengyu (SC) 计划生育 "birth planning," family planning

Jihua Shengyu Zhengce (SC) 计划生育政策 Birth Planning Policy

jin (C) 斤 a catty, a weight measure equal to one-half kilogram

jip-saang-po (C) 接生婆 lay midwife, certified lay midwife, non-certified lay midwife

ji-yin-chaan (C) 自然产 natural birth

jung-lei (C) 總理 "premier," leading members of the management committee of a Jiao festival

jung-naam hing-neui (C) 重男輕女 to value males and belittle females

jyu-yun (C) 主缘 "major contributor" or patron of a written word (inscription) of virtue (goodness and right action); for example, Ding jyu-yun (C) 丁主缘 patron of the written word "Ding"

Kangxi (SC) 康熙 Qing dynasty reign period (1661–1722)

kit-bong (C) 揭榜 "to score highest in the imperial examination," to be recognized as the very best

lau (C) 楼 "mansion," village house with multiple stories and a terrace

leui-dai (C) 里底 "inner area" (also called *seung-bin*, meaning "upper area")

Liu Ma Luo Luo (SC) 六妈罗罗 Six Mamas Luo Luo (WeChat public account)

liushou ertong (SC) 留守儿童 left-behind child(ren)

lok-hau (C) 落后 backward

lou-baan (C) 老板 / 老闆 "old board," shopkeeper, boss

lou-ma (C) 老妈 "old mother," grandmother

lou-sai (C) 老细 "old small," shop-keeper, boss

luohou fengjian mixin (SC) 落后封建迷信 backward feudalist superstitions

lyun-ngoi gwaan-hai (C) 恋爱关系 "love relationships"

man-taan (C) 文壇 "civil altar," inside a temple's main building; also called the "muttering altar"

mong-ba (C) 网吧 Internet café

mong-nguk (C) 望屋 "to see the house," to visit the house of the prospective groom to gather information on his family and village

mou chin gong-ye (C) 冇錢講嘢 "no money to say things (that

matter)," money talks louder than words
mou-taan (C) 武壇 "military altar," outside a temple's main building in a temporary bamboo shelter; also called the "dancing altar"
mu (SC) 亩 unit of area equal to one-fifteenth of a hectare (classifier for fields)

naan-chaan (C) 难产 "difficult birth," a complicated birth that requires a cesarean intervention
nai-jyun nguk (C) 泥砖屋 "clay-brick houses," mud houses
Nanhai (SC) 南海 a well-known district in the city of Foshan, Pearl River Delta
nei (SC) 内 inside
ng wai-saang ge (C) 唔卫生嘅 unhygienic
ngoi-bin (C) 外边 "outer area" (also called *ha-dai*, meaning "lower area")
nung-ga-lok (C) 农家乐 "peasant family happiness," rural hostels

on-lok (C) 安樂 "peace and happiness"

paak-to (C) 拍拖 dating
Pei Yisheng (SC) 裴医生 Dr. Pei (WeChat public account)

qi (SC) 气 vital energy of life force, operates like an invisible gas
qu (SC) 区 district (administrative unit)

renmin gongshe (SC) 人民公社 people's commune (administrative unit)

saam-gaak-sik fa-fan-chi (C) 三格式化粪池 three-chamber septic tank
saam-geuk gai (C) 三脚鸡 "three-footed chicken," three-wheeler
saang-chaan-deui (C) 生产队 production teams (Maoist administrative unit, sheng-chan-dui in SC)
sai-man-jai (C) 细蚊仔 "little mosquitoes," small children
sai-po (C) 細婆 "small wife," a concubine with a lower status
sai-san (C) 洗身 "wash the body"
sangu liupo (SC) 三姑六婆 "three nuns and six grannies," derogatory sixteenth-century term for traditional lay midwives
sei-jai (C) 死仔 "dead son," very bad boy
se-keui geui-wai-wui (C) 社区居委会 neighborhood committees (Reform-era administrative unit, shequ juweihui in SC)
seui lau-loi, ng-hai lau-jau (C) 水流来，唔系流走 "the water coming into the village does not flow away," a feng shui principle that is assured if all village doors face east
seun-chaan (C) 顺产 "smooth birth," a vaginal delivery without major complications
seung-bin (C) 上边 "upper area" (also called *leui-dai*, meaning "inner area")
seung-ji (C) 雙字 double-character written words
seun-si (C) 信士 devout believers
shehui zhuyi hexin jiazhiguan (SC) 社会主义核心价值观 core socialist values (official concept)
shehui zhuyi jingshen wenming (SC) 社会主义精神文明 socialist spiritual civilization (official concept)
shehui zhuyi wenming (SC) 社会主义文明 socialist civilization (official concept)

shehui zhuyi wuzhi wenming (SC) 社会主义物质文明 socialist material civilization (official concept)
sing-sam (C) 誠心 "sincerity"
si-haang (C) 屎坑 "shit pit," latrine
si-haang-seui (C) 屎坑水 "shit-pit water"
sin-hang (C) 善行 charitable deed
sin-jeun (C) 先进 advanced
sin-jeun fo-hok mat-ban (C) 先进科学物品 advanced scientific products
si-tau (C) 事头 "business head," boss
sung-ji (C) 送字 "deliver the [written] words," a ceremony of Jiao festivals
suzhi (SC) 素质 quality (official concept)
suzhi jiaoyu (SC) 素质教育 education for quality (educational policy)
syu-meng (C) 书名 "book name," name used in formal occasions and ritual artifacts such as tomb inscriptions and ancestral tablets

taai giu-ching (C) 太娇情 too frail and delicate
tou-jaap-fei (C) 土杂肥 "mixed-soil fertilizer"
tou-lik (C) 土力 "soil's strength"
tung-sing-chyun (C) 同姓村 single-surname village; also, single lineage village

wai (SC) 外 outside
wai-saang (C) 卫生 hygiene, sanitation
wan, xi, shao (SC) 晚稀少 "later marriage, longer birth interval, fewer births"; mass campaign promoting later-sparser-fewer children
wan-chin (C) 揾钱 "look for money," make money
weiwen (SC) 维稳 "stability maintenance"
wen-ming (SC) 文明 civilization
Wenming Cun (SC) 文明村 Civilized Village (official development program)
wo-hei (C) 和氣 "amiable, peaceful, and polite"
wutong fenmian huxi fa (SC) 无痛分娩呼吸法 "painless labor breathing method"

xian fu qi lai (SC) 先富起来 getting rich first
xiang (SC) 乡 home town (township-level administrative unit used between 1987 and 1993, also used during the pre-Communist period)
Xiangtu Zhongguo (SC) 乡土中国 "*earthbound China,*" original title of a major work by Chinese anthropologist Fei Xiaotong, first published in Chinese in 1947 and in English in 1992 with the title *From the Soil: The Foundations of Chinese Society.*
xiaowo (SC) 小我 small self
xinxing nongcun hezuo yiliao (SC) 新型农村合作医疗 New Rural Cooperative Medical Insurance Scheme
xi-zi-hui (SC) 惜字會 associations for cherishing written words
Xueqiu Mama (SC) 雪求妈妈 Snowball Mama (WeChat public account)

yan-ching (C) 人情 human feeling
yan-hau ching-jiu (C) 人口清醮 "Jiao Ritual for the Population"; *see also* Jiao
yat chi sat juk chin gu han (C) 一次失足千古恨 one wrong step can cause a thousand regrets
yat-nin saam-cha (C) 一年三查 three yearly examinations
yi-ga jeui-kau ge ye do-jo hou do (C) 而家追求嘅嘢多咗好多 today people's material aspirations have increased quite significantly

yi-ga nung-chyun hou wan-chin gwo yi sap nin chin (C) 而家农村好揾钱过二十年前 the countryside nowadays is better to make money and earn a living than two decades earlier

yi-ng-jai (C) 二五仔 traitor, snitch, mole, betrayer

yin-yang (SC) 阴阳 key concepts in Chinese traditional philosophy, used to describe a pair of contrary and complementary forces that are in constant interaction with each other to shape all forms of existence in the universe

yuk-san-chin (C) 肉身钱 "corporeal body money," a traditional form of brideprice payment given by the groom's parents to the bride's parents

yun-sau (C) 缘首 "contribution heads" or "deputies," designated assistants of the management committee of a Jiao festival

zhen (SC) 镇 township (Reform-era administrative unit)

NOTES

INTRODUCTION

1 There is a growing body of literature on the increasing centrality of globalized articulations of technoscience and technocratic expertise in the governance of everyday life (Ong and Collier 2005; Michael 2006; M. Fischer 2007; Bucchi 2009; Morozov 2011, 2013; Prasad 2017). The term "technoscience" refers to the interwovenness of science and technology, or of knowledge and technique in which technology is indispensable for the production of scientific knowledge. To study technoscience is to trace the multiple local processes by which expert scientific knowledge (including the human and social sciences) is constructed and how it comes to circulate and produce particular sorts of social and material orderings. The term "technoscience" was coined in the 1950s, but it started to become popular only in the 1980s due to the growing influence of the field of science, technology, and society (STS) studies. STS scholars such as Bruno Latour (1987) used the term "technoscience" to make several points about the role of science and technology in contemporary late capitalist societies: the intertwinement of scientific and technological development; the power of laboratories and engineering workshops to change the world as it is experienced; the seamless webs that connect scientists, engineers, and societal actors in actual practice; and the propensity of the technoscientific world to create new nature-culture hybrids such as genetically modified organisms. These developments are not circumscribed to Europe and America but have become widespread in different parts of the world, extending across increasingly porous North–South, West–East boundaries (see Anderson 2002; M. Fischer 2007, 2016; Prasad 2017).

2 Of course, as many historians and anthropologists have pointed out, many aspects of this transformation are not new, but its overall scale and scope is unprecedented (see Appadurai 1996, 2020).

3 See Figure 1.9, Sex Ratio at Birth 1982–2017, UNICEF, accessed December 20, 2020, www.unicef.cn/en/figure-19-sex-ratio-birth-19822017. There is broad agreement on the increasingly male-skewed nature of China's SRB by the turn of the millennium, but one needs to bear in mind that national statistics do not include millions of unregistered children. Thus the SRB for this period may have to be adjusted to account for a large number of unregistered girls who are "missing" not because of sex-selective abortion or infanticide, but because they were given for informal adoption and were not registered in *hukou* records (K. Johnson 2004, 2016; Y. Shi and Kennedy 2016).

4 In 2010 all provinces in China had a sex ratio at birth (SRB) higher than 110 males per 100 females except for Xinjiang, Tibet, Beijing, and possibly Shanghai. In six provinces (Hubei, Hunan, Jiangxi, Guangdong, Guangxi, and Guizhou), the SRB oscillated between 120 and 125, and in Anhui, Fujian, and Hainan provinces, it exceeded 125 (N. Feng 2011). There is also evidence of significant class variations across Han populations, with the very wealthy and the very poor having lower sex ratios at birth (Guilmoto and Ren 2011).

5 These genetic tests are banned in mainland China, as are genetic tests that allow sex screening prior to fertilization and implantation. These tests were developed in the late 1990s and were commercialized in the United States as a form of "family balancing" aimed at achieving a more equitable representation of both genders in a family, but in countries like China and India, some evidence suggests that these tests are also being used to realize the cultural ideal of son preference (Bhatia 2018).

6 For a critique, see for example Folbre 1994; Ehrenreich and Hochschild 2002; Carsten 2004; McKinnon and Cannell 2013; Frazer 2016; Bhattacharya 2017.

7 Beck, Giddens, and Lash 1994; Bauman 2001, 2003; Plummer 2003. See also Jamieson 1998 and Illouz 2007, 2012, for a feminist critical reading.

8 See, for example, Carsten 2000, 2004; Povinelli 2006; Godelier 2012; Donner 2008; Brandtstädter and Santos 2009; Donner and Santos 2016, Santos and Harrell 2017; Santos 2016, 2017a; Ahearn 2001; Wardlow 2006; Hirsch 2003; Hirsch and Wardlow 2006; Cole 2009, 2014; Cole and Thomas 2009; Archambault 2017.

9 The May Fourth Movement was an important cultural and political movement in the period between 1915 and 1921. Often referred to as the New Culture Movement, it is generally regarded as an important turning point in China's struggle against imperialism and feudalism. It was a kind of Enlightenment movement that focused on opposing China's old feudal culture and promoting a new culture based on the Western ideals of science and democracy for the sake of building a stronger modern Chinese nation. The movement's reformist spirit had a lasting impact on Chinese politics and culture for much of the twentieth century, and its influence remains strong in the twenty-first century.

10 See, for example, Farrer 2002, 2014; Hansen 2013, 2015; Hansen and Svarverud 2010; V. Fong 2004, 2007; Chao Yang 2017.

11 See also J. Zhang 2017a, 2019; J. Zhang and Sun 2014.

12 See, for example, L. Shi 2017a, 2017b; Evans 1997, 2008, 2017; Guilmoto and Ren 2011; Greenhalgh 2013.

13 See, for example, Farrer 2002, 2014; J. Zhang and Sun 2014; Jankowiak and Li 2017; Engebretsen 2017; Y. Yan 2003, 2006, 2009b, 2015b.

14 Burchell, Gordon, and Miller 1991; Rose 1996, 1999, 2007; Ferguson 1994; Ferguson and Gupta 2002; T. Li 2007; Sigley 2006; D. Bray and Jeffreys 2016; P. Miller and Rose 2008; Greenhalgh and Winckler 2005 ; Lancaster 2010. See also Ortner 2016 for an overview of anthropological approaches to neoliberal economic and governmental formations since the 1980s.

15 See, for example, Wajcman 1991, 2004; F. Fischer 2000, 2009; Bucchi 2009; Feenberg 2010; Eubanks 2017; Sternsdorff-Cisterna 2018.

16 For a critique of the private-public opposition, see for example Rapp and Ginsburg 1995; Carsten 2000, 2004; Yanagisako 2002; Friedman 2007; McKinnon and Cannell 2013; Gottschang 2018; Santos and Harrell 2017; Santos and Gottschang 2020. See also Folbre 1994; Zelizer 2005; Frazer 2016; Bhattacharya 2017.

17 Cowan 1983, 1987; Wajcman 1991, 2000, 2004, 2010, 2016; F. Bray 1997, 2007, 2008, 2009, 2013a, 2013b; Layne et al. 2010; Franklin 2010.

18 Laidlaw 2002, 2014; Mattingly 2012, 2014; Mattingly and Throop 2018; Robbins 2007, 2012, 2013; Faubion 2011; Lambek 2010; Keane 2016; Stafford 2013; Kleinman et al. 2011.

CHAPTER 1: HARMONY CAVE FAMILIES

1 This analytical privileging of cities and urban governance is particularly strong in studies of public policy, demography, and urban planning and development, but it also affects ethnographic studies of labor migrants and rural-urban migration. See, for example, Pun 2005; Jacka 2006; Gaetano and Jacka 2004; Ming 2013; Gaetano 2015; Choi and Peng 2016; Ling 2019; Zavoretti 2017. For examples of studies that take into account the perspective of village communities, see Chu 2010; Lai 2016; May 2010; Murphy 2002, 2020; Oxfeld 2004, 2010, 2014; H. Yan 2008.

2 Interview with Township Official 1, WeChat, June 30, 2018.

3 These figures are not based on official statistics. Local deity temple records are more reliable than official statistics. My figures are based on these records as well as conversations with villagers and village officials between 2013 and 2018. My household survey data from 1999 to 2000 shows a different population configuration. In 2000 Harmony First had a population of about 185 individuals, Harmony Second had about 90, and Harmony Third had about 100. In contrast, Harmony Fourth and Harmony Fifth had a population of about 185 and 100, respectively. See Village Household Survey 2001.

4 Almost all villages in Three Mountains are single-lineage communities with a single patronymic. Harmony Cave, Red Bamboo, New House, and Sand Island are all surnamed Chan, Barrier Pond is surnamed Ho, and Three Mountains is mostly surnamed Leung but has a residential hamlet surnamed Wong. On the

lineage village communities of Guangdong and South China, see Freedman 1958, 1966; J. Watson 1982; Santos 2004, 2006a.

5 Kipnis (2017) refers to these marriage customs as viricentric, rather than virilocal, because they no longer require the couple to set up their regular residence in the husband's village (see also Kipnis 2016).

6 See Harrell 1995, 1997 for more details on demographic and anthropological approaches to genealogical history and generational length.

7 See, for example, J. Watson 1975, 1982; R. Watson 1985; J. Watson and R. Watson 2004; S. Huang 1999; Z. Zheng 2001; Santos 2004, 2006a, 2008; Faure 2007; Baker 1968, 1979; Freedman 1958, 1966.

8 Elsewhere I have written in detail about the economic, demographic, technological, and environmental dimensions of the history of the village (Santos 2010, 2011). Here I focus on spatial mobility and sociality.

9 On the intricate ties between lineage branches and production teams, see the classic ethnographies by A. Chan, Madsen, and Unger 1992 and Potter and Potter 1990.

10 These terms are commonly used in Yellow Flower to classify village space, and this is linked to the fact that most local villages have a long history of continuous settlement that was shaped by processes of population growth and social-spatial differentiation. Most local villages have a core inner area that is said to be the place where the founding ancestors first settled. This inner area may coexist with one or several outer areas that developed later in the history of these villages. In the local Cantonese dialect, the inner area is also called "higher" or "upper area" because it is often situated in a location that is higher in terms of altitude than the outer areas. The other reason for the inner area to be called "higher" or "upper area" is that it is the place where the ancestors first settled, and for this reason, it occupies a more "upstream position" in the generational history of the village, hence it is more strongly associated with the higher-ups called village ancestors. One should be careful not to overstate the position of superiority of the inner area because of its proximity to ancestors. The relation between the inner area and the outer area is both complementary and hierarchical, and it is not always clear who is superior; it all depends on the context and the perspective.

11 This was one of the first achievements of China's modern agricultural research program. It preceded similar developments in Japan, India, and above all the Philippines, under the influence of the International Rice Research Institute, and it was part of a more general rice-farming Green Revolution in Asia (Santos 2010, 2011).

12 Repressive measures applying to all villagers included the enforcement of restrictions on family business activities, which intensified during the 1950s and 1960s with the move toward high socialism. But there were also repressive measures targeting Harmony First families. Many Harmony First families were classified with bad class labels such as "landlords" and "rich peasants" during the

class investigations of the 1950s, and this placed them in a highly disadvantageous position in the local economy.

13 See Aijmer 1980, 1986 and Potter 1968 for an account of similar satellite village communities among mainland Chinese vegetable gardeners working in the New Territories in Hong Kong in the 1960s and 1970s.

14 In the late 1990s, the overall rate of illiteracy for villagers of more than sixteen years old was still 64 percent, and about 70 percent of this adult illiterate population was female (Santos 2004, fig. 34).

15 This lack of spatial mobility in the pre-Communist period was not caused by foot binding, which was never really common in the Yellow Flower region. However, despite the low prevalence of foot binding, local women did not seem to move much beyond their village. My interviews with older villagers suggest that up until the 1970s and 1980s few village women ventured on their own on a regular basis to areas outside the territory of their village and brigade.

16 Interview with high-ranking township official, February 2015.

17 See Pun 2016 for an overview of labor migration in Reform-era China and J. Chan, Selden, and Pun 2020 for an account of the structures of exploitation shaping global chains of factory production in the Pearl River Delta area.

CHAPTER 2: LOVE AND MARRIAGE

1 I draw on the extended case method developed by Max Gluckman (1961) and the Manchester School of Social Anthropology. See also Michael Burawoy (1998) and Don Handelman (2005).

2 See Stacey 1983; M. Wolf 1985; Croll 1981; Hershatter 2011; Harrell and Santos 2017.

3 See White 2006; Greenhalgh 2008; Whyte, Wang, and Cai 2015; Harrell et al. 2011; Harrell and Santos 2017; Mellors 2019.

4 Full Elder Sister explained to me in January 2000 that local pre-1949 customs made it possible to nullify a marriage agreement, but this usually took place at a very early stage of the marriage. The modern practice of divorce was effectively introduced in rural China with the New Marriage Law of 1950, but it started to become more common only in the 1980s and 1990s under the influence of the Second Marriage Law of 1981. Divorce has become more common in the Harmony Cave region in the last decade, but it was still very rare back in the 1990s and the 2000s. If divorced, Full Elder Sister would probably have had to return to her natal village, where she would feel out of place. A better alternative would have been to marry again (and move into her new husband's community), but this would not have been easy, and there was also the question of her four children: who would keep them? Local custom tends to favor the male side regarding child custody.

5 On earlier technical procedures of sterilization, see Leo Orleans (1979).

6 See Greenhalgh 1994, 2008; Scharping 2003; Short et al. 2000; Nian et al. 2010.

7 See, for example, Robert Porter, Justin L. Kaplan, and Barbara P. Homeier, eds., 2009, *The Merck Manual Home Health Handbook* (Hoboken, NJ: John Wiley and Sons), 1604.

8 On Cantonese popular medical traditions, see Marjorie Topley (2011, pt. V).

9 This submission of eros to family and reproduction remains an important feature of the local ethical system, and although the younger generations today are constructing forms of sexuality decoupled from reproduction, there remains a strong taboo on talking openly about sexuality. For an interesting historical discussion of Chinese discourses of sexuality since 1949, see Evans 1997. Charlotte Furth (1994, 125–46) has noted the historical linkages between the rise of an ethical regime that submits eros to family and procreation and the ascendancy of neo-Confucianism in the fifteenth century.

10 In Harmony Cave, the first cases of (outgoing) brideprice payments reaching ¥10,000 (US$1,500) or more occurred in the late 1990s and the 2000s and involved families from the richer agnatic group of the village: Harmony First team. These brideprice payments were more expensive than the going rate of brideprice at the time because the matchmaking negotiations leading to these marriages did not follow the usual ritual procedures, and the family of the groom was willing to pay as much money as required to get things done quickly. The wife of Fortune Hero cost a brideprice of ¥10,000 (US$1,500) in 1999, the wife of Cassia Forest cost ¥12,000 (US$1,800) in 2000, and the wife of Fortune Country cost ¥15,000 (US$2,200) in 2002.

11 See Engebretsen 2017 and Y. Yan 2021 for an account of emerging forms of resistance to marriage heteronormativity in urban China.

12 For example, the wife of one of Bright Gold's close village brothers, Fortune Big, gave birth to nine daughters and had one midterm abortion (also of a daughter) before having a son. Unable to raise so many children, the parents ended up giving up four daughters for local adoption. Three daughters were given to families living in Yellow Flower; one was given to a family based in the neighboring township of Dragonpath. These local adoptions have gained increasing significance under the Birth Planning Policy because villagers have to find ways of hiding, concealing, and/or disguising "unplanned children." These adoptions usually entail the complete transfer of rights of custody to the family adopting the child, and these arrangements may or may not involve procedures of official registration or legalization, at least initially. In some cases, the family who gives the child for adoption wants to remain directly involved in the upbringing of the child—for example, by pledging to contribute to a share of the expenses of the child's formal education.

13 See, for example, Callon and Latour 1981; Callon 1986; Latour 1986; Law 1992.

CHAPTER 3: WOMEN AND CHILDBIRTH

1 See, for example, X. Liu et al. 2016; J. Liang et al. 2018; Owen and Razak 2019; News.China.com 2019. The NHFPC was responsible for the coordination of the

ten-year (2011–20) national plan for women's development, and one of the key goals of this plan was to curb cesarean section rates by means of a system of C-section quotas for public hospitals. The NHFPC was also responsible for implementing the WHO and United Nations Children's Fund (UNICEF)-guided Baby-Friendly Hospital Initiative. This initiative, first launched in 1991, was subject to various revisions over the years (WHO and UNICEF 1991, 2009, 2018), including provisions on promoting natural childbirth and gradually reducing nonmedical indications for cesarean section rates year by year. See Gottschang 2018 for a fascinating ethnography of the Baby-Friendly Hospital Initiative in China.

2 Other quantitative studies of rising cesarean rates include Klemetti et al. 2010; Mi and Liu 2014; X. Feng et al. 2012; Hellerstein et al. 2015, 2016; Z. He et al. 2016; Y. Zhang et al. 2017; X. Wang et al. 2017. Anthropologist Jun Zhang has acquired a large database from a major public hospital in the city of Guangzhou that points to an average cesarean rate of 38.5 percent between 2015 and 2017. This database includes detailed information on more than 30,000 deliveries taking place between January 2015 and April 2017. The parents of these babies are not necessarily Guangzhou natives, but at least one of the four addresses provided to the hospital (including contact address and address of household registration of both parents) is located in one of the city's ten administrative districts. The cesarean rate of this hospital between January 2015 and April 2017 oscillated between a minimum rate of 29 percent and a maximum rate of 39.7 percent. In April 2017 the cesarean rate was still as high as 39.6 percent (Santos and Zhang forthcoming).

3 I use the term "medicalization" to refer to the rise of scientific medicine as a major institution of social control as well as to the expansion of its jurisdiction to almost all aspects of daily life in the name of health (Lock 2004; Conrad 2007). This transformation has a long global history with very different trajectories depending on the context and the period. Some authors use the term "biomedicalization" to refer to the increasing technoscientization of biomedical practices and related public health interventions from the 1980s onward (Clarke 2010). Here I use the term "technocratic medicalization" to refer to the increasing power of biomedical expert discourses and technologies in everyday life practices and processes of governance (Davis-Floyd 1992, 1994). I argue that the shift to technocratic medicalization has started to become more visible globally during the 1970s and 1980s due to signficant technoscientific developments, the global flow of information via new digital technologies, and the increasing centrality of technoscientific institutions and capitalism.

4 See also Jordan 1978; Ehrenreich and English (1975) 2010; Oakley 1980, 1986; E. Martin 1987; Davis-Floyd 1992, 1994, 2017; Davis-Floyd and Sargent 1997.

5 See also Jordan 1978; Oakley 1980, 1986; Rapp and Ginsburg 1995; Oakley and Houd 2013; Davis-Floyd 1992, 1994, 2017; Davis-Floyd and Sargent 1997; Davis-Floyd and Cheyney 2019; Rothman 2007, 2016; Van Hollen 2003; Donner 2003, 2008; Clarke 2008; Brubaker and Dillaway 2009; McCourt 2009; Cosminsky

2016; Gottschang 2017, 2018, 2020; Santos 2020; Shirai 2016, 2020; Santos and Gottschang 2020.

6 Cowan 1983; Cockburn and Ormrod 1983; Cockburn 1985; F. Bray 1997, 2007; Rapp 1987, 1999; Wajcman 1991, 2004, 2016. See also, for example, Lerman et al. 2003; Franklin 2010; Layne et al. 2010. For useful reviews of the literature on gender and technology, see Bray 2007; Wajcman 2000, 2010.

7 The depiction of "traditional" midwives as obstacles to progress and reproductive modernity is a discourse that emerged during the May Fourth Movement period, but there is a long recorded history of imperial elite discourses referring to the skills of "traditional" lay midwives in a highly derogatory manner. As early as the sixteenth century, the expression "three nuns and six grannies" (SC: *sangu liupo*) was already widely used to refer to women with so-called disreputable professions such as midwives (Furth 1999).

8 See T. Johnson 2011; T. Johnson and Wu 2014; M. Li 2020.

9 See M. Li 2020; Yip 1992; T. Johnson 2011; T. Johnson and Wu 2014.

10 See Sidel 1973; Lucas 1982; T. Johnson and Wu 2014.

11 See Croll 1978, 245–46; Lucas 1982; Goldstein 1998; Hershatter 2007a, 2011, 154–81; Ahn 2013; Fang 2016. See also Mo 2016 for a fictional account.

12 The term "barefoot doctors" refers to health-care providers who underwent basic medical training and worked in rural villages in China.

13 Chinese concerns with birth control and population planning started well before the launching of the Birth Planning Policy (Harrell et al. 2011; Mellors 2019), but this policy was the first to enforce a medicalized system of birth quotas that defined the hospital as the normative location of childbirth for reasons of birth control.

14 Harvey and Buckley 2009; X. Feng et al. 2011; T. Johnson and Wu 2014; Cheung and Mander 2018.

15 Santos 2016; T. Johnson and Wu 2014; Fang 2016; Cheung and Mander 2018.

16 Harvey and Buckley 2009; Cheung and Mander 2018; Gottschang 2020.

17 Harris et al. 2009; X. Zhu et al. 2018; Harvey and Buckley 2009; Cheung 2009; Cheung and Pan 2011; Cheung and Mander 2018.

18 T. Johnson and Wu 2014; Cheung and Mander 2018; Harvey and Buckley 2009; X. Zhu et al. 2018; Cheung 2009.

19 T. Johnson and Wu 2014; Cheung and Mander 2018; X. Zhu et al. 2018; Cheung 2009; Ministry of Health, People's Republic of China 2011. The end of home births was celebrated in state media as a major achievement that prevented the horrors of midwife-assisted deliveries at home (see, for example, *People's Daily* 2002; News QQ 2005).

20 Ethnographers working in lineage village communities in Hong Kong in the 1970s noted the centrality of mothers-in-law in the provision of child care (see, for example, E. Johnson 1975, 233).

21 Researcher's field notes, September 2015.

22 The interviews quoted in this chapter are only a small sample of a much larger body of materials collected through longitudinal field research since 1999. In

addition to group discussion materials, my data includes field notes describing childbirth negotiations, as well as individual interview materials referring to the childbirth experiences of more than thirty-five village mothers of different generations. I also have interview materials referring to the biographical and professional trajectories of ten village midwives and three barefoot doctors of different generations, including village midwives and barefoot doctors who were trained before and during the Reform period.

23 Collective interview, Focus Group 1A, September 2015.

24 Collective interview, Focus Group 1B, September 2015.

25 Village Household Survey, Harmony Cave, 1950s–2010s.

26 Cowan 1983, 1987. See also Wajcman 1991, 2016.

27 Collective interview, Focus Group 2A, December 2016.

28 I never witnessed a young mother using an actual case to illustrate her point.

29 On the effects of the Birth Planning Policy on rural childbirth practices, see Greenhalgh 1994; Santos 2016.

30 On the natural birth movement, see Craven 2010; Rothman 2016; Davis-Floyd 2017; Davis-Floyd and Cheyney 2019. See also Shirai 2016, 2020 for the situation in Japan.

31 Individual interview, Saam-dai, September 2017. On the challenges of promoting less medicalized birth models in China, see, for example, Cheung, Mander, and Cheng 2005a, 2005b; X. Zhang 2010; Cheung and Pan 2011; Cheung and Mander 2018.

32 This is a reminder that "medicalization" and "medical pluralism" are not mutually exclusive. On medical pluralism, see Leslie 1976; Lock and Nichter 2002.

33 Ahn 2013; Goldstein 1998; Michaels 2014.

34 Hellerstein et al. 2016; E. Wang 2016, 2017; Santos 2020. In 2019 the central government announced a pilot program to introduce pharmacological pain-relief medication in public hospitals (see News.China.com 2019).

35 There are also cases of vaginal deliveries with forceps or vacuum extractors, but my sample does not include any such case. In China, rates of episiotomy in vaginal deliveries are very high, close to 100 percent in some hospitals (Harvey and Buckley 2009, 60). In June 2016, anthropologist Jun Zhang and I interviewed several medical doctors working in the city of Guangzhou, and our sources confirmed that rates of episiotomy in public hospitals are very high, well above 70 percent in most public hospitals. Performing episiotomy does not require the mother's consent, and the surgery is usually performed without the use of any anesthesia (interview with Medical Doctor 1, June 2016, Guangzhou).

36 Individual interview, Saam-dai, September 2017. See also Harvey and Buckley 2009, 62.

37 Elective prescheduled cesareans are more common among urban middle-class mothers, and one important factor leading to this phenomenon is the increasingly advanced age of primiparous women in urban contexts (S. Tang et al. 2006). Urban middle-class mothers often have their first birthing experience

when they are already in their thirties, and many doctors consider that "advanced age pregnant women" (SC: *gaoling chanfu*)—meaning "pregnant women over thirty"—are too old to handle the risks of a vaginal delivery. This perception of age as an objective biological limitation is widely shared by urban middle-class mothers and is an important factor shaping their willingness to undergo a prescheduled cesarean (Santos and Zhang forthcoming). These "structures of feeling" (Williams 1977) are very different from those constructed by rural mothers of Candy's generation. All rural mothers of this generation in my sample had their first birth experience when they were in their early and mid-twenties, and there is a strong sense that doing things otherwise would be unnatural. Rural mothers who favored an elective cesarean for a first birth were not concerned with the risks of age.

38 For a comparison with India, see Donner 2003, 2008; Van Hollen 2003.

39 Santos and Zhang forthcoming; Bogg et al. 2010; Cai et al. 1998. Cesarean births are covered, to various degrees, by either government health insurance schemes (SC: *gongfei yiliao*) or social health insurance schemes such as the Urban Employee Basic Medical Insurance Scheme (SC: *chengzhen zhigong jiben yiliao baoxian*) and the New Rural Cooperative Medical Insurance Scheme. Reimbursement is not guaranteed, but there is the possibility of applying for reimbursement, even though not every family is aware of this possibility and not every family is successful in handling the necessary paperwork to get reimbursed.

40 Individual interview, Mou-dai, June 2013; individual interview, Mou-dai, September 2015; collective interview, Focus Group 1A, September 2015.

41 One needs to make a distinction between maternal and infant mortality. Stories of late-term miscarriages or of young infants dying during childbirth or soon after childbirth appear quite frequently in my interview materials. By contrast, stories of mothers dying during childbirth are relatively rare. These materials suggest relatively low rates of childbirth-related maternal mortality in the 1970s and 1980s in rural northern Guangdong.

42 There is some evidence suggesting that "self-delivery" may have been more common in earlier periods of human history than previously acknowledged. For a provocative discussion, see Odent 2015.

43 Individual interview, June 2013; individual interview, September 2015.

44 Collective interview, Focus Group 1A, September 2015.

45 Greenhalgh 1994; Santos 2016. See also Greenhalgh and Winckler 2005.

46 See Santos 2016. For a comparative discussion, see Harrell et al. 2011. The most popular certified midwife in Yellow Flower told me that she assisted an average of about 800 to 1,000 deliveries per year in the 1980s (interview with Certified Midwife 1). This is an extraordinary amount of births. Martha Ballard, the celebrated New England midwife who wrote a diary recording her life and professional deambulations in the late 1700s and the early 1800s, performed a total of 816 deliveries between 1785 and 1812, or an average of 31.4 deliveries per year (see Ulrich 1991, intro.).

47 Mou-dai was not the only lay midwife operating in the vegetable garden allotments in Foshan and Guangzhou. There were many other lay midwives, and not all from the township of Yellow Flower.

48 For a critique of "magic-bullet approaches" in national and global public health agendas, see Biehl and Petryna 2013. For a critique of "magic-bullet approaches" in Chinese maternal and infant health-care agendas, see Gottschang 2018.

49 See, for example, Q. Wang 2011; Y. Chen 2013; Y. Zheng 2015; Lin and Zhou 2016; S. Jiang 2016; Ma 2016a, 2016b; X. Pan 2017.

50 See, for example, the following WeChat public accounts (all names in standard Chinese—see Glossary for translations): Liu Ma Luo Luo, Di Yi Fu Chan, Da J Xiao D, Dian Dian Jia De Tu Xiao Dou, Ding Xiang Ma Ma, Ba Ma Ying, Pei Yisheng, Guo Ma Xiu Lian Ji, and Xueqiu Mama.

51 See, for example, Sohu.com 2017; News.sina.com 2017; Toutiao.com 2017.

CHAPTER 4: GRANDPARENTS AND LABOR MIGRATION

1 On the notion of "sociotechnical ensembles" see the work of Wiebe Bijker (2010). My usage of this concept in connection to child rearing is inspired by the work of Wiebe Bijker (2010) and other science, technology, and society (STS) studies scholars such as Ruth Cowan (1983), Annemarie Mol (2008), and Annemarie Mol, Ingunn Moser, and Jeanette Pols (2015). This conceptualization is compatible with a well-established anthropological tradition developed from the 1950s onward that approaches child rearing in any given context as a collective endeavor that involves multiple actors, institutions, ideals, artifacts, and procedures well beyond the narrow confines of the nuclear family of daddy, mommy, and me (Mead and Wolfenstein 1955; Ward 1970; Topley 1974; E. Goody 1982; Stafford 1995; Rogoff 2003; Gottlieb 2009; Hrdy 2009; Constable 2018).

2 The ideal of the "patrilineal joint family" refers to a corporate vision of the family that includes a senior couple, their male children and spouses, and their grandchildren and even great-grandchildren. This ideal remains very salient in China, but it is not always achieved. Even historically, few patrilineal joint families were able to hold tight together. The joint family would eventually split into smaller conjugal units either in the same house or in separate houses, but these smaller units would maintain tight obligations to one another as an imagined joint family (Harrell n.d.; Cohen 1976; Skinner 1997, 2003; Santos 2009).

3 See Chinanews.com 2015. For a more detailed discussion, see Murphy 2020.

4 See, for example, Jing 2000; V. Fong 2004; Gottschang 2007, 2018; Kipnis 2009, 2011; Kuan 2015; Naftali 2016; Harrell and Santos 2017; Zhong 2019. On the rise of global ideologies of intensive parenting and mothering, see Ehrenreich and English 1979; Badinter 1981; Hardyment 1995; Hays 1996; Furedi 2002; Douglas and Michaels 2004; Warner 2006; Faircloth, Hoffman, and Layne 2013.

5 On grandparenting and multigenerational parenting in China see, for example, Goh 2011; Silverstein, Cong, and Li 2006, 2007; Z. Cong and Silverstein 2012; F. Chen and Liu 2012; F. Chen, Liu, and Mair 2011.

6 See the works of Francesca Bray (1997, 2013a), Gail Hershatter (2011), Jacob Eyferth (2009), and Hill Gates (2015) for a critique of the neglect of women's productive activities in standard accounts of late imperial China. F. Bray (1997, 270) suggests that this historiographical bias was probably shaped by "the Western cultural predilection for construing female identity in terms of biological reproduction and its control."

7 Santos 2008, 2011, 2013, 2016; Santos and Donzelli 2009. For similar processes in other parts of Guangdong, see also Potter and Potter 1990; Aijmer and Ho 2000; Ku 2003; Oxfeld 2010, 2017.

8 See also Silverstein, Cong, and Li 2006, 2007; Z. Cong and Silverstein 2012. Beyond rural areas, grandparents in China are widely regarded as a vital source of child-care support that allows the middle generation to find better ways of coping with the dual burden of work and family.

9 Chinese sociologist Yunkang Pan (2002) refers to this somewhat exploitative relationship of dependency as a phenomenon of "(treating the senior generation as) cows with inexhaustible milk, and (seeing themselves as) lambs that never grow up" (SC: *ji bu wan nai de niu, zhang bu da de gaoyang*).

10 For an account of increasing work-life balance tensions in China after the turn of the millennium, see Santos et al. 2021.

11 For a comparison with working-class mothers in Hong Kong in the 1990s, see D. Martin 1997.

12 See, for example, Yue et al. 2016, Yue et al. 2017; Chang et al. 2019. See Normile 2017 for a good summary of Rozelle's findings in *Science* magazine.

13 Goode 1963; Cowgill and Holmes 1972; Giddens 1991, 1992, 1999; Beck and Beck-Gernsheim 2002.

CHAPTER 5: FLUSH TOILETS

1 F. Bray 1984, 1986; King (1911) 2004; L. Zhou 2004; X. Du 2018.

2 F. Bray 1984, 289–98; L. Zhou 2004, 178–214; King (1911) 2004; X. Du 2018.

3 Xue 2005; Yu 2010; L. Zhou 2004, 180–85; X. Du 2018.

4 J. Zhu 1988; L. Zhou 2004; Rogaski 2004; Xue 2005; Yu 2010; Furth 2010; X. Huang 2016. See also Dong 2005 for a comparison with the situation in Taiwan under Japanese occupation.

5 On "socialist civilization," see, for example, Dynon 2008, 2014; Pieke 2016.

6 See also J. Zhu 1988; Srinivas 2002; Molotch 2003; Szczygiel 2016; Dong 2005; Dombroski 2015; Kawa 2016.

7 To make sense of these large-scale civilizational tensions, I draw theoretically on traditions initiated by Marcel Mauss ([1929] 1969, 1950, 2006) and Norbert Elias ([1939] 1994) to reconnect with what the historian Fernand Braudel ([1979] 1992) famously called "material civilization" (see also F. Bray 1997). Like Braudel, I use this concept as a corrective to approaches that focus only on the ideational dimensions of civilizational processes, and in contrast to official party ideologies of "socialist civilization" (Dynon 2008, 2014), I do not believe that it is

productive to develop clear-cut distinctions between "material civilization" and "spiritual civilization," because all civilizational processes are simultaneously material and ideational.

8 See Lili Lai (2016) for an account of a similar transformation in southern Henan.

9 These manual water pumps became popular in the 1980s with the marketization of borehole well technologies for household usage. Before these nonautomated water supply technologies became widely available, most local households did not have their own individual water supply, but got groundwater from communal wells using a rope and bucket (see X. Wu 2008).

10 Electricity and gas are considered expensive in rural China.

11 A Bourdieusian analysis of the intersections between local toilet practices and social stratification would reveal the exact extent of these internal variations (see Sterne 2003).

12 Rockefeller 1996; George 2008; Black and Fawcett 2008; Jewitt 2011.

13 Rockefeller 1996; George 2008; Black and Fawcett 2008; Dombroski 2015; Kawa 2016. See also Hope Ngo, 2020, "How Hong Kong Cleaned Up Its Toxic Harbor," BBC Future Planet, accessed December 18, 2020. www.bbc.com/future/article/20200629-the-toxic-past-of-hong-kongs-iconic-victoria-harbour.

14 Lemonnier 1992, 1993; F. Bray 1997, n.d. Elsewhere I have tried to integrate this anthropological tradition with the study of changes in patterns of human-environment relations (Santos 2011). Here I am not concerned with these linkages between technology and ecology, sociotechnical ensembles and ecological systems.

15 See, for example, Mackenzie and Wajcman 1999; Bijker et al. 2012; Bijker and Law 1992; Latour 1996, 2005.

16 Mauss and Durkheim 1969; Mauss (1929) 1969, 2006. See also Febvre (1930) 1973; Schlanger 2006; Arnason 2010.

17 This dualistic ideology is based on official socialist narratives of civilizational progress calling for the need to promote a harmonious relationship between developments in "material civilization" (meaning material and economic development) and developments in "spiritual civilization" (meaning good socialist values); Dynon 2008.

18 See Santos 2011, Dombroski 2015, and Kawa 2016 for a reappraisal of such alternative models of human waste management.

CHAPTER 6: POPULAR RELIGION

1 "Popular religion" in the Chinese context refers to a composite religious system including rituals of the Confucian, Buddhist, and Daoist traditions in local practices of ancestor worship and deity cults with local shamanistic traditions and with various mantic systems for reading landscape, faces, hands, and times (Feuchtwang 2001). The term "popular religion" has been criticized for its elitist connotations (Lagerwey 2010, 153), but the term is useful for capturing a large number of ritual practices that are neither recognized by the central government

as an official religion nor organized under an institutionalized religious organization. Such ritual practices are not circumscribed to the countryside but are particularly salient and visible in rural areas (X. Li 2001; Feuchtwang 2001; Goossaert 2004; Goossaert and Palmer 2011; I. Johnson 2017).

2 The anthropological literature on China's contemporary moral landscape emphasizes these growing tensions and contradictions (Stafford 2013; Hsu and Madsen 2019; Madsen 2020; Y. Yan 2021), revealing a mixed picture of negative developments (X. Liu 2000; Y. Yan 2009a, 2010, 2012, 2015b, 2018; Osburg 2013, 2018) and other more positive developments (Ku 2003; Oxfeld 2004, 2017; Jankowiak 2004; Fleischer 2009, 2018).

3 Research in the cognitive sciences contests the conventional philosophical view of moral reasoning as a rule-following activity based on universal laws (M. Johnson 1995; Harris 2000, 2012), suggesting that moral reasoning involves constructive activities that rely to a large extent on the human cognitive capacity for imagination. Moral reasoning is a constructive imaginative activity because it uses imaginatively structured concepts and because it requires imagination to discern what is morally relevant in situations, to understand empathetically how others experience things, and to envision alternative courses of action in a particular case.

4 Faubion 2011; Das 2007; Fassin 2012, 2014; Laidlaw 1995, 2002, 2014; Keane 2016; Lambek 2010; Lambek et al. 2015; Robbins 2007, 2012, 2013; Mattingly 2012, 2014; Mattingly and Throop 2018; Kleinman et al. 2011; Stafford 2013.

5 See, for example, Mauss (1925) 2016, 1950, 2006; Malinowski 1965a, 1965b; Lévi-Strauss (1976) 1983, 1982.

6 One of the first articulations of the notion of "socialist spiritual civilization" is a letter written in 1980 by the vice president of the Chinese Academy of Sciences (C. Li 1980).

7 Siu 1990; Dean 2003; X. Li 2001; Tam 2006; Lagerwey 2010, 95–152; Aijmer and Ho 2000, 187–236.

8 Present-day Jiao ritual practices in the Yellow Flower region display many elements explicitly associated with Buddhist and shamanist traditions (Tam 2006; Tan and Zeng 2010). The rituals are complex and their performance usually unfolds simultaneously in two separate altars: the "civil altar" (C: *man-taan*) inside the temple's main building and the "military altar" (C: *mou-taan*) set on a temporary bamboo shelter outside. Village folks often refer to these altars as the "muttering altar" and the "dancing altar," respectively, because most performances in the first altar entail Buddhist recitations and most performances in the second altar include Daoist rites and shamanic acts of various kinds, including theatrical dances *en travesti* (men in female roles). In addition to what goes on inside these two altars, a few acrobatic shows (fire walking, climbing knife ladders) take place outdoors at different times during the festivities.

9 The reason why local Jiao rituals are called "Jiao for the Population" is not clear. Although it is tempting to link this designation to the increasing salience of "population" in Chinese political rhetoric, this linkage is not warranted, because

the designation was already in use during the pre-Communist period. In all likelihood, the designation is linked to the region's long-standing concerns with epidemics and population health.

10 Since then, four other major Jiao festivals took place: 2004, 2009, 2014, and 2018. Jiao festivals are usually held in the autumn, soon after the second rice harvest of the local double rice-cropping cycle.

11 The leader of this committee was a charismatic retired civil servant from Harmony Cave (he also presided over the Jiao festivals of 2004, 2009, 2014, and 2018). Another Harmony Cave villager led the Jiao festivals of 1989 and 1994, but his mounting gambling debts in the late 1990s forced him to flee the township just before his death in 2000.

12 These ritual contests are open ascending-price auctions, like those described by James Laidlaw (1995, 334–45, 349–53) for an urban Jain community in northwest India, in which participants bid openly against one another, with each subsequent bid higher than the previous bid; the auctioning of each written word ends when no participant is willing to bid further, at which point the highest bidder is declared as the winner of the contest.

13 The Confucian tradition, for example, is well known for its active role in the cultivation of the sacredness of the written word, and this emphasis has led it to promote "associations for cherishing written words" (SC: *xizi hui*) in the late imperial period (Liang 1994). The Daoist and Buddhist traditions are also well known for their active role in the cultivation of the art of calligraphy (Goossaert 2004).

14 French anthropologist Pierre Bourdieu (1992) has analyzed such processes of ritual institution of symbolic power. Here I am highlighting the important role played by material culture and technical procedures in rites of institution.

15 This is a reminder of the continuing existence in Guangdong of an unofficial vernacular writing tradition whose origins go back to the late imperial period (Snow 2004).

16 The overwhelming majority of the present adult literate population in Harmony Cave and surrounding villages has attained literacy only at the primary-school level. In 2001, 29 percent of all adult males of Harmony Cave were still illiterate. Moreover, the average level of education among literate males was low: more than 60 percent had not moved beyond elementary school, and a mere 8 percent had reached senior high school (none had reached university).

17 See also Puett 2015 for a remarkably clear summary of this ethical tradition.

REFERENCES

Abu-Lughod, Lila. 1990. "The Romance of Resistance: Tracing Transformations of Power through Bedouin Women." *American Ethnologist* 17 (1): 41–55.

ACWF (All China Women's Federation). 2013. "Woguo nongcun liushou ertong, chengxiang liudong ertong zhuangkuang yanjiu baogao" (Research report on the situation of left-behind children and migrant children in the Chinese countryside). *Zhongguo Funü Xinwen* (China Women's News). Accessed February 6, 2016. http://acwf.people.com.cn/n/2013/0510/c99013-21437965.html.

Ahearn, Laura. 2001. *Invitations to Love: Literacy, Love Letters, and Social Change in Nepal.* Ann Arbor: University of Michigan Press.

Ahn, Byungil. 2013. "Reinventing Scientific Medicine for the Socialist Republic: The Soviet Psycho-Prophylactic Method of Delivery in 1950s China." *Twentieth Century China* 38 (2): 139–55.

Aijmer, Goran. 1980. *Economic Man in Shatin: Vegetable Gardeners in a Hong Kong Valley.* London: Curzon Press.

———. 1986. *Atomistic Society in Sha Tin: Immigrants in a Hong Kong Valley.* Gothenburg: Acta Universitatis Gothoburgensis.

Aijmer, Goran, and Virgil K. Y. Ho. 2000. *Cantonese Society in a Time of Change.* Hong Kong: Chinese University Press.

Althusser, Louis. 1971. *Lenin and Philosophy and Other Essays.* New York: Monthly Review Press.

Anderson, Warwick. 2002. "Postcolonial Technoscience." *Social Studies of Science* 32:643–58.

Andrews, Bridie, and Mary Brown Bullock. 2014. *Medical Transitions in Twentieth-Century China.* Bloomington: Indiana University Press.

Appadurai, Arjun. 1996. *Modernity at Large: Cultural Dimensions of Globalization.* Minneapolis: University of Minnesota Press.

———. 2013. *The Future as Cultural Fact: Essays on the Global Condition*. London: Verso.

———. 2020. "Globalization and the Rush to History." *Global Perspectives* 1 (1): 11656.

Archambault, Julie Soleil. 2017. *Mobile Secrets: Youth, Intimacy and the Politics of Pretense in Mozambique*. Chicago: University of Chicago Press.

Arnason, Johann P. 2010. "Domains and Perspectives of Civilizational Analysis." *European Journal of Social Theory* 13, no. 1 (February 1): 5–13.

Attané, Isabel. 2012. "Being a Woman in China Today: A Demography of Gender." *China Perspectives* 4:5–15.

Attias-Donfut, Claudine, and Martine Segalen. 1998. *Grand-parents: La Famille à Travers les Generations*. Paris: Odile Jacob.

———. 2002. "The Construction of Grandparenthood." *Current Sociology* 50:281–94.

Babiarz, Kimberly S., Karen Eggleston, Grant Miller, and Qiong Zhang. 2015. "An Exploration of China's Mortality Decline under Mao: A Provincial Analysis, 1950–80." *Population Studies (Camb)* 69 (1): 39–56.

Badinter, Elisabeth. 1981. *The Myth of Motherhood: A Historical View of the Maternal Instinct*. London: Souvenir Press.

Baker, Hugh D. R. 1968. *Chinese Lineage Village: Sheung Shui*. Stanford, CA: Stanford University Press.

———. 1979. *Chinese Family and Kinship*. London: Macmillan.

Bauman, Zygmunt. 2001. *The Individualized Society*. Cambridge: Polity Press.

———. 2003. *Liquid Love: On the Frailty of Human Bonds*. Cambridge: Polity Press.

Beck, Ulrich. 1992. *Risk Society: Towards a New Modernity*. London: Sage.

———. 2009. *World at Risk*. Cambridge: Polity Press.

———. 2016. *The Metamorphosis of the World*. Cambridge: Polity Press.

Beck, Ulrich, and Elisabeth Beck-Gernsheim. 1995. *The Normal Chaos of Love*. London: Polity Press.

———. 2002. *Individualization: Institutionalized Individualism and Its Social and Political Consequences*. London: Sage.

———. 2013. *Distant Love*. Cambridge: Polity Press.

Beck, Ulrich, Anthony Giddens, and Scott Lash. 1994. *Reflexive Modernization: Politics, Tradition and Aesthetics in the Modern Social Order*. Stanford, CA: Stanford University Press.

Berlin, Isaiah. (1953) 2013. *The Hedgehog and the Fox*. Princeton, NJ: Princeton University Press.

Bétran, Ana P., et al. 2016. "The Increasing Trend in Caesarean Section Rates: Global, Regional and National Estimates: 1990–2014." *PLoS One* 11 (2): e0148343.

Bhatia, Rajani. 2018. *Gender before Birth. Sex Selection in a Transnational Context*. Seattle: University of Washington Press.

Bhattacharya, Tithi, ed. 2017. *Social Reproduction Theory: Remapping Class, Recentering Oppression*. Chicago: University of Chicago Press.

Biehl, João, and Adriana Petryna. 2013. "Critical Global Health." In *When People Come First: Critical Studies in Global Health*, edited by João Biehl and Adriana Petryna, 1–20. Princeton, NJ: Princeton University Press.

Bijker, Wiebe E. 2010. "How Is Technology Made? That Is the Question!" *Cambridge Journal of Economics* 34 (1): 63–76.

Bijker, Wiebe E., et al., eds. 2012. *The Social Construction of Technological Systems: New Directions in the Sociology and History of Technology*. Anniversary ed. Cambridge, MA: MIT Press.

Bijker, Wiebe E., and John Law, eds. 1992. *Shaping Technology/Building Society: Studies in Sociotechnical Change*. Cambridge, MA: MIT Press.

Black, Maggie, and Ben Fawcett. 2008. *The Last Taboo: Opening the Door on the Global Sanitation Crisis*. London: Earthscan.

Blumenthal, David, and Michael Hsiao. 2005. "Privatization and Its Discontents: The Evolving Chinese Health Care System." *New England Journal of Medicine* 353 (11): 1165–70.

———. 2015. "Lessons from the East: China's Rapidly Evolving Health Care System." *New England Journal of Medicine* 372 (14): 1281–85.

Boellstorff, Tom. 2015. *Coming of Age in Second Life: An Anthropologist Explores the Virtually Human*. 2nd ed. Princeton, NJ: Princeton University Press.

Bogg, Lennart, et al. 2010. "Dramatic Increase of Cesarean Deliveries in the Midst of Health Reforms in Rural China." *Social Science and Medicine* 70 (10): 1544–49.

Bourdieu, Pierre. 1977. *Outline of a Theory of Practice*. New York: Cambridge University Press.

———. 1979. *Algeria 1960: "The Disenchantment of the World," "The Sense of Honour," "The Kabyle House or the World Reversed."* New York: Cambridge University Press.

———. 1980. *Le Sens Pratique*. Paris: Les Editions de Minuit.

———. 1992. *Language and Symbolic Power*. Cambridge, MA: Polity Press.

———. 1993. *The Field of Cultural Production: Essays on Art and Literature*. New York: Columbia University Press.

———. 1998. *Practical Reason. On the Theory of Action*. Stanford, CA: Stanford University Press.

———. 2002. *Masculine Domination*. Stanford, CA: Stanford University Press.

———. 2013. *Algerian Sketches*. Cambridge. MA: Polity Press.

Bourdieu, Pierre, and Abdelmalek Sayad. 1964. *Le Deracinement: La Crise de l'Agriculture en Algerie*. Paris: Les Editions de Minuit.

Brackbill, Yvonne, June Rice, and Diony Young. 1984. *Birth Trap: The Legal Low-down on High-Tech Obstetrics*. St. Louis, MO: C. V. Mosby.

Brandtstädter, Susanne. 2003. "With Elias in China: 'Civilizing Process,' Local Restorations and Power in Contemporary Rural China." *Anthropological Theory* 3 (1): 87–105.

Brandtstädter, Susanne, and Gonçalo Santos, eds. 2009. *Chinese Kinship: Contemporary Anthropological Perspectives*. London: Routledge.

Braudel, Fernand. (1979) 1992. *The Structures of Everyday Life: The Limits of the Possible*. Berkeley: University of California Press.

Bray, David, and Elaine Jeffreys, eds. 2016. *New Mentalities of Government in China*. New York: Routledge.

Bray, Francesca. 1984. *Science and Civilization in China: Volume 6, Biology and Biological Technology, Part 2, Agriculture*. Cambridge, UK: Cambridge University Press.

———. 1986. *The Rice Economies: Technology and Development in Asian Societies*. Berkeley: University of California Press.

———. 1997. *Technology and Gender: Fabrics of Power in Late Imperial China*. Berkeley: University of California Press.

———. 2007. "Gender and Technology." *Annual Review Anthropology* 36:37–53.

———. 2008. "Constructing Intimacy: Technology, Family and Gender in East Asia." *East Asian Science, Technology and Society* 2 (2): 151–65.

———. 2009. "Becoming a Mother in Late Imperial China: Maternal Doubles and the Ambiguities of Fertility." In *Chinese Kinship: Contemporary Anthropological Perspectives*, edited by Susanne Brandtstädter and Gonçalo Santos, 181–203. London: Routledge.

———. 2013a. *Technology, Gender and History in Imperial China: Great Transformations Reconsidered*. New York: Routledge.

———. 2013b. "Tools for Virtuous Action: Technology, Skills and Ordinary Ethics." In *Ordinary Ethics in China Today*, edited by Charles Stafford, 175–93. LSE Monographs on Social Anthropology. London: Bloomsbury.

———. n.d. "American Modern: The Foundation of Western Civilization." Accessed December 26, 2020. www.anth.ucsb.edu/faculty/bray/toilet/.

Brown, Melissa. 2017. "Dutiful Help: Masking Rural Women's Economic Contributions." In *Transforming Patriarchy: Chinese Families in the Twenty-First Century*, edited by Gonçalo Santos and Stevan Harrell, 39–58. Seattle: University of Washington Press.

Brubaker, Sarah Jane, and Heather E. Dillaway. 2009. "Medicalization, Natural Childbirth and Birthing Experiences." *Sociology Compass* 3 (1): 31–48.

Bucchi, Massimiano. 2009. *Beyond Technocracy: Science, Politics, and Citizens*. Dordrecht, Netherlands: Springer.

Burawoy, Michael. 1998. "The Extended Case Method." *Sociological Theory* 16 (1): 4–33.

Burchell, Graham, Colin Gordon, and Peter Miller, eds. 1991. *The Foucault Effect: Studies in Governmentality*. Chicago: University of Chicago Press.

Cai, Wen-Wei, James Marks, Charles Chen, You-Xien Zhuang, Leo Morris, and Jeffrey Harris. 1998. "Increased Cesarean Section Rates and Emerging Patterns of Health Insurance in Shanghai, China." *American Journal of Public Health* 88 (5): 777–80.

Cai, Yong. 2013. "China's New Demographic Reality: Learning from the 2010 Census." *Population and Development Review* 39 (3): 371–96.

Callahan, William. 2013. *China Dreams: 20 Visions of the Future*. Oxford: Oxford University Press.

Callon, Michel. 1986. "Some Elements of a Sociology of Translation: Domestication of the Scallops and the Fishermen of St Brieuc Bay." In *Power, Action and Belief: A New Sociology of Knowledge?* edited by John Law, 196–223. London: Routledge.

Callon, Michel, and Bruno Latour. 1981. "Unscrewing the Big Leviathan, or How Actors Macrostructure Reality, and How Sociologists Help Them to Do So?" In *Advances in Social Theory and Methodology*, edited by K. Knorr-Cetina and A. Cicourel, 277–303. London: Routledge and Kegan Paul.

Cao, Cong, and Richard P. Suttmeier. 2017. "Challenges of S&T System Reform in China." *Science* 355 (6329): 1019–21.

Carsten, Janet, ed. 2000. *Cultures of Relatedness: New Approaches to the Study of Kinship*. Cambridge, UK: Cambridge University Press.

Carsten, Janet. 2004. *After Kinship*. Cambridge, UK: Cambridge University Press.

Chan Lineage Association. 2010. "Written Genealogy of CHAN Yeung-mun." Manuscript, author's personal collection.

Chan, Anita, Richard Madsen, and Jonathan Unger. 1992. *Chen Village under Mao and Deng*. Expanded and updated ed. Berkeley: University of California Press.

Chan, Jenny, Mark Selden, and Pun Ngai. 2020. *Dying for an iPhone: Apple, Foxconn and the Lives of China's Workers*. London: Pluto Press.

Chan, Kam Wing. 2010. "The Household Registration System and Migrant Labor in China: Notes on a Debate." *Population and Development Review* 36 (2): 357–64.

Chan, Selina C. 2011. "Cultural Governance and Place-Making in Taiwan and China." *China Quarterly* 206:372–90.

Chan, Selina C., and Graham Lang. 2015. *Building Temples in China: Memories, Tourism, and Identities*. Abingdon, UK: Routledge.

Chang, Fang, et al. 2019. "Understanding the Situation of China's Left-Behind Children: A Mixed-Methods Analysis." *Developing Economies* 57 (1): 3–35.

Chen, Feinian, and Guangya Liu. 2012. "The Health Implications of Grandparents Caring for Grandchildren in China." *Journals of Gerontology Series B: Psychological Sciences and Social Sciences* 67 (1): 99–112.

Chen, Feinian, Guangya Liu, and Christine A. Mair. 2011. "Intergenerational Ties in Context: Grandparents Caring for Grandchildren in China." *Social Forces* 90 (2): 571–94.

Chen, Hu, et al. 2017. "Household Biogas CDM Project Development in Rural China." *Renewable and Sustainable Energy Reviews* 67:184–91.

Chen, Meixuan. 2013. "'Eating Huaqiao' and the Left Behind: The Moral Socioeconomic Consequences of the Return of Overseas Chinese to a South China Village." PhD diss., Department of Anthropology, University College London.

Chen, Yongmei. 2013. *Anchan, Zuo Yuezi, Xinshenger Huli Yibentong* (*Safe Birth, Postnatal Confinement, Infant Care Comprehensive Manual*). Beijing: Zhongguo Nongye Chubanshe.

Cheung, Ngai Fen. 2009. "Chinese Midwifery: The History and Modernity." *Midwifery* 25:228–41.

Cheung, Ngai Fen, and Rosemary Mander. 2018. *Midwifery in China*. London: Routledge.

Cheung, Ngai Fen, Rosemary Mander, and Linan Cheng. 2005a. "The 'Doula-Midwives' in Shanghai." *Evidence-Based Midwifery* 3 (2): 73–79.

———. 2005b. "'Informed Choice' in the Context of Caesarean Decision-making in China." *Evidence-Based Midwifery* 3 (1): 33–38.

Cheung, Ngai Fen, and Anshi Pan. 2011. "The Challenge of Promoting Normality and Midwifery in China." In *Promoting Normal Birth: Research, Reflections, and Guidelines*, edited by Sylvie Donna, 190–203. Chester-le-Street, UK: Fresh Heart Publishing.

Chinanews.com. 2015. "Baipishu cheng Zhongguo jin qianwan liushou ertong 'yiniandaotou jianbudao ba ma'" (White paper says China's close to ten million left-behind children go a full year without seeing their parents). June 18. Accessed July 22, 2015. www.chinanews.com/gn/2015/06-18/7353603.shtml.

Choi, Susanne Y. P., and Yinni Peng. 2016. *Masculine Compromise: Migration, Family, and Gender in China*. Berkeley: University of California Press.

Chu, Julie Y. 2010. *Cosmologies of Credit: Transnational Mobility and the Politics of Destination in China*. Durham, NC: Duke University Press.

Chun, Lin. 2006. *The Transformation of Chinese Socialism*. Durham, NC: Duke University Press.

———. 2013. *China and Global Capitalism: Reflections on Marxism, History, and Contemporary Politics*. New York: Palgrave Macmillan.

Clarke, Adele. 2008. "Introduction: Gender and Reproductive Technologies in East Asia." *East Asian Science, Technology, and Society* 2:303–26.

———. 2010. "Epilogue: Thoughts on Biomedicalization in Its Traditional Travels." In *Biomedicalization: Technoscience, Health, and Illness in the U.S.*, edited by Adele E. Clarke, Laura Mamo, Jennifer Ruth Fosket, Jennifer R. Fishman, and Janet K. Shim, 380–406. Durham, NC: Duke University Press.

Clifford, James. 1988. *The Predicament of Culture: Twentieth-Century Ethnography, Literature, and Art*. Cambridge, MA: Harvard University Press.

Cockburn, Cynthia. 1985. *Machinery of Dominance: Women, Men and Technical Know-How*. London: Pluto Press.

Cockburn, Cynthia, and Susan Ormrod. 1983. *Gender and Technology in the Making*. London: Sage.

Cohen, Myron L. 1976. *House United, House Divided: The Chinese Family in Taiwan*. New York: Columbia University Press.

Cole, Jennifer. 2009. "Love, Money and Economies of Intimacy in Tamatave Madagascar." In *Love in Africa*, edited by Jennifer Cole and Lynn Thomas, 109–34. Chicago: University of Chicago Press.

———. 2014. "Working Mis/understandings: The Tangled Relationship between Kinship, Franco-Malagasy Bi-national Marriage and the French State." *Cultural Anthropology* 29 (3): 527–51.

Cole, Jennifer, and Lynn Thomas, eds. 2009. *Love in Africa*. Chicago: University of Chicago Press.

Cong, Yali. 2004. "Doctor-Family-Patient Relationship: The Chinese Paradigm of Informed Consent." *Journal of Medicine and Philosophy* 29 (2): 149–78.

Cong, Zhen, and Merril Silverstein. 2012. "Custodial Grandparents and Intergenerational Support in Rural China." In *Experiencing Grandparenthood: An Asian Perspective*, edited by Kalyani K. Mehta and Leng Leng Thang, 109–28. Dordrecht, Netherlands: Springer.

Connelly, Matthew. 2008. *Fatal Misconception: The Struggle to Control World Population*. Cambridge, MA: Harvard University Press.

Conrad, Peter. 2007. *The Medicalization of Society: On the Transformation of Human Conditions into Treatable Disorders*. Baltimore: John Hopkins University Press.

Constable, Nicole. 2009. "The Commodification of Intimacy: Marriage, Sex, and Reproductive Labor." *Annual Review of Anthropology* 38:49–64.

———. 2018. "Assemblages and Affect: Migrant Mothers and the Varieties of Absent Children." *Global Networks* 18 (1): 168–85.

Cosminsky, Sheila. 2016. *Midwives and Mothers: The Medicalization of Childbirth on a Guatemalan Plantation*. Berkeley: University of California Press.

Cowan, Ruth Schwarz. 1983. *More Work for Mother: The Ironies of Household Technology from the Open Hearth to the Microwave*. New York: Basic Books.

———. 1987. "The Consumption Junction: A Proposal for Research Strategies in the Sociology of Technology." In *The Social Construction of Technological Systems: New Directions in the Sociology and History of Technology*, edited by Wiebe E. Bijker, Thomas P. Hughes, and Trevor J. Pinch, 261–80. Cambridge, MA: MIT Press.

Cowgill, Donald O., and Lowell D. Holmes, eds. 1972. *Aging and Modernization*. New York: Appleton-Century-Crofts.

Craven, Christa. 2010. *Pushing for Midwives: Homebirth Mothers and the Reproductive Rights Movement*. Philadelphia: Temple University Press.

Croll, Elisabeth J. 1978. *Feminism and Socialism in China*. London: Routledge and Kegan Paul.

———. 1981. *The Politics of Marriage in Contemporary China*. Cambridge, UK: Cambridge University Press.

———. 2006. "The Intergenerational Contract in the Changing Asian Family." *Oxford Development Studies* 34 (4): 473–91.

Dant, Tim. 2006. "Materiality and Civilization: Things and Society." *British Journal of Sociology* 57 (2): 289–308.

Das, Veena. 2007. *Life and Words: Violence and Descent into the Ordinary*. Berkeley: University of California Press.

Davis, Deborah, 2014a. "On the Limits of Personal Autonomy: PRC Law and the Institution of Marriage." In *Wives, Husbands, and Lovers: Marriage and Sexuality in Hong Kong, Taiwan, and Urban China*, edited by Deborah Davis and Sara Friedman, 41–61. Stanford, CA: Stanford University Press.

———. 2014b. "Privatization of Marriage in Post-Socialist China." *Modern China* 40 (6): 551–77.

Davis, Deborah, and Sara Friedman, eds. 2014. *Wives, Husbands, and Lovers: Marriage and Sexuality in Hong Kong, Taiwan, and Urban China*. Stanford, CA: Stanford University Press.

Davis-Floyd, Robbie E. 1992. *Birth as an American Rite of Passage*. Berkeley: University of California Press.

———. 1994. "The Technocratic Body: American Childbirth as Cultural Expression." *Social Science and Medicine* 38:1125–40.

———. 2017. *Ways of Knowing about Birth: Mothers, Midwives, Medicine, and Birth Activism*. Long Grove, IL: Waveland Press.

Davis-Floyd, Robbie E., and Melissa Cheyney, eds. 2019. *Birth in Eight Cultures*. Long Grove, IL: Waveland Press.

Davis-Floyd, Robbie E., and Carolyn F. Sargent, eds. 1997. *Childbirth and Authoritative Knowledge: Cross-Cultural Perspectives*. Berkeley: University of California Press.

Dean, Kenneth. 2003. "Local Communal Religion in Contemporary South-East China." *China Quarterly* 174 (1): 338–58.

Dombroski, Kelly. 2015. "Multiplying Possibilities: A Postdevelopment Approach to Hygiene and Sanitation in Northwest China." *Asia Pacific Viewpoint* 56 (3): 321–44.

Dong, Yiqiu. 2005. *Diguo yu Biansuo: Rizhi Shiqi Taiwan Biansuo Xingjian ji Wuwu Chuli (Empire and Toilets: Construction of Toilets and Sewage Treatment in Taiwan under the Japanese)*. Taipei: Taiwan Guji Chuban Youxian Gongsi.

Donner, Henrike. 2003. "The Place of Birth: Childbearing and Kinship in Calcutta Middle-Class Families." *Medical Anthropology* 22 (4): 303–41.

———. 2008. *Domestic Goddesses: Maternity, Globalization and Middle-Class Identity in Contemporary India*. Farnham, UK: Ashgate.

Donner, Henrike, and Gonçalo Santos. 2016. "Love, Marriage, and Intimate Citizenship in Contemporary China and India: An Introduction." *Modern Asian Studies* 50 (4): 1123–46.

Douglas, Susan, and Meredith Michaels. 2004. *The Mommy Myth: The Idealization of Motherhood and How It Has Undermined Women*. New York: Simon and Schuster.

Drucker, Donna J. 2020. *Contraception: A Concise History*. Cambridge, MA: MIT Press.

Du, Fenglian, and Xiao-yuan Dong. 2013. "Women's Employment and Child Care Choices in Urban China during the Economic Transition." *Economic Development and Cultural Change* 62 (1): 131–55.

Du, Xinhao. 2018. *Jinzhi: Zhongguo Chuantong Feiliao Zhishi yu Jishu Shijian Yanjiu (10–19 Shiji) (Golden Juice: Research on Chinese Traditional Fertilizer Knowledge and Techniques in Practice [10th–19th Centuries])*. Beijing: Zhongguo Nongye Kexue Jishu Chubanshe.

Duan, Chenrong, and Ge Yang. 2008. "The Situation of the Left-Behind Children in Rural China" (Woguo Nongcun Liu shou Ertong Zhuang kuang Yan Jiu). *Population Research (Ren Kou Yan Jiu)* 32 (3): 15–25.

Duara, Prasenjit. 2001. "The Discourse of Civilization .and PanAsianism." *Journal of World History* 12 (1): 99–130.

Durkheim, Emile. 1895. "Revue critique: L'Origine du mariage dans l'espèce humaine, d'après Westermarck." *Revue Philosophique* 40:606–23.

———. 1898. "Review of Ernest Grosse, Die Formen der Familie und die Formen der Wirthschaft." *Année Sociologique* 1:319–32.

———. 1900. "Review of C.-V. Starke, La famille dans les différentes sociétés, Paris: Giard et Brière, 1899." *Année Sociologique* 3:365–70.

———. 1921. "La famille conjugale." *Revue Philosophique* 90:1–14.

Dynon, Nicholas. 2008. "'Four Civilizations' and the Evolution of Post-Mao Chinese Socialist Ideology." *China Journal* 60:83–109.

———. 2014. "Civilisation-State: Modernising the Past to Civilise the Future in Jiang Zemin's China." *China: An International Journal* 12 (1): 22–42.

Ehrenreich, Barbara, and Deirdre English. (1975) 2010. *Witches, Midwives, and Nurses: A History of Women Healers.* 2nd ed. New York: Feminist Press.

———. 1979. *For Her Own Good: 150 Years of the Experts' Advice to Women.* New York: Anchor Books.

Ehrenreich, Barbara, and Arlie Hochschild, eds. 2002. *Global Woman: Nannies, Maids, and Sex Workers in the New Economy.* New York: Henry Holt.

Eisenstadt, Shmuel N. 2003. *Comparative Civilizations and Multiple Modernities.* Leiden: Brill.

Elias, Norbert. (1939) 1994. *The Civilizing Process.* Oxford: Blackwell.

Engebretsen, Elisabeth. 2017. "Under Pressure: Lesbian-Gay Contract Marriages and Their Patriarchal Bargains." In *Transforming Patriarchy. Chinese Families in the Twenty-First Century,* edited by Gonçalo Santos and Stevan Harrell, 163–81. Seattle: University of Washington Press.

Escobar, Arturo. 2018. *Designs for the Pluriverse: Radical Interdependence, Autonomy, and the Making of Worlds.* Durham, NC: Duke University Press.

———. 2020. *Pluriversal Politics: The Real and the Possible.* Durham, NC: Duke University Press.

Eubanks, Virginia. 2017. *Automating Inequality: How High-Tech Tools Profile, Police, and Punish the Poor.* New York: St. Martins Press.

Evans, Harriet. 1997. *Women and Sexuality in China.* Cambridge: Polity Press.

———. 2008. *The Subject of Gender: Daughters and Mothers in Urban China.* Lanham, MD: Rowman and Littlefield.

———. 2017. "Patriarchal Investments: Expectations of Male Authority and Support in a Poor Beijing Neighborhood." In *Transforming Patriarchy: Chinese Families in the Twenty-First Century,* edited by Gonçalo Santos and Stevan Harrell, 182–99. Seattle: University of Washington Press.

Eyferth, Jacob. 2009. *Eating Rice from Bamboo Roots: The Social History of a Community of Handicraft Papermakers in Rural Sichuan, 1920–2000.* Harvard East Asian Monographs, Cambridge, MA.

Faircloth, Charlotte, Diane M. Hoffman, and Linda L. Layne, eds. 2013. *Parenting in Global Perspective: Negotiating Ideologies of Kinship, Self and Politics.* Abingdon, UK: Routledge.

Fang, Xiaoping. 2016. "Bamboo Steamers and Red Flags: Building Discipline and Collegiality among China's Traditional Rural Midwives in the 1950s." Manuscript presented at SHOT in Asia Conference, Singapore.

FAO. 1977. *China: Recycling of Organic Wastes in Agriculture.* Rome: UN Food and Agriculture Organization.

Farrer, James. 2002. *Opening Up: Youth Sex Culture and Market Reform in Shanghai.* Chicago: University of Chicago Press.

———. 2014. "Love, Sex, and Commitment: Delinking Premarital Intimacy from Marriage in Urban China." In *Wives, Husbands, and Lovers: Marriage and Sexuality in Hong Kong, Taiwan, and Urban China*, edited by Deborah S. Davis and Sara L. Friedman, 62–96. Stanford, CA: Stanford University Press.

Fassin, Didier, ed. 2012. *A Companion to Moral Anthropology.* Chichester, UK: Wiley-Blackwell.

Fassin, Didier. 2014. "The Ethical Turn in Anthropology: Promises and Uncertainties." *HAU: Journal of Ethnographic Theory* 4 (1): 429–35.

Faubion, James. 2011. *An Anthropology of Ethics.* Cambridge, UK: Cambridge University Press.

Faure, David. 2007. *Emperor and Ancestor: State and Lineage in South China.* Stanford, CA: Stanford University Press.

Febvre, Lucien. (1930) 1973. "Civilisation: Evolution of a Word and a Group of Ideas." In *A New Kind of History and Other Essays*, edited by Peter Burke, 219–57. New York: Harper and Row.

Feenberg, Andrew. 2010. *Between Reason and Experience: Essays in Technology and Modernity.* Cambridge, MA: MIT Press.

Fei, Xiaotong. 1939. *Peasant Life in China: A Field Study of Country Life in the Yangtze Valley.* London: G. Routledge.

———. 1948. *Xiangtu Zhongguo (Earthbound China).* Shanghai: Guancha She.

———. 1992. *From the Soil: The Foundations of Chinese Society.* Berkeley: University of California Press (English translation of *Xiangtu Zhongguo*).

Fei, Xiaotong, and Chang Chih-I. 1945. *Earthbound China: A Study of Rural Economy in Yunnan.* Chicago: University of Chicago Press.

Feng, Nailin. 2011. *Zhongguo 2010 Nian Renkou Pucha Ziliao* (Materials from the 2010 Population Census of the People's Republic of China). Beijing: China Statistics Press.

Feng, Xinglin, Ling Xu, Yan Guo, and Carine Ronsmans. 2011. "Socioeconomic Inequalities in Hospital Births in China between 1988 and 2008." *Bulletin of World Health Organization* 89 (6): 432–41.

———. 2012. "Factors Influencing Rising Caesarean Section Rates in China between 1988 and 2008." *Bulletin of the World Health Organization* 90 (1): 30–39.

Ferguson, James. 1994. *The Anti-politics Machine: Development, Depoliticization, and Bureaucratic Power in Lesotho.* Minneapolis: University of Minnesota Press.

———. 2011. "Novelty and Method. Reflections on Global Fieldwork." In *Multi-Sited Ethnography: Problems and Possibilities in the Translocation of Research Methods*, edited by Simon Coleman and Pauline Von Hellerman, 194–207. London: Routledge.

Ferguson, James, and Akhil Gupta. 2002. "Spatializing States: Toward an Ethnography of Neoliberal Governmentality." *American Ethnologist* 29 (4): 981–1002.

Feuchtwang, Stephan. 2001. *Popular Religion in China.* London: Curzon Press.

Fischer, Frank. 2000. *Citizens, Experts, and the Environment: The Politics of Local Knowledge*. Durham, NC: Duke University Press.

———. 2009. *Democracy and Expertise: Reorienting Policy Inquiry*. Oxford, UK: Oxford: University Press.

Fischer, Michael. 2007. "Four Genealogies for a Recombinant Anthropology of Science and Technology." *Cultural Anthropology* 22 (4): 539–615.

———. 2016. "Anthropological STS in Asia." *Annual Review of Anthropology* 45:181–98.

Fleischer, Friederike. 2009. *Between Technology of Self and Technology of Power: The Volunteer Phenomenon in Guangzhou, China*. Max Planck Institute for Social Anthropology, Working Paper 11, Halle (Saale), Germany.

———. 2018. *Soup, Love, and a "Helping Hand": Social Relations and Support in Guangzhou, China*. New York: Berghahn Books.

Folbre, Nancy. 1994. *Who Pays for the Kids? Gender and the Structures of Constraint*. London: Routledge.

Fong, Mei. 2016. *One Child: The Story of China's Most Radical Experiment*. Boston: Houghton Mifflin Harcourt.

Fong, Vanessa. 2004. *Only Hope: Coming of Age Under China's One-Child Policy*. Stanford, CA: Stanford University Press.

———. 2007. "Parent-Child Communication Problems and the Perceived Inadequacies of Chinese Only-Children." *Ethos* 35:85–127.

Foucault, Michel. 1977. *Discipline and Punish: The Birth of the Prison*. New York: Random House.

———. 1978. *The History of Sexuality. Volume 1, An Introduction*. New York: Random House.

———. 1979. *Microfísica do Poder*. Rio de Janeiro: Edições Graal.

———. 1988. "Technologies of the Self." In *Technologies of the Self: A Seminar with Michel Foucault*, edited by Luther H. Martin, Huck Gutman, and Patrick H. Hutton, 16-49. Amherst: University of Massachusetts Press.

———. 1991. "Governmentality." In *The Foucault Effect: Studies in Governmentality*, edited by Graham Burchell, Colin Gordon, and Peter Miller, 87–104. Chicago: University of Chicago Press.

———. 2009. *Security, Territory, Population: Lectures at the Collège de France 1977–1978*. New York: Picador.

Franklin, Sarah. 2010. "Revisiting Reprotech: Firestone and the Question of Technology." In *Further Adventures of the Dialectic of Sex: Critical Essays on Shulamith Firestone*, edited by Mandy Merck and Stella Sandford, 29–60. New York: Palgrave Macmillan.

Frazer, Nancy. 2016. "Contradictions of Capital and Care." *New Left Review* 100:99–117.

Freedman, Maurice. 1958. *Lineage Organisation in South-Eastern China*. London: Athlone Press.

———. 1966. *Chinese Lineage and Society: Fukien and Kwangtung*. London: Athlone Press.

Friedman, Sara. 2004. "Embodying Civility: Civilizing Processes and Symbolic Citizenship in Southeastern China." *Journal of Asian Studies* 63 (3): 687–718.

———. 2007. *Intimate Politics: Marriage, the Market, and State Power in South-Eastern China.* Cambridge, MA: Harvard University Asia Center.

Furedi, Frank. 2002. *Paranoid Parenting: Why Ignoring the Experts May Be Best for Your Child.* Chicago: Chicago Review Press.

Furth, Charlotte. 1987. "Concepts of Pregnancy, Childbirth, and Infancy in Ch'ing Dynasty China." *Journal of Asian Studies* 46 (1): 7–35.

———. 1994. "Rethinking Van Gulik: Sexuality and Reproduction in Traditional Chinese Medicine." In *Engendering China: Women, Culture, and the State*, edited by Christina K. Gilmartin, Gail Hershatter, Lisa Rofel, and Tyrene White. Cambridge, MA: Harvard University Press.

———. 1999. *A Flourishing Yin: Gender in China's Medical History: 960–1665.* Berkeley: University of California Press.

———. 2010. "Hygienic Modernity in Chinese East Asia." In *Health and Hygiene in Chinese East Asia: Policies and Publics in the Long Twentieth Century*, edited by C. Furth and A. Leung, 1–23. Durham, NC: Duke University Press.

Gaetano, Arianne. 2015. *Out to Work: Migration, Gender, and the Changing Lives of Rural Women in Contemporary China.* Honolulu: University of Hawai'i Press.

Gaetano, Arianne, and Tamara Jacka, eds. 2004. *On the Move: Women and Rural-to-Urban Migration in Contemporary China.* New York: Columbia University Press.

Gammeltoft, Tine. 2014. *Haunting Images: A Cultural Account of Selective Reproduction in Vietnam.* Berkeley: University of California Press.

Gates, Hill. 2015. *Footbinding and Women's Labor in Sichuan.* Abingdon, UK: Routledge.

Geertz, Clifford, 1973. "Deep Play: Notes on the Balinese Cockfight." In *The Interpretation of Cultures*, by Clifford Geertz, 412–53. London: Fontana Press.

Gell, Alfred. 1988. "Technology and Magic." *Anthropology Today* 4 (2): 6–9.

George, Rose. 2008. *The Big Necessity: The Unmentionable World of Human Waste and Why It Matters.* New York: Holt.

Giddens, Anthony. 1991. *Modernity and Self-Identity: Self and Society in the Late Modern Age.* Stanford, CA: Stanford University Press.

———. 1992. *The Transformation of Intimacy: Sexuality, Love, and Eroticism in Modern Societies.* Cambridge, MA: Polity Press.

———. 1999. *Runaway World: How Globalization Is Reshaping Our Lives.* London: Profile Books.

Gluckman, Max. 1961. "Ethnographic Data in British Social Anthropology." *Sociological Review* 9, no. 1, 5–17.

Godelier, Maurice. 2012. *The Metamorphoses of Kinship.* London: Verso.

Goh, Esther. 2011. *China's One-Child Policy and Multiple Caregiving: Raising Little Suns.* Abingdon, UK: Taylor and Francis.

Goldstein, Joshua. 1998. "Scissors, Surveys, and Psycho-Prophylactics: Prenatal Health Care Campaigns and State Building in China, 1949–1954." *Journal of Historical Sociology* 11 (2): 153–84.

Goode, William. 1963. *World Revolution and Family Patterns*. New York: Free Press.

Goody, Esther N. 1982. *Parenthood and Social Reproduction: Fostering and Occupational Roles in West Africa*. Cambridge, UK: Cambridge University Press.

Goody, Jack. 2006. *The Theft of History*. Cambridge, UK: Cambridge University Press.

Goossaert, Vincent. 2004. *Dans les Temples de la Chine: Histoires des Cultes, Vie des Communautés*. Paris: Albin Michel.

Goossaert, Vincent, and David Palmer. 2011. *The Religious Question in Modern China*. Chicago: University of Chicago Press.

Gottlieb, Alma. 2009. "Who Minds the Baby? Beng Perspectives on Mothers, Neighbours, and Strangers as Caretakers." In *Substitute Parents: Biological and Social Perspective on Alloparenting across Human Societies*, edited by Gillian Bentley and Ruth Mace, 115–38. New York: Berghahn Books.

Gottschang, Suzanne. 2007. "Maternal Bodies, Breast-Feeding, and Consumer Desire in Urban China." *Medical Anthropology Quarterly* 21:64–80.

———. 2017. "Taking Patriarchy Out of Postpartum Recovery?" In *Transforming Patriarchy: Chinese Families in the Twenty-First Century*, edited by Gonçalo Santos and Stevan Harrell, 201–18. Seattle: University of Washington Press.

———. 2018. *Formulas for Motherhood in a Chinese Hospital*. Ann Arbor: University of Michigan Press.

———. 2020. "Reproductive Modernities in Policy: Maternal Mortality, Midwives, and Cesarean Sections in China, 1900s–2000s." *Technology and Culture* 61 (2): 617–44.

Gow, Michael. 2017. "The Core Socialist Values of the Chinese Dream: Towards a Chinese Integral State." *Critical Asian Studies* 49 (1): 91–116.

Greenhalgh, Susan. 1988. "Fertility as Mobility: Sinic Transitions." *Population and Development Review* 14 (4): 629–74.

———. 1994. "Controlling Births and Bodies in Village China." *American Ethnologist* 21 (1): 1–30.

———. 2003. "Science, Modernity, and the Making of China's One-Child Policy." *Population and Development Review* 29 (2): 163–96.

———. 2008. *Just One Child: Science and Policy in Deng's China*. Berkeley: University of California Press.

———. 2010. *Cultivating Global Citizens: Population in the Rise of China*. The Edwin O. Reischauer Lectures 2008. Cambridge, MA: Harvard University Press.

———. 2013. "Patriarchal Demographics? China's Sex Ratio Reconsidered." *Population and Development Review* 38:130–49.

———. 2020. "Introduction: Governing through Science; The Anthropology of Science and Technology in Contemporary China." In *Can Science and Technology Save China?* edited by Susan Greenhalgh and Li Zhang, 1–24. Ithaca, NY: Cornell University Press.

Greenhalgh, Susan, and Edwin A. Winckler. 2005. *Governing China's Population: From Leninist to Neoliberal Biopolitics*. Stanford, CA: Stanford University Press.

Greenhalgh, Susan, and Li Zhang, eds. 2020. *Can Science and Technology Save China? Utopian Dreams, Dystopian Realities*. Ithaca, NY: Cornell University Press.

Guilmoto, Christophe Z., and Qiang Ren. 2011. "Socio-economic Differentials in Birth Masculinity in China." *Development and Change* 42 (5): 1269–96.

Gupta, Akhil, and James Ferguson. 1992. "Beyond 'Culture': Space, Identity, and the Politics of Difference." *Cultural Anthropology* 7 (1): 6–23.

Handelman, Don. 2005. "The Extended Case: Interactional Foundations and Prospective Dimensions." *Social Analysis* 49 (3): 61–84.

Hansen, Mette Halskov. 2013. "Learning Individualism: Hesse, Confucius, and Pep-Rallies in a Chinese Rural High School." *China Quarterly*, no. 213, 60–77.

———. 2015. *Educating the Chinese Individual: Life in a Rural High School*. Seattle: University of Washington Press.

Hansen, Mette Halskov, and Rune Svarverud, eds. 2010. *iChina: The Rise of the Individual in Modern Chinese Society*. Copenhagen: Nordic Institute of Asian Studies Press.

Hardyment, Christina. 1995. *Perfect Parents. Baby-Care Advice Past and Present*. Oxford: Oxford University Press.

Harrell, Stevan. 1995. "Introduction." In *Cultural Encounters on China's Ethnic Frontiers*, edited by Stevan Harrell, 3–36. Seattle: University of Washington Press.

———. 1997. *Human Families*. Boulder, CO: Westview Press.

———. 2020. "From Conquest of Nature to Ecological Civilization: Development, Revolution, and Science in Chinese Communist Party Ideology." Unpublished manuscript presented at Sci-Tech Asia Virtual Seminar, November 11. https://scitechasia.org/?p=1034.

———. n.d. "Patriliny, Patriarchy, Patrimony: Surface Features and Deep Structures in the Chinese Family System." Manuscript, available at author's web page. https://faculty.washington.edu/stevehar/PPP.html.

Harrell, Stevan, and Gonçalo Santos. 2017. "Introduction." In *Transforming Patriarchy: Chinese Families in the Twenty-First Century*, edited by Gonçalo Santos and Stevan Harrell, 3–36. Seattle: University of Washington Press.

Harrell, Stevan, Wang Yuesheng, Han Hua, Gonçalo Santos, and Zhou Yingying. 2011. "Fertility Decline in Rural China: A Comparative Analysis." *Journal of Family History* 36 (1): 15–36.

Harris, Amanda, Suzanne Belton, Lesley Barclay, and Jenny Fenwick. 2009. "Midwives in China: 'Jie sheng po' to 'zhu chan shi'." *Midwifery* 25 (2): 203–12.

Harris, Paul. 2000. *The Work of Imagination*. Chichester, UK: Wiley-Blackwell.

———. 2012. *Trusting What You're Told: How Children Learn from Others*. Cambridge, MA: Harvard University Press.

Harvey, Travis A., and Lila Buckley. 2009. "Childbirth in China." In *Childbirth across Cultures. Ideas and Practices of Pregnancy, Childbirth and the Postpartum*, edited by Helaine Selin and Pamela K. Stone, 55–69. New York: Springer.

Hays, Sharon. 1996. *The Cultural Contradictions of Motherhood*. New Haven, CT: Yale University Press.

He, Zhifei, Zhaohui Cheng, Tailai Wu, Yan Zhou, Junguo Chen, Qian Fu, and Zhanchun Feng. 2016. "The Costs and Their Determinant of Cesarean Section and Vaginal Delivery: An Exploratory Study in Chongqing Municipality, China." *BioMed Research International*, https://doi.org/10.1155/2016/5685261.

Hecht, Gabrielle. 1998. *The Radiance of France: Nuclear Power and National Identity after World War II*. Cambridge, MA: MIT Press.

Hellerstein, Susan, Sarah Feldman, and Tao Duan. 2015. "China's 50% Caesarean Delivery Rate: Is It Too High?" *BJOG: An International Journal of Obstetrics and Gynaecology* 122 (2): 160–64.

———. 2016. "Survey of Obstetric Care and Cesarean Delivery Rates in Shanghai, China." *Birth Issues in Perinatal Care* 43 (3): 193–99.

Hershatter, Gail. 2007a. "Birthing Stories: Rural Midwives in 1950s China." In *Dilemmas of Victory: The Early Years of the People's Republic of China*, edited by Jeremy Brown and Paul G. Pickowicz, 337–58. Cambridge, MA: Harvard University Press.

———. 2007b. *Women in China's Long Twentieth Century*. Berkeley: University of California Press.

———. 2011. *The Gender of Memory: Rural Women and China's Collective Past*. Berkeley: University of California Press.

Herzfeld, Michael. (1997) 2016. *Cultural Intimacy: Social Poetics and the Real Life of States, Societies, and Institutions*. 3rd ed. London: Routledge.

Hirsch, Jennifer. 2003. *Courtship after Marriage: Sexuality and Love in Mexican Transnational Families*. Berkeley: University of California Press.

Hirsch, Jennifer, and Holly Wardlow, eds. 2006. *Modern Loves: The Anthropology of Romantic Courtship and Companionate Marriage*. Ann Arbor: University of Michigan Press.

Hornborg, Alf. 2019. *Nature, Society, and Justice in the Anthropocene: Unraveling the Money-Energy-Technology Complex*. Cambridge, UK: Cambridge University Press.

Hrdy, Sarah. 2009. *Mothers and Others: The Evolutionary Origins of Mutual Understanding*. Cambridge, MA: Belknap Press of Harvard University Press.

Hsu, Becky Yang, and Richard Madsen, eds. 2019. *The Chinese Pursuit of Happiness: Anxieties, Hopes, and Moral Tensions in Everyday Life*. Berkeley: University of California Press.

Huang, Shuping. 1999. *Guangdong Zuqun yu Quyu Wenhua Yanjiu*. (*Research on Guangdong Regional Ethnic Culture*). Guangzhou: Guangdong Gaodeng Jiaoyu Chubanshe.

Huang, Xuelei. 2016. "Deodorizing China: Odour, Ordure, and Colonial (Dis)order in Shanghai, 1840s–1940s." *Modern Asian Studies* 50 (3): 1092–122.

Hui, Yuk. 2016. *The Question Concerning Technology in China: An Essay in Cosmotechnics*. Falmouth, UK: Urbanomic Media.

Ikels, Charlotte. 1996. *The Return of the God of Wealth: The Transition to a Market Economy in Urban China*. Stanford, CA: Stanford University Press.

Illouz, Eva. 2007. *Cold Intimacies. The Making of Emotional Capitalism*. Cambridge, MA: Polity Press.

———. 2012. *Why Love Hurts: A Sociological Explanation*. Cambridge, MA: Polity Press.

Jacka, Tamara. 2006. *Rural Women in Urban China: Gender, Migration, and Social Change*. Armonk, NY: M. E. Sharpe.

Jacques, Martin. 2009. *When China Rules the World*. London: Penguin.

Jamieson, Lynn. 1998. *Intimacy: Personal Relationships in Modern Societies*. Cambridge, MA: Polity Press.

Jankowiak, William. 1995. "Love and Passion in Chinese Society." In *Romantic Passion: The Universal Emotion?* edited by William Jankowiak. New York: Columbia University Press.

———. 2004. "Market Reforms, Nationalism and the Expansion of Urban China's Moral Horizon." *Urban Anthropology and Studies of Cultural Systems and World Economic Development* 33:167–210.

———. 2016. *Family Life in China*. London: Polity Press.

Jankowiak, William, and Li Xuan. 2017. "Emergent Conjugal Love, Mutual Affection, and Female Marital Power." In *Transformations of Chinese Patriarchy: Contemporary Anthropological Perspectives*, edited by Gonçalo Santos and Stevan Harrell, 146–62. Seattle: University of Washington Press.

Jasanoff, Sheila, ed. 2004. *States of Knowledge: The Co-production of Science and Social Order*. New York: Routledge.

———. 2016. *The Ethics of Invention. Technology and the Human Future*. New York: W. W. Norton.

Jewitt, Sarah. 2011. "Geographies of Shit: Spatial and Temporal Variations in Attitudes towards Human Waste." *Progress in Human Geography* 35 (5): 608–26.

Jiang, Quanbao, Qun Yu, Shucai Yang, and Jesús J. Sánchez-Barricarte. 2017. "Changes in Sex Ratio at Birth in China: A Decomposition by Birth Order." *Journal of Biosocial Science* 49 (6): 826–841. https://doi.org/10.1017/S0021932016000547.

Jiang, Shuqing. 2016. *Hao Xin Qing Bei Yun. (Good Mood for Pregnancy)*. Nanjing: Yilin Chubanshe.

Jing, Jun, ed. 2000. *Feeding China's Little Emperors: Food, Children, and Social Change*. Stanford, CA: Stanford University Press.

Johnson, Elisabeth. 1975. "Women and Childbearing in Kwan Mun Hau Village: A Study of Social Change." In *Women in Chinese Society*, edited by Margery Wolf and Roxanne Witke, 215–42 Stanford, CA: Stanford University Press.

Johnson, Ian. 2017. *The Souls of China. The Return of Religion After Mao*. New York: Penguin.

Johnson, Kay Ann. 2004. *Wanting a Daughter, Needing a Son: Abandonment, Adoption, and Orphanage Care in China*. St. Paul, MN: Yeong and Yeong Book Co.

———. 2016. *China's Hidden Children: Abandonment, Adoption, and the Human Costs of the One-Child Policy*. Chicago: University of Chicago Press.

Johnson, Mark. 1995. *Moral Imagination: Implications of Cognitive Science for Ethics*. Chicago: University of Chicago Press.

Johnson, Tina Phillips. 2011. *Childbirth in Republican China: Delivering Modernity.* Lanham, MD: Lexington Books.

Johnson, Tina Phillips, and Yi-Li Wu. 2014. "Maternal and Child Health in Nineteenth- to Twenty-First-Century China." In *Medical Transitions in Twentieth-Century China*, edited by Bridie Andrews and Mary Brown Bullock, 51–68. Bloomington: Indiana University Press.

Jordan, Brigitte. 1978. *Birth in Four Cultures: A Crosscultural Investigation of Childbirth in Yucatan, Holland, Sweden, and the United States.* Montreal: Eden Press Women's Publications.

Kandiyoti, Deniz. 1988. "Bargaining with Patriarchy." *Gender and Society* 2 (3): 274–90.

Kappa, Seno. 2011. *Kuishi Cesuo (Taking a Peep at Toilets).* Beijing: Sanlian Shudian.

Kawa, Nicholas. 2016. "What Happens When We Flush?" *Anthropology Now* 8 (2): 34–43.

Keane, Webb. 2016. *Ethical Life: Its Natural and Social Histories.* Princeton, NJ: Princeton University Press.

King, Franklin H. (1911) 2004. *Farmers of Forty Centuries: Organic Farming in China, Korea, and Japan.* Mineola, NY: Dover.

Kipnis, Andrew. 2006. "Suzhi: A Keyword Approach." *China Quarterly* 186:295–313.

———. 2009. "Education and the Governing of Child-Centered Relatedness." In *Chinese Kinship. Contemporary Anthropological Perspectives*, edited by Susanne Brandtstädter and Gonçalo Santos, 204–22. London: Routledge.

———. 2011. *Governing Educational Desire: Culture, Politics, and Schooling in China.* Chicago: University of Chicago Press.

———. 2016. *From Village to City: Social Transformation in a Chinese County Seat.* Chicago: University of Chicago Press.

———. 2017. "Urbanisation and the Transformation of Kinship Practice in Shandong." In *Transforming Patriarchy. Chinese Families in the Twenty-First Century*, edited by Gonçalo Santos and Stevan Harrell, 113–28. Seattle: University of Washington Press.

Kleinman, Arthur, et al. 2011. *Deep China: The Moral Life of the Person.* Berkeley: University of California Press.

Klemetti, Reija, et al. 2010. "Cesarean Section Delivery among Primiparous Women in Rural China: An Emerging Epidemic." *American Journal of Obstetrics and Gynecology* 202 (1): 65.e1–6.

Kohrman, Matthew. 2005. *Bodies of Difference: Experiences of Disability and Institutional Advocacy in the Making of Modern China.* Stanford, CA: Stanford University Press.

Ku, Hok Bun. 2003. *Moral Politics in a South Chinese Village: Responsibility, Reciprocity and Resistance.* Lanham, MD: Rowman and Littlefield.

Kuan, Teresa. 2015. *Love's Uncertainty: The Politics and Ethics of Child Rearing in Contemporary China.* Berkeley: University of California Press.

Kubat, Aleksandra. 2018. "Morality as Legitimacy under Xi Jinping: The Political Functionality of Traditional Culture for the Chinese Communist Party." *Journal of Current Chinese Affairs* 47 (3): 47–86.

Lagerwey, John. 2010. *China: A Religious State*. Hong Kong: Hong Kong University Press.

Lai, Lili. 2016. *Hygiene, Sociality, and Culture in Contemporary Rural China: The Uncanny New Village*. Amsterdam: Amsterdam University Press.

Laidlaw, James. 1995. *Riches and Renunciation: Religion, Economy, and Society among the Jains*. Oxford: Clarendon Press.

———. 2002. "For an Anthropology of Ethics and Freedom." *Journal of the Royal Anthropological Institute* 8 (2): 311–32.

———. 2014. *The Subject of Virtue: An Anthropology of Ethics and Freedom*. Cambridge, UK: Cambridge University Press.

Lamanna, Mary Ann. 2002. *Emile Durkheim on the Family*. London: Sage.

Lambek, Michael. 2010. "Introduction." In *Ordinary Ethics: Anthropology, Language and Action*, edited by Michael Lambek, 1–36. New York: Fordham University Press.

Lambek, Michael, Veena Das, Didier Fassin, and Webb Keane. 2015. *Four Lectures on Ethics: Anthropological Perspectives*. Chicago: Hau Books.

Lancaster, Roger N. 2010. "Republic of Fear: The Rise of Punitive Governance in America." In *The Insecure American: How We Got Here and What We Should Do About It*, edited by Hugh Gusterson and Catherine Besteman, 63-76. Berkeley: University of California Press.

Laporte, Dominique. 2010. *History of Shit*. Cambridge, MA: MIT Press.

Latour, Bruno. 1986. "The Powers of Association." In *Power, Action and Belief*, edited by John Law, 264–80. London: Routledge.

———. 1987. *Science in Action*. Cambridge, MA: Harvard University Press.

———. 1994. "On Technical Mediation." *Common Knowledge* 3 (2): 29–64.

———. 1996. *Aramis, or the Love of Technology*. Cambridge, MA: Harvard University Press.

———. 2005. *Reassembling the Social: An Introduction to Actor-Network-Theory*. London: Oxford University Press.

Law, John. 1992. "Notes on the Theory of the Actor-Network: Ordering, Strategy and Heterogeneity." *Systems Practice* 5:379–93.

Law, Pui-lam, and Peng Yinni. 2006. "The Use of Mobile Phones among Migrant Workers in Southern China." In *New Technologies in Global Societies*, edited by Pui-Lam Law, Leopoldina Fortunati, and Shanhua Yang, 245–25. Singapore: World Scientific.

———. 2008. "Mobile Networks: Migrant Workers in Southern China." In *Handbook of Mobile Communication Studies*, edited by James E. Katz, 55–64. Cambridge, MA: MIT Press.

Layne, Linda, Sharra Vostral, and Kate Boyer, eds. 2010. *Feminist Technology*. Urbana: University of Illinois Press.

Lemonnier, Pierre. 1992. *Elements for an Anthropology of Technology*. Ann Arbor: Museum of Anthropology, University of Michigan.

Lemonnier, Pierre, ed. 1993. *Technological Choices: Transformation in Material Cultures since the Neolithic*. London: Routledge.

Lerman, Nina, Arwen Mohun, and Ruth Oldenziel, eds. 2003. *Gender and Technology: A Reader.* Baltimore: John Hopkins University Press.

Leslie, Charles, ed. 1976. *Asian Medical Systems.* Berkeley: University of California Press.

Lévi-Strauss, Claude. (1976) 1983. "The Scope of Anthropology [1960]." In *Structural Anthropology*, vol. 2, by Claude Lévi-Strauss, 3–32. Chicago: University of Chicago Press.

———. 1982. *The Way of the Masks.* Seattle: University of Washington Press.

Li, Chang. 1980. "'Building Socialist Spiritual civilization,' Letter from Li Chang, Vice-President of the Chinese Academy of Sciences, to a Member of the Party Central Committee, December 1980." In *Sources of Chinese Tradition: Volume 2: From 1600 Through the Twentieth Century*, edited by William Theodore de Bary, 493–94. New York: Columbia University Press.

Li, Hongtian, Susan Hellerstein, Yubo Zhou, et al. 2020. "Trends in Cesarean Delivery Rates in China, 2008–2018." *Journal of American Medical Association* 323 (1): 89–91.

Li, Hongtian, Shusheng Luo, Leonardo Trasande, et al. 2017. "Geographic Variations and Temporal Trends in Cesarean Delivery Rates in China, 2008–2014." *Journal of the American Medical Association* 317 (1): 69–76.

Li, Minghui. 2020. "Childbirth Transformation and New Style Midwifery in Beijing, 1926–1937." *History of the Family* 25 (3): 406–31.

Li, Tania. 2007. *The Will to Improve: Governmentality, Development, and the Practice of Politics.* Durham, NC: Duke University Press.

Li, Xiyuan. 2001. "Xiangcun Minjian Xinyang: Tixi yu Xiangzheng (Country Folk Beliefs: System and Symbol). PhD diss., Department of Anthropology, Sun Yat-sen University, Guangzhou.

Li, Yifei, et al. 2015. "Zhongguo Liushou Ertong Xinling Zhuangkuang Baipishu (2015 Nian)" (The Mental Condition of China's Left-behind Children [Year 2015]). White paper, Shangxue Lushang Ertong Xinling Guanai Zhongxin (On the Road to School Center for the Mental Care of Children), Beijing.

Liang, Juan, et al. 2018. "Relaxation of the One Child Policy and Trends in Caesarean Section Rates and Birth Outcomes in China between 2012 and 2016: Observational Study of Nearly Seven Million Health Facility Births." *British Medical Journal (clinical research ed.)* 360:k817.

Liang, Qizi. 1994. "Qingdai de Xizi Hui" (Societies for Cherishing Written Characters in the Qing Dynasty). *Xin Shixue (New History)* 5 (2): 83–115.

Lin, Zouyan, and Yuru Zhou. 2016. *Huaren Yu'er Baike (Encyclopedia of Child Care for Chinese People).* Beijing: Beijing Lianhe Chubanshe.

Ling, Minhua. 2019. *The Inconvenient Generation: Migrant Youth Coming of Age on Shanghai's Edge.* Stanford, CA: Stanford University Press.

Liu, Ke, Li-Ming You, Shao-Xian Chen, Yuan-Tao Hao, Xiao-Wen Zhu, Li-Feng Zhang, and Linda H. Aiken. 2012. "The Relationship between Hospital Work Environment and Nurse Outcomes in Guangdong, China: A Nurse Questionnaire Survey." *Journal of Clinical Nursing* 21 (9–10): 1476–85.

Liu, Xiaomei, Courtney D. Lynch, Wayne W. Cheng, and Mark B. Landon. 2016. "Lowering the High Rate of Caesarean Delivery in China: An Experience from Shanghai." *BJOG: An International Journal of Obstetrics and Gynaecology* 123 (10): 1620–28.

Liu, Xin. 2000. *In One's Own Shadow: An Ethnographic Account of the Condition of Post-reform Rural China*. Berkeley: University of California Press.

———. 2017. "In Pursuit of Boy Babies, Families Send Samples to HK for Sex Tests, Abort Girls." *China Global Times*, January 16. www.globaltimes.cn/content/1029065.shtml.

Liu, Yajun, Guanghui Li, Yi Chen, Xin Wang, Yan Ruan, Liying Zou, and Weiyuan Zhang. 2014. "A Descriptive Analysis of the Indications for Caesarean Section in Mainland China." *BMC Pregnancy and Childbirth* 14 (1): 410.

Lock, Margaret. 2004. "Medicalization and the Naturalization of Social Control." In *Encyclopedia of Medical Anthropology*, edited by C. R. Ember and M. Ember, 116–25. New York: Springer.

Lock, Margaret, and Mark Nichter. 2002. "Introduction: From Documenting Medical Pluralism to Critical Interpretations of Globalized Health Knowledge, Policies, and Practices." In *New Horizons in Medical Anthropology: Essays in Honor of Charles Leslie*, edited by Mark Nichter and Margaret Lock, 1–34. London: Routledge.

Lucas, AnElissa. 1982. *Chinese Medical Modernization Comparative Policy Continuities, 1930–1980s*. New York: Praeger.

Lumbiganon, Pisake, et al. 2010. "Method of Delivery and Pregnancy Outcomes in Asia: The WHO Global Survey on Maternal and Perinatal Health 2007–08." *Lancet* 375:490–99.

Ma, Liangkun, ed. 2016a. *Xie he Zhuanjia + Xie he Mama Quan Ganhuo Fenxiang: Chan Jian (Cooperate with Experts, Cooperate with Circle of Moms' Substantial Sharing: Antenatal Examination)*. Beijing: Zhongguo Qinggongye Chubanshe.

———, ed. 2016b. *Xie he Zhuanjia + Xie he Mamaquan Ganhuo Fenxiang: Huaiyun (Cooperate with Experts, Cooperate with Circle of Moms' Substantial Sharing: Pregnancy)*. Beijing: Zhongguo Qinggongye Chubanshe.

MacIntyre, Alasdair. 1981. "The Nature of the Virtues." *Hastings Center Report* 11 (2): 27–34.

Mackenzie, Donald, and Judy Wajcman, eds. 1999. *The Social Shaping of Technology*. 2nd ed. London: Open University Press.

Madsen, Richard. 2020. "Inequality, Culture War, and Imperiled Common Good: America and China." Paper presented at Third Meeting of the Culture and the Common Good Research Group, May, Initiative for US-China Dialogue on Global Issues, Georgetown University, Washington, DC.

Mahmood, Saba. 2005. *Politics of Piety: The Islamic Revival and the Feminist Subject*. Princeton, NJ: Princeton University Press.

Malinowski, Bronislaw. 1965a. *Coral Gardens and Their Magic*. Vol. 1, *Soil-Tilling and Agricultural Rites in the Trobriand Islands*. Bloomington: Indiana University Press.

———. 1965b. *Coral Gardens and Their Magic*. Vol. 2, *The Language of Magic and Gardening*. Bloomington: Indiana University Press.

Mannheim, Karl. 1952. "The Problem of Generations." In *Essays on the Sociology of Knowledge: Collected Works*, Vol. 5, edited by Karl Mannheim, 276–322. New York: Routledge.

Mao, Tse-Tung (Mao Zedong). (1945) 1965. "The Foolish Old Man Who Removed the Mountains." In *Selected Works of Mao Tse-Tung*, vol. 3, 271–74. Beijing: Foreign Languages Press.

Marcus, George E. 1998. *Ethnography through Thick and Thin*. Princeton, NJ: Princeton University Press.

Martin, Diana. 1997. "Motherhood in Hong Kong: The Working Mother and Childcare in the Parent-Centred Hong Kong Family." In *Hong Kong: The Anthropology of a Chinese Metropolis*, edited by Grant Evans and Maria Tam, 198–221. London: Curzon Press.

Martin, Emily. 1987. *The Woman in the Body*. Boston: Beacon Press.

Massey, Doreen. 1994. *Space, Place and Gender*. Minneapolis: University of Minnesota Press.

Mattingly, Cheryl. 2012. "Two Virtue Ethics and the Anthropology of Morality." *Anthropological Theory* 12 (2): 161–84.

———. 2014. *Moral Laboratories: Family Peril and the Struggle for a Good Life*. Berkeley: University of California Press.

Mattingly, Cheryl, and Jason Throop. 2018. "The Anthropology of Ethics and Morality." *Annual Review of Anthropology* 47:475–92.

Mauss, Marcel. (1925) 2016. *The Gift*. Expanded ed., selected, annotated, and translated by Jane I. Guyer. Chicago: Hau Books.

———. (1929) 1969. "Les civilisations: Elements et formes." In *Oeuvres. 2. Representations collectives et diversite des civilisations*, by Marcel Mauss, 456–79. Paris: Les Editions de Minuit.

———. 1950. "Les techniques du corps." In *Sociologie et Anthropologie*, by Marcel Mauss, 363–86. Paris: Presses Universitaires de France.

———. 2006. *Techniques, Technology, and Civilisation*. Edited and introduced by Nathan Schlanger. Oxford, UK: Berghahn Books.

Mauss, Marcel, and Emile Durkheim. 1969. "Note sur la notion de civilisation." In *Oeuvres. 2. Representations collectives et diversite des civilisations*, by Marcel Mauss, 451–55. Paris: Les Editions de Minuit.

May, Shannon. 2010. "Bridging Divides and Breaking Homes: Young Women's Lifecycle Labor Mobility as a Family Managerial Strategy." *China Quarterly* 204:899–920.

McCourt, Christine. 2009. *Childbirth, Midwifery and Concepts of Time*. New York: Berghahn Books.

McKinnon, Susan, and Fenella Cannell, eds. 2013. *Vital Relations: Modernity and the Persistent Life of Kinship*. Santa Fe, NM: SAR Press.

Mead, Margaret, and Martha Wolfenstein, eds. 1955. *Childhood in Contemporary Cultures*. Chicago: University of Chicago Press.

Mellors, Sarah. 2019. "Less Reproduction, More Production: Birth Control in the Early People's Republic of China, 1949–1958." *East Asian Science, Technology and Society* 13 (3): 367–89.

Mennell, Stephen. 2007. *The American Civilizing Process.* London: Polity Press.

Mi, Jie, and Fangchao Liu. 2014. "Rate of Caesarean Section Is Alarming in China." *The Lancet* 383 (9927): 1463–64.

Michael, Mike. 2006. *Technoscience and Everyday Life: The Complex Simplicities of the Mundane.* London: Open University Press.

Michaels, Paula. 2014. *Lamaze. An International History.* Oxford, UK: Oxford University Press.

Miller, Peter, and Nikolas Rose. 2008. *Governing the Present: Administering Economic, Social and Personal Life.* London: Polity Press.

Miller, Suellen, Edgardo Abalos, Monica Chamillard, et al. 2016. "Beyond Too Little, Too Late and Too Much, Too Soon: A Pathway towards Evidence-based, Respectful Maternity Care Worldwide." *Lancet* 388 (10056): 2176–92.

Ming, Holly H. 2013. *The Education of Migrant Children and China's Future: The Urban Left Behind.* London: Routledge.

Ministry of Health, People's Republic of China. 2011. "Report on Women and Children's Health Development (2011)." www.gov.cn/gzdt/att/att/site1/20110921/001e3741a4740fe3bdbf02.pdf.

Mitchell, Timothy. 2002. *Rule of Experts: Egypt, Techno-politics, Modernity.* Berkeley: University of California Press.

Mo, Yan. 2016. *Frog: A Novel.* Translated by Howard Goldblatt. New York: Penguin.

Mol, Annemarie. 2008. *The Logic of Care: Health and the Problem of Patient Choice.* Abingdon, UK: Routledge.

Mol, Annemarie, Ingunn Moser, and Jeannette Pols, eds. 2015. *Care in Practice: On Tinkering in Clinics, Homes and Farms.* New York: Columbia University Press.

Molotch, Harvey. 2003. *Where Stuff Comes From: How Toasters, Toilets, Cars, Computers, and Many Other Things Come to Be as They Are.* London: Routledge.

Moore, Jason, ed. 2016. *Anthropocene or Capitalocene? Nature, History, and the Crisis of Capitalism.* Oakland, CA: PM Press.

Morgan, Lynn, and Elizabeth Roberts. 2012. "Reproductive Governance in Latin America." *Anthropology and Medicine* 19 (2): 241–54.

Morgan, Lynn, and Meredith Wilson, eds. 1999. *Fetal Subjects, Feminist Positions.* Philadelphia: University of Pennsylvania Press.

Morozov, Evgeny. 2011. *The Net Delusion: The Dark Side of Internet Freedom.* New York: Public Affairs.

———. 2013. *To Save Everything, Click Here: The Folly of Technological Solutionism.* New York: Public Affairs.

Murphy, Rachel. 2002. *How Migrant Labor Is Changing Rural China.* Cambridge, UK: Cambridge University Press.

———. 2020. *The Children of China's Great Migration.* Cambridge, UK: Cambridge University Press.

Naftali, Orna. 2014. *Children, Rights, and Modernity in China: Raising Self-Governing Citizens. Studies in Childhood and Youth.* New York: Palgrave Macmillan.

———. 2016. *Children in China.* Cambridge, UK: Polity Press.

Nedostup, Rebecca. 2010. *Superstitious Regimes. Religion and the Politics of Chinese Modernity.* Cambridge, MA: Harvard University Press.

News.China.com. 2019. "Guojia wei jian wei: 900 yu jia yiyuan jiang kaizhan wutong fenmian shidian" (National Health and Medical Commission: more than 900 hospitals will launch pilot programs for painless delivery). August 22. http://news.china.com.cn/2019-08/22/content_.

News QQ. 2005. "Jieshengpo yong tu fa qiang la jiang yunfu zigong fanchu ti wai niang can ju" (Traditional midwife using local method to pull the womb of a pregnant woman results in tragedy). November 15. Accessed November 5, 2017. https://news.qq.com/a/20051115/001461.htm.

News.sina.com. 2017. "Yulin zhuimang chanfu jiashu yu yuanfang dacheng diaojie xieyi?" (Has the family of the laboring woman who encountered death in a hospital in Yulin city reached an agreement with the hospital?). September 11. Accessed September 24, 2018. http://news.sina.com.cn/c/2017-09-11/doc-ifyktzim9407200.shtml.

Nian, Cui, Xiaozhang Liu, Xiaofang Pan, Qing Yang, and Minxiang Li. 2010. "Factors Influencing the Declining Trend of Vasectomy in Sichuan, China." *Southeast Asian Journal of Tropical Medicine Public Health* 41 (4): 1008–20.

Nie, Mao, et al. 2008. *Shangcun: Zhongguo Nongcun Liushou Ertong Yousi Lu* (Wounded Village: A Record of Worries of Rural China's Left-Behind Children). Beijing: Renmin Ribao Chubanshe.

Normile, Dennis. 2017. "One in Three Chinese Children Faces an Education Apocalypse: An Ambitious Experiment Hopes to Save Them." *Science Magazine*, September 21. Accessed January 8, 2019. www.sciencemag.org/news/2017/09/one-three-chinese-children-faces-education-apocalypse-ambitious-experiment-hopes-save.

Oakley, Ann. 1980. *Women Confined: Towards a Sociology of Childbirth.* New York: Schocken Books.

———. 1986. *The Captured Womb: A History of the Medical Care of Pregnant Women.* Oxford: Blackwell.

Oakley, Ann, and Susanne Houd. 2013. *Helpers in Childbirth: Midwifery Today.* London: Routledge.

Odent, Michel. 2004. *The Cesarean.* London: Free Association Books.

———. 2015. *Do We Need Midwives?* New York: Pinter and Martin.

Ong, Aihwa, and Stephen J. Collier, eds. 2005. *Global Assemblages: Technology, Politics, and Ethics as Anthropological Problems.* Chichester, UK: Wiley-Blackwell.

Orleans, Leo. 1979. *Chinese Approaches to Family Planning.* London: MacMillan.

Ortner, Sherry B. 1995. "Resistance and the Problem of Ethnographic Refusal." *Comparative Studies in Society and History* 37 (1): 173–93.

———. 2006. *Anthropology and Social Theory: Culture, Power, and the Acting Subject.* Durham, NC: Duke University Press.

———. 2016. "Dark Anthropology and Its Others: Theory Since the Eighties." *HAU: Journal of Ethnographic Theory* 6 (1): 47–73.

Osburg, John. 2013. *Anxious Wealth: Money and Morality Among China's New Rich.* Stanford, CA: Stanford University Press.

———. 2018. "Making Business Personal: Corruption, Anti-Corruption, and Elite Networks in Post-Mao China." *Current Anthropology* 59:S18, S149–59.

Owen, Lara, and Aidila Razak. 2019. "Why Chinese Mothers Turned away from C-sections." *BBC News*, March 2. www.bbc.com/news/world-asia-china-46265808.

Oxfeld, Ellen. 2004. "'When You Drink Water, Think of Its Source': Morality, Status, and Reinvention in Rural Chinese Funerals." *Journal of Asian Studies* 63:961–90.

———. 2010. *Drink Water, but Remember the Source: Moral Discourse in a Chinese Village.* Berkeley: University of California Press.

———. 2017. *Bitter and Sweet: Food, Meaning, and Modernity in Rural China.* Berkeley: University of California Press.

Palmer, Michael. 2007. "The Transformation of Family Law in Post-Deng China: Marriage, Divorce and Reproduction." *China Quarterly* 191:675–95.

Pan, Xiaoyu. 2017. *Quan Huli: Hao Yun an Chan Bai Ke (Complete Nursing: Good Pregnancy and Safe Birth).* Beijing: Beijing Llianhe Chubanshe.

Pan, Yunkang. 2002. *Jiating Shehuixue (Family Sociology).* Beijing: Zhongguo Shehui Chubanshe.

Parish, William L., and Martin King Whyte. 1978. *Village and Family in Contemporary China.* Chicago: University of Chicago Press.

People's Daily. 2002. "Traditional Midwifery Phased Out in China's Rural Areas." September 30. Accessed November 5, 2017. www.china.org.cn/english/Life/44748.htm.

Perry, Elizabeth J. 2011. "From Mass Campaigns to Managed Campaigns: Constructing a 'New Socialist Countryside.'" In *Mao's Invisible Hand*, edited by Elizabeth J. Perry and Sebastian Heilmann, 30–61. Cambridge, MA: Harvard University Press.

Pfaffenberger, Bryan. 1992. "Social Anthropology of Technology." *Annual Review of Anthropology* 21:491–516.

Pieke, Frank N. 2016. *Knowing China: A Twenty-First-Century Guide.* Cambridge, UK: Cambridge University Press.

Plummer, Ken. 2003. *Intimate Citizenship. Private Decisions and Public Dialogues.* Seattle: University of Washington Press.

Potter, Jack M. 1968. *Capitalism and the Chinese Peasant.* Berkeley: University of California Press.

Potter, Jack M., and Sulamith H. Potter. 1990. *China's Peasants: The Anthropology of a Revolution.* Cambridge, UK: Cambridge University Press.

Povinelli, Elizabeth A. 2006. *The Empire of Love: Toward a Theory of Intimacy, Genealogy, and Carnality.* Durham, NC: Duke University Press.

Prasad, Amit. 2017. "Introduction: Global Assemblages of Technoscience." *Science, Technology and Society* 22 (1): 1–5.

Puett, Michael. 2015. "Ritual and Ritual Obligations: Perspectives on Normativity from Classical China." *Journal of Value Inquiry* 49:543–50.

Pun, Ngai. 2005. *Made in China: Women Factory Workers in a Global Workplace.* Durham, NC: Duke University Press.

———. 2016. *Migrant Labor in China: Postsocialist Transformations.* Cambridge, UK: Polity Press.

Rapp, Rayna. 1987. "Moral Pioneers: Women, Men and Fetuses on a Frontier of Reproductive Technology." *Women Health* 13 (1–2): 101–16.

———. 1999. *Testing Women, Testing the Fetus: The Social Impact of Amniocentesis in America.* New York: Routledge.

Rapp, Rayna, and Faye Ginsburg, eds. 1995. *Conceiving the New World Order: The Global Politics of Reproduction.* Berkeley: University of California Press.

Redfield, Peter, and Steven Robins. 2016. "Toilets for Africa: Humanitarian Design Meets Sanitation Activism in Khayelitsha, Cape Town." In *World Anthropologies in Practice: Situated Perspectives, Global Knowledge,* edited by John Gledhill, 173–88. London: Bloomsbury Academic.

Robbins, Joel. 2007. "Between Reproduction and Freedom: Morality, Value, and Radical Cultural Change." *Ethnos* 72 (3): 293–314.

———. 2012. "On Becoming Ethical Subjects: Freedom, Constraint, and the Anthropology of Morality." *Anthropology of This Century* 5, http://aotcpress.com/articles/ethical-subjects-freedom-constraint-anthropology-morality/.

———. 2013. "Beyond the Suffering Subject: Toward an Anthropology of the Good." *Journal of the Royal Anthropological Institute* 19:447–62.

Rockefeller, Abby. 1996. "Civilization and Sludge. Notes on the History of the Management of Human Excreta." *Current World Leaders* 39 (6): 99–113.

Rogaski, Ruth. 2004. *Hygienic Modernity. Meanings of Health and Disease in Treaty-Port China.* Berkeley: University of California Press.

Rogoff, Barbara. 2003. *The Cultural Nature of Human Development.* Oxford: Oxford University Press.

Rose, Nikolas. 1996. *Inventing Our Selves. Psychology, Power, and Personhood.* Cambridge, UK: Cambridge University Press.

———. 1999. *Powers of Freedom: Reframing Political Thought.* Cambridge, UK: Cambridge University Press.

———. 2007. *The Politics of Life Itself: Biomedicine, Power, and Subjectivity in the Twenty-First Century.* Princeton, NJ: Princeton University Press.

Rothman, Barbara K. 2007. "Laboring Now: Current Cultural Constructions of Pregnancy, Birth, and Mothering." In *Laboring On: Birth in Transition in the United States,* edited by Wendy Simons, Barbara K. Rothman, and Bari M. Norman, 29–93. New York: Routledge.

———. 2016. *A Bun in the Oven: How the Food and Birth Movements Resist Industrialization.* New York: New York University Press.

Santos, Boaventura de Sousa. 2014. *Epistemologies of the South: Justice against Epistemicide.* Boulder, CO: Paradigm Publishers.

———. 2018. *The End of the Cognitive Empire.* Durham, NC: Duke University Press.

Santos, Gonçalo D. 2004. "The Process of Kinship and Identity in a Common-Surname Village in Southeastern China." PhD diss., ISCTE-IUL, Lisbon.

———. 2006a. "The Anthropology of Chinese Kinship. A Critical Overview." *European Journal of East Asian Studies* 5:275–333.

———. 2006b. "Os 'Camponeses' e o 'Imperador': Reflexões Etnográficas sobre Orizicultura Intensiva e Estratificação Social no Sudeste da China." (The 'Farmers' and the 'Emperor': Ethnographic Reflections on Intensive Rice Farming and Social Stratification in Southeastern China." *Etnográfica* 10 (1): 41–70.

———. 2008. "On 'Same-Year Siblings' in Rural South China." *Journal of the Royal Anthropological Institute* 14:535–53.

———. 2009. "The 'Stove-Family' and the Process of Kinship in Rural South China." In *Chinese Kinship: Contemporary Anthropological Perspectives*, edited by Susanne Brandtstädter and Gonçalo Santos, 112–36. Abingdon, UK: Routledge.

———. 2010. "L'Agriculture Traditionnelle Chinoise Est-elle Verte et Jusqu'où?" (How Green Is Chinese Traditional Agriculture?) In *L'Empreinte de la Technique: Comment les Technologies Changent les Societés? Colloque de Cerisy (The Imprint of Technology: How Do Technologies Change Societies? Cerisy Colloquium)*, edited by Thierry Gaudin and Élie Faroult, 117–39. Paris: L'Harmattan.

———. 2011. "Rethinking the Green Revolution in South China: Technological Materialities and Human-Environment Relations." *East Asian Science, Technology and Society* 5:479–504.

———. 2013. "Technologies of Ethical Imagination." In *Ordinary Ethics in China Today*, edited by Charles Stafford, 194–221. London: Bloomsbury.

———. 2016. "On Intimate Choices and Troubles in Rural South China." *Modern Asian Studies* 50 (4): 1298–326.

———. 2017a. "Love, Family, and Gender in 21st Century China." In *Socialism with Neoliberal Characteristics. Social Support and Kinship in China and Vietnam*, edited by Kirsten W. Endres and Chris Hann, 31–35. Halle, Germany: Max Planck Institute for Social Anthropology.

———. 2017b. "Multiple Mothering and Labor Migration in Rural South China." In *Transforming Patriarchy: Chinese Families in the Twenty-First Century*, edited by Gonçalo Santos and Stevan Harrell, 91–128. Seattle: University of Washington Press.

———. 2018. "Technological Choices and Modern Material Civilization: Reflections on Everyday Toilet Practices in Rural South China." In *Anthropology and Civilizational Analysis*, edited by Johann Arnason and Chris Hann, 259–80. New York: State University of New York Press.

———. 2020. "Birthing Stories and Techno-moral Change across Generations: Coping with Hospital Births and High-Tech Medicalization in Rural South China, 1960s–2010s." *Technology and Culture* 61 (2): 581–616.

Santos, Gonçalo, and Aurora Donzelli. 2009. "Rice Intimacies: Reflections on the 'House' in Upland Sulawesi and South China." *Archiv für Völkerkunde* 57–58:37–64.

Santos, Gonçalo, and Suzanne Gottschang. 2020. "Rethinking Reproductive Technologies and Modernities in Time and Space." *Technology and Culture* 61 (2): 549–58.

Santos, Gonçalo, and Stevan Harrell, eds. 2017. *Transforming Patriarchy: Chinese Families in the Twenty-First Century.* Seattle: University of Washington Press.

Santos, Gonçalo, and Stevan Harrell. 2019. "21 Shiji Zhongguo Jiating de Quanli Goucheng Xingtai. 'Nanquan Jiazhang Zhi' Zuo Wei Yi Zhong Fenxi Kuangjia" (Changing power configurations in 21st century Chinese families: Using patriarchy as an analytical category). *Zhongguo Xueshu* 41:79–124.

Santos, Gonçalo, Yichen Rao, Jack L. Xing, and Jun Zhang. 2021. "Capitalism, Overwork, and Polanyi's Dialectics of Freedom. Emerging Visions of Work-Life Balance in Contemporary Urban China." In *Work, Society, and Self: Chimeras of Freedom in the Era of Neoliberalism*, edited by Chris Hann, 132–57. New York: Berghahn Books.

Santos, Gonçalo, and Jun Zhang. Forthcoming. "Who Is Requesting Cesarean Delivery? The Politics and Ethics of Childbirth Medicalization in Late Reform China." Unpublished manuscript.

Scharping, Thomas. 2003. *Birth Control in China, 1949–2000: Population Policy and Demographic Development.* London: Routledge.

Schlanger, Nathan. 2006. "Introduction: Technological Commitments; Marcel Mauss and the Study of Techniques in the French Social Sciences." In *Techniques, Technology, and Civilisation*, by Marcel Mauss, 1–30. New York: Berghahn Books.

Scott, James C. 1985. *Weapons of the Weak: Everyday Forms of Peasant Resistance.* New Haven, CT: Yale University Press.

———. 1990. *Domination and the Arts of Resistance: Hidden Transcripts.* New Haven, CT: Yale University Press.

———. 1998. *Seeing Like a State: How Certain Schemes to Improve the Human Condition Have Failed.* New Haven, CT: Yale University Press.

———. 2009. *The Art of Not Being Governed: An Anarchist History of Upland Southeast Asia.* New Haven, CT: Yale University Press.

Segalen, Martine. 2001. "The Shift of Kinship Studies in France: The Case of Grandparenting." In *Relative Values: Reconfiguring Kinship Studies*, edited by Sarah Franklin and Susan McKinnon, 246–75. Durham, NC: Duke University Press.

———. 2009. "On Papies and Mammies: The Invention of a New Relative in Contemporary European Kinship." Goody Lecture, Max Planck Institute for Social Anthropology, Halle, Germany. www.eth.mpg.de/4423203/Goody_Lecture_2016.pdf.

Shi, Lihong. 2017a. "From Care Providers to Financial Burdens: The Changing Role of Sons and Reproductive Choice in Rural Northeast China." In *Transforming Patriarchy. Chinese Families in the 21st Century*, edited by Gonçalo Santos and Stevan Harell, 59–73. Seattle: University of Washington Press.

———. 2017b. *Choosing Daughters: Family Change in Rural China.* Stanford, CA: Stanford University Press.

Shi, Yaojiang, and John James Kennedy. 2016. "Delayed Registration and Identifying the 'Missing Girls' in China." *China Quarterly* 228:1018–38.

Shirai, Chiaki. 2016. *Umi Sodate to Josan no Rekishi: Kindaika no 200 nen o Furi Kaeru (History of Childbirth, Childrearing, and Midwifery in Japan)*. Tokyo: Igakushoin.

———. 2020. "Historical Dynamism of Childbirth in Japan: Medicalization and Its Normative Politics, 1868–2017." *Technology and Culture* 61 (2): 559–80.

Short, Susan, Ma Linmao, and Yu Wentao. 2000. "Birth Planning and Sterilization in China." *Population Studies* 54:279–91.

Sidel, Ruth. 1973. *Women and Child Care in China: A Firsthand Report*. Harmondsworth, UK: Penguin.

Sigley, Gary. 2006. "Chinese Governmentalities: Government, Governance and the Socialist Market Economy." *Economy and Society* 35 (4).

Silverstein, Merril, Zhen Cong, and Shuzhuo Li. 2006. "Intergenerational Transfers and Living Arrangements of Older People in Rural China: Consequences for Psychological Well-Being." *Journal of Gerontology: Social Sciences* 61 (5): S256–66.

———. 2007. "Grandparents Who Care for Their Grandchildren in Rural China: Benefactors and Beneficiaries." In *New Perspectives on China and Aging*, edited by Ian G. Cook and Jason L. Powell, 49–71. New York: Nova Science Publishers.

Siu, Helen F. 1990. "Recycling Tradition: Culture, History, and Political Economy in the Chrysanthemum Festivals of South China." *Comparative Studies in Society and History* 32 (4): 765–94.

———. 1993. "The Reconstitution of Brideprice and Dowry in South China." In *Chinese Families in the Post-Mao Era*, edited by Deborah Davis and Stevan Harrell, 165–88. Berkeley: University of California Press.

Skinner, G. William. 1997. "Family Systems and Demographic Processes." In *Anthropological Demography: Toward a New Synthesis*, edited by D. I. Kertzer and T. E. Fricke, 53–95. Chicago: University of Chicago Press.

———. 2003. "Family and Reproduction in Southeastern China: A Comparison of Cantonese, Hakka, and Yao." *Asian Anthropology*, no. 2, 1–47.

Sleeboom-Faulkner, Margaret, ed. 2010. *Frameworks of Choice: Predictive and Genetic Testing in Asia*. Amsterdam: Amsterdam University Press.

Snow, Don. 2004. *Cantonese as Written Language: The Growth of a Written Chinese Vernacular*. Hong Kong: Hong Kong University Press.

Sohu.com. 2017. "Zhuzhi yisheng tingzhi gongzuo peihe diaocha, yiyuan zai tiaolou chanfu chancheng zhong jinzhi le ma?" (The doctor-in-charge stopped working to help the investigation, was the hospital responsible and diligent in the case of the laboring woman who jumped out of the window during labor?). September 6. Accessed September 24, 2018. www.sohu.com/a/190151955_114988.

Srinivas, Tulasi. 2002. "Flush with Success: Bathing, Defecation, Worship, and Social Change in South India." *Space and Culture* 5 (4): 368–86.

Stacey, Judith. 1983. *Patriarchy and Socialist Revolution in China*. Berkeley: University of California Press.

Stafford, Charles. 1995. *The Roads of Chinese Childhood: Learning and Identification in Angang.* Cambridge, UK: Cambridge University Press.

———. 2010. "The Punishment of Ethical Behavior." In *Ordinary Ethics: Anthropology, Language and Action*, edited by Michael Lambek, 187–206. New York: Fordham University Press.

———, ed. 2013. *Ordinary Ethics in China.* London: Bloomsbury.

Sterne, Jonathan. 2003. "Bourdieu, Technique, and Technology." *Cultural Studies* 17 (3–4): 367–89.

Sternsdorff-Cisterna, Nicolas. 2018. *Food Safety After Fukushima: Scientific Citizenship and the Politics of Risk.* Honolulu: University of Hawai'i Press.

Stockman, Norman, Norman Bonney, and Sheng Xuewen. 1995. *Women's Work in East and West: The Dual Burden of Employment and Family Life.* London: UCL Press.

Sufang, Guo, Sabu S. Padmadas, Fengmin Zhao, James J. Brown, and R. William Stones. 2007. "Delivery Settings and Caesarean Section Rates in China." *Bulletin of the World Health Organization* 85 (10): 755–62.

Swartz, Teresa T. 2009. "Intergenerational Family Relations in Adulthood: Patterns, Variations, and Implications in the Contemporary United States." *Annual Review of Sociology* 25:191–212.

Szczygiel, Marta E. 2016. "From Night Soil to Washlet: The Material Culture of Japanese Toilets." *Electronic Journal of Contemporary Japanese Studies* 16 (3). www.japanesestudies.org.uk/ejcjs/vol16/iss3/szczygiel.html.

Takeshita, Chikako. 2012. *The Global Biopolitics of the IUD: How Science Constructs Contraceptive Users and Women's Bodies.* Cambridge, MA: MIT Press.

Tam, Wai Lun. 2006. "Local Religion in Contemporary China." In *Chinese Religions in Contemporary Societies*, edited by James Miller, 57–83. Santa Barbara, CA: ABC-CLIO Press.

Tan, Weilun, and Hanxiang Zeng, eds. 2010. *Yingde de Chuantong Difang Shehui yu Minzu (The Traditional Local Society and People of Yingde).* Chengdu: Sichuan Daxue Chubanshe.

Tang, Shenglan, Xiaoyan Li, and Zhuochun Wu. 2006. "Rising Cesarean Delivery Rate in Primiparous Women in Urban China: Evidence from Three Nationwide Household Health Surveys." *American Journal of Obstetrics and Gynecology* 195 (6): 1527–32.

Thornton, Arland. 2005. *Reading History Sideways: The Fallacy and Enduring Impact of the Developmental Paradigm on Family Life.* Chicago: University of Chicago Press.

Topley, Marjorie. 1974. "Cosmic Antagonisms: A Mother-Child Syndrome." In *Religion and Ritual in Chinese Society*, edited by Arthur Wolf, 233–50. Stanford, CA: Stanford University Press.

———. 2011. *Cantonese Society in Hong Kong and Singapore. Gender, Religion, Medicine and Money: Essays by Marjorie Topley.* Edited and introduced by Jean DeBernardi. Hong Kong: Hong Kong University Press.

Toutiao.com. 2017. "Diaocha: Yulin chanfu bei moshi de shengyin; Zhishao liu ci tichu poufuchan" (Investigation: The sound of the laboring woman of Yulin was ignored; She proposed C-section at least six times). September 13. Accessed September 25, 2018. www.toutiao.com/a6465153118240768526/.

Tsing, Anna L. 1994. *In the Realm of the Diamond Queen: Marginality in an Out-of-the-way Place*. Princeton, NJ: Princeton University Press.

———. 2005. *Friction: An Ethnography of Global Connection*. Princeton, NJ: Princeton University Press.

———. 2017. *The Mushroom at the End of the World: On the Possibility of Life in Capitalist Ruins*. Princeton, NJ: Princeton University Press.

Tsing, Anna L., Jennifer Deger, Alder Keleman Saxena, and Feifei Zhou. 2020. *Feral Atlas: The More-Than-Human Anthropocene*. Stanford, CA: Stanford University Press/Stanford Digital Project, http://feralatlas.org/, https://doi.org/10.21627/2020fa.

Ulrich, Laurel Thatcher. 1991. *A Midwife's Tale: The Life of Martha Ballard, Based on Her Diary, 1785–1812*. New York: Vintage Books.

Van Buren, Ariane (1979) 1997. *The Chinese Biogas Manual: Popularising Technology in the Countryside*. London: Intermediate Technologies.

Van Hollen, Cecilia. 2003. *Birth on the Threshold: Childbirth and Modernity in South India*. Berkeley: University of California Press.

Veblen, Thorstein. (1899) 1934. *The Theory of the Leisure Class*. New York: Penguin.

Village Household Survey. 2001. "Harmony Cave Household Survey, 1999–2000." Unpublished manuscript, author's personal collection.

Vogel, Ezra. 1990. *One Step Ahead in China: Guangdong under Reform*. Cambridge, MA: Harvard University Press.

Wajcman, Judy. 1991. *Feminism Confronts Technology*. Cambridge, MA: Polity Press.

———. 2000. "Reflections on Gender and Technology Studies: In What State Is the Art?" *Social Studies of Science* 30 (3): 447–64.

———. 2004. *TechnoFeminism*. Cambridge, MA: Polity Press.

———. 2010. "Feminist Theories of Technology." *Cambridge Journal of Economics* 34 (1): 143–52.

———. 2016. *Pressed for Time: The Acceleration of Life in Digital Capitalism*. Chicago: University of Chicago Press.

Wallis, Cara. 2013. *Technomobility in China: Young Migrant Women and Mobile Phones*. New York: New York University Press.

Wang, Eileen. 2016. "Choice, Control and Childbirth: Cesarean Deliveries on Maternal Request in Shanghai, China." PhD diss. in anthropology, University of Pennsylvania, Philadelphia.

———. 2017. "Requests for Cesarean Deliveries: The Politics of Labor Pain and Pain Relief in Shanghai, China." *Social Science and Medicine* 173 (Suppl. C): 1–8.

Wang, Qi. 2011. *Huaiyun, Anchan, Yuezi: Yi Ji Shen* (*Pregnancy, Safe Birth, Postnatal Confinement: Do's and Don'ts*). Beijing: Zhongguo Renkou Chubanshe.

Wang, Xin, Susan Hellerstein, Lei Hou, Liying Zou, Yan Ruan, and Weiyuan Zhang. 2017. "Caesarean Deliveries in China." *BMC Pregnancy and Childbirth* 17:54.

Ward, Barbara. 1970. "Temper Tantrums in Kau Sai: Some Speculations upon Their Effects." In *Socialization: The Approach from Social Anthropology*, edited by

Philip Mayer, 107–25. London: Tavistock (Association of Social Anthropology Monographs).

Wardlow, Holly. 2006. *Wayward Women: Sexuality and Agency in New Guinea Society.* Berkeley: University of California Press.

Warner, Judith. 2006. *Perfect Madness: Motherhood in the Age of Anxiety.* New York: Riverhead Books.

Watson, James L. 1975. *Emigration and the Chinese Lineage: The Mans in Hong Kong and London.* Berkeley: University of California Press.

———. 1982. "Chinese Kinship Reconsidered: Anthropological Perspectives on Historical Research." *China Quarterly* 92:589–622.

Watson, James L., and Rubie S. Watson. 2004. *Village Life in Hong Kong: Politics, Gender, and Ritual in the New Territories.* Hong Kong: Chinese University of Hong Kong.

Watson, Rubie S. 1985. *Inequality among Brothers: Class and Kinship in South China.* Cambridge: Cambridge University Press.

White, Tyrene. 2006. *China's Longest Campaign: Birth Planning in the People's Republic, 1949–2005.* Ithaca, NY: Cornell University Press.

———. 2010. "Domination, Resistance, and Accommodation in China's One-Child Campaign." In *Chinese Society: Change, Conflict, and Resistance*, 3rd ed., edited by Elizabeth J. Perry and Mark Selden, 171–96. New York: Routledge.

WHO (World Health Organization). 1985. "Appropriate Technology for Birth." *The Lancet* 326 (8452): 436–37.

———. 2016. "Standards for Improving Quality of Maternal and Newborn Care in Health Facilities." Accessed January 6, 2019. http://apps.who.int/iris/bitstream/10665/249155/1/9789241511216-eng.pdf?ua=1.

WHO (World Health Organization) and APOHSP (Asia Pacific Observatory on Health Systems and Policies). 2015. "People's Republic of China Health System Review." Accessed January 6, 2019. https://iris.wpro.who.int/handle/10665.1/11408.

WHO (World Health Organization) and HRP (Human Reproduction Programme). 2015. "WHO Statement on Caesarean Section Rates." Accessed January 6, 2019. www.who.int/reproductivehealth/publications/maternal_perinatal_health/cs-statement/en/.

WHO (World Health Organization) and UNICEF (United Nations Children's Fund). 1991. "The Baby-Friendly Hospital Initiative. Monitoring and Reassessment: Tools to Sustain Progress." Accessed March 7, 2018. http://apps.who.int/iris/handle/10665/65380.

———. 2009. "Baby-Friendly Hospital Initiative. Revised, Updated and Expanded for Integrated Care." Accessed January 7, 2019. www.who.int/nutrition/publications/infantfeeding/bfhi_trainingcourse/en/.

———. 2018. "Protecting, Promoting, and Supporting Breastfeeding in Facilities Providing Maternity and Newborn Services: The Revised Baby-Friendly Hospital Initiative." Accessed January 10, 2019. https://apps.who.int/iris/bitstream/handle/10665/272943/9789241513807-eng.pdf?ua=1.

Whyte, Martin King, and William L. Parish. 1984. *Urban Life in Contemporary China*. Chicago: University of Chicago Press.

Whyte, Martin King, Feng Wang, and Irvine Yong Cai. 2015. "Challenging Myths About China's One-Child Policy." *China Journal* 74 (74):144–59.

Williams, Raymond. 1977. *Marxism and Literature*. Oxford, UK: Oxford University Press.

Wolf, Arthur P. 1974. "Gods, Ghosts, and Ancestors." In *Religion and Ritual in Chinese Society*, edited by Arthur P. Wolf, 131–82. Stanford, CA: Stanford University Press.

Wolf, Jacqueline. 2018. *Cesarean Section: An American History of Risk, Technology, and Consequence*. Baltimore: John Hopkins University Press.

Wolf, Margery. 1970. "Child Training and the Chinese Family." In *Family and Kinship in Chinese Society*, edited by Maurice Freedman, 37-62. Stanford, CA: Stanford University Press.

———. 1972. *Women and the Family in Rural Taiwan*. Stanford, CA: Stanford University Press.

———. 1985. *Revolution Postponed: Women in Contemporary China*. Stanford, CA: Stanford University Press.

Wu, Xiujie. 2008. "Men Purchase, Women Use: Coping with Domestic Electrical Appliances in Rural China." *East Asian Science, Technology and Society* 2 (2): 211–34.

Wu, Yi-Li. 2010. *Reproducing Women. Medicine, Metaphor, and Childbirth in Late Imperial China*. Berkeley: University of California Press.

Xia, Zuzhang. 2013. *Domestic Biogas in a Changing China: Can Biogas Still Meet the Energy Needs of China's Rural Households?* London: International Institute for Environment and Development.

Xiang, Biao. 2007. *Global "Body Shopping": An Indian Labor System in the Information Technology Industry*. Princeton, NJ: Princeton University Press.

Xue, Yong. 2005. "'Treasure Nightsoil as if It Were Gold': Economic and Ecological Links between Urban and Rural Areas in Late Imperial Jiangnan." *Late Imperial China* 26 (1): 41–71.

Yan, Hairong. 2008. *New Masters, New Servants: Migration, Development, and Women Workers in China*. Durham, NC: Duke University Press.

Yan, Yunxiang. 1997. "The Triumph of Conjugality: Structural Transformation of Family Relations in a Chinese Village." *Ethnology* 36 (3): 191–212.

———. 2003. *Private Life under Socialism: Love, Intimacy, and Family Change in a Chinese Village, 1949-1999*. Stanford, CA: Stanford University Press.

———. 2006. "Girl Power: Young Women and the Waning of Patriarchy in Rural North China." *Ethnology* 45, no. 2 (Spring): 105–23.

———. 2009a. "The Good Samaritan's New Trouble: A Study of the Changing Moral Landscape in Contemporary China." *Social Anthropology* 17 (1): 9–24.

———. 2009b. *The Individualization of Chinese Society*. London: Berg.

———. 2010. "The Chinese Path to Individualization." *British Journal of Sociology* 61 (3): 489–512.

———. 2012. "Food Safety and Social Risk in Contemporary China." *Journal of Asian Studies* 71 (3): 705–29.

———. 2013a. "The Drive for Success and the Ethics of the Striving Individual." In *Ordinary Ethics in China Today*, edited by Charles Stafford, 263–91. London: Bloomsbury.

———. 2013b. "How Far Away Can We Move from Durkheim? Reflections on the New Anthropology of Morality." *Anthropology of this Century* 2, http://aotcpress.com/articles/move-durkheim-reflections-anthropology morality/.

———. 2015a. "Moral Hierarchy and Social Egoism in a Networked Society: The *Chaxugeju* Thesis Revisited." *Korean Journal of Sociology* 49 (3): 39–58.

———. 2015b. "Parent-Driven Divorce and Individualisation among Urban Chinese Youth." *International Social Science Journal* 64 (213–214). https://doi.org/10.1111/issj.12048.

———. 2016. "Intergenerational Intimacy and Descending Familism in Rural North China." *American Anthropologist* 118 (2): 244–257.

———. 2017. "Doing Personhood in Chinese Culture." *Cambridge Journal of Anthropology* 35 (2): 1–17.

———. 2018. "Neo-familism and the State in Contemporary China." *Urban Anthropology and Studies of Cultural Systems and World Economic Development* 47 (3–4).

———. 2021. "The Politics of Moral Crisis in Contemporary China." *China Journal*, no. 85, published electronically December 2, 2020.

Yanagisako, Sylvia. 2002. *Producing Culture and Capital: Family Firms in Italy*. Princeton, NJ: Princeton University Press.

Yang, C. K. 1961. *Religion in Chinese Society*. Berkeley: University of California Press.

Yang, Chao. 2017. *Television and Dating in Contemporary China: Identities, Love and Intimacy*. Singapore: Palgrave Macmillan.

Yen, Yuehping. 2005. *Calligraphy and Power in Contemporary Chinese Society*. London: Routledge.

Yingde Xian. 1965. "Yingde Xian Jiban Qingkuang" (General Situation of Yingde County). Yingde: Zhong Gong Yingde Xian Wei Ban Gong Shi.

Yingde Xianzhi. 2006. "Yingde Xianzhi" (Yingde County Annals). Guangzhou: Guangdong Renmin Chubanshe.

Yip, Ka-che. 1992. "Health and Nationalist Reconstruction: Rural Health in Nationalist China, 1928–1937." *Modern Asian Studies* 26 (2): 395–415.

Yu, Xinzhong. 2010. "The Treatment of Night-Soil and Waste in Modern China." In *Health and Hygiene in Chinese East Asia: Policies and Publics in the Long Twentieth Century*, edited by Charlotte Furth and Angela K. Leung, 51–72. Durham, NC: Duke University Press.

Yue, Ai, Yaojiang Shi, Renfu Luo, Jamie Chen, James Garth, Jimmy Zhang, Alexis Medina, Sarah Kotb, and Scott Rozelle. 2017. "China's Invisible Crisis: Cognitive Delays among Rural Toddlers and the Absence of Modern Parenting." *China Journal* 78 (1): 50–80.

Yue, Ai, Sean Sylvia, Yaojiang Shi, Renfu Luo, and Scott Rozelle. 2016. *The Effect of Maternal Migration on Early Childhood Development in Rural China*. Working Paper, Freeman Spogli Institute for International Studies, Stanford University, California.

Zavoretti, Roberta. 2017. *Rural Origins, City Lives: Class and Place in Contemporary China*. Seattle: University of Washington Press.

Zelizer, Viviana A. 2005. *The Purchase of Intimacy*. Princeton, NJ: Princeton University Press.

Zeng, Yi, and Therese Hesketh. 2016. "The effects of China's Universal Two-Child Policy." *The Lancet* 388 (10054): 1930–38.

Zhang, Hong. 2017. "Recalibrating Filial Piety: Realigning the State, Family, and Market Interests in China." In *Transforming Patriarchy: Chinese Families in the Twenty-First Century*, edited by Gonçalo Santos and Stevan Harrell, 234–50. Seattle: University of Washington Press.

Zhang, Jun. 2017a. "(Extended) Family Car, Filial Consumer-Citizens: Becoming Properly Middle Class in Post-Socialist South China." *Modern China* 43 (1): 36–65.

———. 2017b. "Materializing a Form of Urban Governance: When Street Building Intersected with City Building in Republican Canton (Guangzhou), China." *History and Technology* 33 (2): 153–74.

———. 2019. *Driving toward Modernity. Cars and the Lives of the Middle Class in Contemporary China*. Ithaca, NY: Cornell University Press.

Zhang, Jun, and Gonçalo Santos. 2018. "From Agricultural Commodities to Domestic Waste: Sociotechnical Transformation of Human Excreta Management in Republican Canton." Paper presented at the Fifth AAS (Association for Asian Studies)-in Asia Conference, New Delhi.

Zhang, Jun, and Peidong Sun. 2014. "When Are You Going to Get Married? Parental Matchmaking and Middle-Class Women in Contemporary Urban China." In *Wives, Husbands, and Lovers: Marriage and Sexuality in Hong Kong, Taiwan, and Urban China*, edited by D. Davis and S. Friedman, 118–44. Stanford, CA: Stanford University Press.

Zhang, Jun, Yinghui Liu, Susan Meikle, et al. 2008. "Cesarean Delivery on Maternal Request in Southeast China," *Obstetrics & Gynecology* 111 (5): 1077–82.

Zhang, Xiaying. 2010. "Dangqian Zhongguo Zhuchanshi Mianlin de Kunjing yu Tiaozhan" (Current Difficulties and Challenges Faced by Professional Midwives in Present-Day China). *Yixue yu Zhexue (Linchuang Juece Luntan Ban)* 10 (415): 68–69.

Zhang, Yihui, Ning Gu, Zhiqun Wang, et al. 2017. "Use of the 10-Group Classification System to Analyze How the Population Control Policy Change in China Has Affected Cesarean Delivery." *International Journal of Gynecology and Obstetrics* 138 (2): 158–63.

Zhang, Yong, Tong De, and Liang Xiongfei. 2018. "New Perspective on Regional Inequality: Theory and Evidence from Guangdong, China." *Journal of Urban Planning and Development* 144 (1).

Zheng, Yuqiao. 2015. *Zheng Yuqiao Yu'er Baihuo* (*Zheng Yuqiao's Encyclopedia of Childcare*). Beijing: Huaxue Gongye Chubanshe.

Zheng, Zhenman. 2001. *Family Lineage Organization and Social Change in Ming and Qing Fujian*. Translated by Michael Szonyi. Honolulu: University of Hawai'i Press.

Zhong, Yishan. 2019. "Mothering with Mobile Communication Technologies in Urban China." MPhil. diss. in anthropology, University of Hong Kong, Hong Kong.

Zhou, Lianchun. 2004. *Xueyin Xunzong: Cesuo de Lishi Jingji Fengsu* (*Looking for Traces of the Toilet: History, Economy, and Social Customs*). Hefei: Anhui Renmin Chubanshe.

Zhou, Viola. 2018. "A Chinese Doctor Refuses to Do a C-section: He Was Beaten Up." *Inkstone*, October 18. www.inkstonenews.com/health/chinese-doctor-beaten-refusing-do-c-section/article/2168586.

Zhu, Jiaming, ed. 1988. *Zhongguo: Xuyao Cesuo Geming* (*China: Needs a Toilet Revolution*). Shanghai: Sanlian Shudian Shanghai Fendian.

Zhu, Xiu, Jiasi Yao, Jianyu Lu, Ruyan Pang, and Hong Lu. 2018. "Midwifery Policy in Contemporary and Modern China: From the Past to the Future." *Midwifery* 66:97–102.

Zigon, Jarrett. 2009. "Within a Range of Possibilities: Morality and Ethics in Social Life." *Ethnos* 74 (2): 251–76.

INDEX

CPSIA information can be obtained
at www.ICGtesting.com
Printed in the USA
BVHW030239080821
613667BV00001B/2

9 780295 747385